RISING UP

Life Stories of Belizean Women

Canadian Cataloguing in Publication Data
Henderson, Peta, 1937 -
       Rising Up: Life stories of Belizean women by women of the Orange Walk District.

ISBN 0-920813-78-X

1. Women - Belize - Orange Walk District - Social conditions.
2. Women - Belize - Orange Walk District - Interviews.
I. Houghton, Ann Bryn
II. Title.

HQ1470.5.Z8074 1993   305.4'097282'6
                                                       C93-094272-8

Editor for the Press: Makeda Silvera
Editor: P.K. Murphy
Copy Editor: Martha Sharpe
Printed and bound in Canada by Union Labour.

Published by:
Sister Vision Press
P.O. Box 217
Station E,
Toronto, Ontario
Canada M6H 4E2

RISING UP

Life Stories of Belizean Women

*By Women of the
Orange Walk District*

EDITED BY

Peta Henderson

AND

Ann Bryn Houghton

Sister Vision

Black Women and Women of Colour Press

*For the women of Belize
in their struggles to rise up*

Contents

Contents

Foreword
Cynthia Ellis Topsey

The stories of women's lives are woven into a tapestry of joy and pain with which many of us can relate. It is an important way in which to invite other people into our world created by the Europeans and their slaves, and the many other people who have sought refuge on this space of the earth called Belize.

The book gives some impression of what it means to be born woman in Belize. Women created of many colours and combinations of various ethnic groups of Maya, Garifuna, Kekchi, Creole and Mestizo, to name a few.

Belize, still fairly untouched and unspoilt, and often referred to as virgin country, is about to be discovered. Hopefully, this book will quench your thirst to learn more about this tiny English-speaking nation in Central America, where the people are both rich and poor at the same time.

We are rich with the natural resources which we have, of numerous rivers and streams and forests. We are poor in terms of our inability to harness these resources in order to feed ourselves and to heal ourselves of the dependency on the outer world.

As women, we scream out at abuse of every kind to our space, but often too silently. Women have limited access to services such as health, especially in rural communities.

The gynaecologists, for example, are located in Belize City. Our fertility rate is one of the highest per capita in the English speaking Caribbean. The highest female morbidity rates in Belize are abortion related.

9

We need to validate and celebrate the richness of Belizean women who have more than survived in spite of the odds. The over one hundred practising traditional healers and birth attendants in rural communities need to be supported and encouraged as people who continue to make valuable contributions in their communities. There are women who have made their yards schools for young children, teaching them about plants, food processing and healing.

There are women in Garifuna communities who have taught children the language and songs and stories. There are women who have enforced fierce pride in being Belizean.

There are women, Mayan women, who hold fast to their tradition of weaving colourful embroidery patterns of stories relating to their connection with nature and earth. Yet we women have not been able to effectively position ourselves to improve the quality of our lives.

What do Belizean women want? What does any human being want?

Self-respect and the opportunity to develop one's creative potential. As women, we need to cope with back breaking and time consuming domestic work such as making corn tortilla and cassava bread. We no longer want to be marginalized, getting the lowest paid jobs, when we get any jobs at all. We need support with child care services, for example.

As a people, we have been studied, written about, and re-searched... What needs to happen as well is for women and commu-nity based organizations to develop leadership and the capability of addressing their problems independently.

We hail the efforts of the United Nations Decade for Women 1975-1985, which helped to place women's issues on the global agenda. The challenge now is to assist women in developing their capacity to negotiate with existing economic and social structures which affect and control their lives. At the same time, we women need to take leadership in shaping and deciding the course of our lives. This includes our relationship with our children and with the world. Women in Belize do not wish to be viewed as victims.

Women in Belize would like to develop the capacity to cope and manage our lives in spite of the onslaught from outside forces. Resting blame on others is not necessarily going to help us in dealing with unemployment, hunger and disease.

Life, of course, needs to be balanced, because we are part of a global community. Although we believe that sisterhood is global, our differences need to be acknowledged and celebrated.

These stories reflect on what women can do for themselves when they get sick and tired of abuse. This book is another important attempt to harness the courage and creative fighting spirit of Belizean women.

It challenges us to struggle on in solidarity as women who, in our own way, make a difference. By breaking down barriers of dependency, we can clear our own paths.

Belize Rural Women's Association
Belmopan, Belize
January, 1993

Preface
Peta Henderson

In a rented Land Rover one hot mid-day in April 1968, I drove into the village of San Miguel[1] in the Orange Walk district of what was then British Honduras, now the independent nation of Belize. The previous year, Tate and Lyle, a British-based multinational, had constructed a modern sugar factory near Orange Walk Town. I was a graduate student and I was looking for a village in that area where I could investigate how this invasion of the international capitalist market was affecting the culture and livelihood of the rural populace of Maya-Mestizo *milperos*.

I directed my inquiries to the local Creole policeman who suggested that I talk to one of the teachers in the local primary school, a young woman in her late twenties named Celia. Since it was lunchtime, Celia asked if I would like to come home with her to meet her family. Living with her were her younger sister, Alicia, 18, and their parents Don Gaspar and Dona Mercedes. In my halting Spanish, I explained that I was a graduate student at McGill University in Montreal, Canada, who had come to British Honduras to do research for master's thesis. Without hesitation, they invited me to live with them while I was doing my work.

Like most houses in San Miguel, their home was a single-room thatched roof structure, partitioned into sleeping and living areas. A separate kitchen building and bathhouse were in back. Here, Dona Mercedes, the mother of ten adult children, washed, cooked and cared for her children. After lunch, she used to like to sit outside her kitchen and listen to Mexican soaps broadcast from the radio station in Chetumal, the Mexican border town.

Don Gaspar made his living growing corn and sugar cane. He was a small man, a descendant of one of the Yucatecan Maya groups which moved south into British Honduras during the so-called War of the Castes in the mid-nineteenth century. When he was younger he was a *chiclero*, cutting *chicle* in the bush as a contracted labourer, but an accident had put a stop to that.

In those days Chetumal was a half-day boat ride down the Rio Hondo from San Miguel, and much licit and illicit trafficking took place on both sides of the river under the surveillance of the local police officer who kept close watch on comings and goings. Today the passenger boats have disappeared, replaced by customs patrol boats, and most people travel by road.

During my first visit to San Miguel I stayed for four months. Thus began an association which has lasted over twenty years. At the deepest level, it is as sister, daughter and friend, not as professional anthropologist, that I think about myself in relation to the people of San Miguel.

The paradoxes of my work and the limits of my professional training should have been obvious to me from my first visit. As a woman, I spent much of my time in the company of women. I got to know the women personally, sitting in their kitchens, attending their prayer meetings and helping with small chores, but I never considered what contributions they might make to my research.

My interest was in sugar cane and this was the business of men. The problem was that men's work took them outside the village. Every morning at four, Don Gaspar would ride his small mare out to his fields, returning to eat at midday and then riding out again until late afternoon. It was not considered proper that I should accompany the men. On the one occasion when I visited Don Gaspar's *milpa*, special arrangements were made to transport me by horse-drawn cart, although I knew how to ride horseback and could have walked. Most of the time, in order to interview a cane farmer, I had to catch him between four in the afternoon and dusk, after he had returned from the bush and taken his daily bath, or on weekends if he was not working. Such was my academic training, which defined "socio-economic change" in terms of men's, not women's, experience and perceptions.

I didn't return to San Miguel until May 1984, sixteen years after my first visit, although I corresponded regularly with Celia. Her letters had kept me informed of developments, but I was still unprepared for the extent of the changes which had resulted from several years of high sugar cane prices in the seventies. In the interim, my family had built a large, two-story frame house. They had an electrical generator which they turned on for a couple of hours at six in the evening to catch the Mexican soaps on television. Small water tanks now made daily trips to the village well unnecessary for those who had substituted a laminated run-off surface for thatch roofs. Trucks, tractor-trailers and pick-ups rumbled through the village, scattering pigs, dogs and chickens as they raced to complete their deliveries of sugar cane to the factory before the end of the season. A large communications satellite had been erected behind the community centre.

Yet beneath the surface, there were many continuities between 1968 and 1984; women still washed, cooked, bore children and discussed the number they had played in the daily lottery. Men still talked of the weather, corn and sugar cane.

For me, too, there was both change and continuity. Besides being sixteen years older, I was no longer a struggling graduate student but a greying university professor. My fluency in Spanish had improved, though marginally. My research interests had been affected by the Vietnam War and the women's movement, as well as ten years of teaching. I had co-authored a book about the origins of gender inequality. Yet despite my changed appearance and status, I found my relationship with the family and community fundamentally unchanged. I decided to return to San Miguel as soon as I could to pursue the research where I had left off in 1968, but focusing more directly on how women had experienced their lives over the past quarter century.

In shifting my focus to the female experience, it struck me that the life history approach might be an appropriate method since it would encourage the women to tell their stories in their own way. In the spring of 1988, I returned with the single goal of recording the life histories and making black-and-white images of the daily lives of women living in San Miguel. On this occasion, I was accompanied by a former student, Bryn Houghton, who worked in Orange Walk Town among the urbanized English-speaking population. Bryn was of a different generation than I and she helped me to make the change from a traditional male-oriented "scientific" perspective to the more woman-centred narrative approach that is reflected here. This book is the result of our joint work. We interviewed approximately twenty-five women of all ages, although not all the interviews are included in this volume. We hope that those who were left out will not feel slighted; some selection was necessary for practical reasons of space.

The women I worked with are in no sense representative in a scientific sense. I chose them because I already knew them or because I knew something of their background. I consciously tried to choose women of different ages, marital status, occupation and socio-economic status. I assured each woman of anonymity and confidentiality and offered each modest financial compensation for her time and effort.[2]

For most of the women this was a novel experience. I tried to encourage them to tell stories and to reflect on their lives and emotions, rather than to simply recount the facts. Once we had agreed to work together, I spent about a week with each woman, observing and photographing her work, talking with her as she washed clothes and went about her daily round. I learned to make tortillas and tamales, to shell coconuts, and to bake bread. I went to school with the teacher and to the clinic with the health worker. After a day or two together, we would begin to record at a time convenient for her. In most cases, we had three or four two-hour sessions, although some were shorter. It was not easy to find time. Most women work hard and there were many interruptions from children, men and animals. Sometimes we were inhibited by a lack of privacy, as when only a curtain separated us from a husband or son.

Having reviewed the tapes, I returned to the village in October of the same year hoping to meet again with all the women before beginning the translation. I saw all but two of the women: Gabriela and Estella were unavailable. In the case of the others, although time constraints prevented us from reviewing the entire tapes, I played back portions that I had found interesting and significant and asked the women to comment on what they had said. I also asked them if there was anything else that they wanted to tell me and raised a few additional questions of my own.

Despite my desire to make the interviews an interactive process, there was an unavoidable built-in asymmetry. In the context of village life, I am hard to categorize. Why would this unmarried gringa woman spend so much time talking with them about their lives? How could I explain the mixture of personal and professional interest that had motivated my return to San Miguel after so many years? On one occasion I recall, Clara asked me whether I would consider marrying someone from San Miguel and settling down in Belize. I replied, quite honestly, that I didn't think that I would, that my work and friends are in the United States. But my answer was inadequate because it failed to acknowledge the real differences which are class-based as well as cultural. However close I felt to the women, those differences were always present, if unacknowledged. There were also difficulties in communication: Belizean village Spanish has its own specialized vocabulary and I was acutely aware that I did not always choose the words that would have triggered the culturally-grounded response I was looking for.

In a few cases, especially with those who were close to me in age – Clara, Cristina, Magdalena – I thought that our relationship developed to a level in which some real confidence was established. Some of them seemed to enjoy this opportunity to relive their experiences with men, money and mothers-in-law. Some of them told me that they found it easier to talk to me – an outsider – than to women in their own community whom they suspected would gossip. In life history research, there is a fine line between the role of interviewer and that of confidante-friend; there were times when I thought I had crossed that line. I wish I had crossed it more often for I have come to believe that oral history, as a specifically feminist methodology, may be most effective where it involves a real sharing of experience and participation by all parties.

While in Belize, we became acquainted with the Belize Rural Women's Association, which uses oral history interviewing in small groups as an organizational tool for the collective empowerment of women. As participants in a BRWA workshop in June 1988, Bryn and I observed this technique in action and saw how the awareness of shared experiences and skills can be translated into a powerful force for community change and development spearheaded by women. I am indebted to the staff and members of the Belize Rural Women's Association, and especially to Cynthia Ellis and Lucia Engleton, for sharing their approach to oral history and inviting our participation in their activities.

I am grateful to the to the Evergreen State College for granting me leave during the spring and fall of 1988 and the winter of 1989 to begin work on this project. Many people have been involved since its inception. My colleagues, Nancy Allen and Sandra Lewis Nisbet, gave me the initial encouragement to undertake a work that would represent a somewhat radical departure from my prior training and orientation. Bob Haft and Paul Sparks helped to teach me the fundamentals of black-and-white photography and eased access to the darkroom. Tomas Black and Mal Pina Chan in Photo Services provided professional support in printing the images. Allegra Hinkle, Director of Media Loan, was generous in providing access to transcription equipment. Andrea Winship in the Inter-Library Loan Department helped me to locate sources on Belize. Sue Pittman and Jill Drennon were wonderfully efficient and helpful in the final stages of manuscript preparation.

Martha Tapia and Renee Bourbeau did a truly professional job of translating from the tape transcription in Spanish. Students Ruth Smith and Greg Free helped with the tedious process of tape transcription. Many other Evergreen students and faculty have provided comments and encouragement over the past three years when I have presented versions of the material.

I would like to thank Sue-Ellen Jacobs, of the University of Washington Programme in Women Studies, who, in the early stages of planning the project, offered expert advice based on her own experience with the oral history of women in the Northwest fishing industry.

My colleagues, Stephanie Coontz and Nancy Allen read drafts of the Preface, Introduction and Conclusion and offered thoughtful and constructive suggestions. Special thanks go to Stephanie for the personal support and encouragement to persevere with this project and to Bryn Houghton for her participation in it as co-editor.

Most importantly, I want to express my gratitude and affection to the Belizeans who have contributed to this work, most particularly the women of the village of "San Miguel." They were promised anonymity, but they know who they are. To my Belizean family, especially "Celia," I once again express my love and thanks.

---

[1] *The names of people and villages have been changed to protect the identity of the storytellers.*

[2] *One woman refused compensation. Bryn did not offer compensation to the women she interviewed in Orange Walk Town.*

Preface
Ann Bryn Houghton

I was introduced to this project in the spring quarter of my senior year at The Evergreen State College. Peta Henderson was my professor and I became intrigued with her projected oral history work in Belize when she discussed it in class. I explored with Peta the prospects for joining her as a research partner and she accepted my proposal. The experience was and continues to be profound for me and one for which I am very grateful.

I bring to this project a non-traditional assortment of experiences and skills. My undergraduate degree is in Women's Studies and Anthropology. I am an activist and a feminist and have gained my education as much through political work as through academic study.

My feminist and political concerns influenced and provided a strong base for my research. As an activist, I am committed to creating a world where all people have self-determination and equal access to resources and political power. I am particularly interested in supporting women in their struggles for self-determination. This interest was one of the primary reasons I wanted to do this oral history project. Oral history provides a vehicle for women to do the consciousness-raising that I believe to be necessary for collective empowerment and action. I also believe we must document and acknowledge women's lives and the contributions they made to their families and communities.

A major influence on my work has been my involvement with Safeplace, a feminist collective in Olympia, Washington, which serves survivors of sexual assault and domestic violence. Because of this work, I was especially interested in exploring the ways Belizean women define, cope with and resist abuse.

My interest in issues of abuse encouraged me to investigate the Orange Walk chapter of the national group, Belize Women Against Violence (WAV). I attended meetings, helped them paint their new office, and co-facilitated a workshop where we discussed some of the differences and similarities of doing the work in the United States and Belize. Through WAV I met three of the women represented in this book: Felicia, Sister Grace and Lotty.

I do not support many of the development and economic practices conducted in the Third World by the industrialized nations. Often such foreign policy is a thinly veiled attempt to serve the needs of the industrialised nations. The impact of global capitalism, however, is complex and may even influence an individual's life in a positive way. I was interested in discussing with Belizean women how the sugar industry and development affects their lives, both economically and socially.

Unlike Peta, I had done little academic research in anthropology previous to this project. I had completed several short-term anthropology projects in college and had gained interviewing skills through counselling classes and activities in women's groups. Additionally, Peta and I jointly developed skills in life history interviewing techniques in the months before we went to Belize. Although Peta had already developed the theoretical framework for the project before my involvement, I designed my own research plan. We did most of our fieldwork, transcribing and editing independently and collaborated on much of the final manuscript.

My inexperience led me to make many mistakes. My desire for a diverse sampling caused me to interview too many women. Several narrations lack the depth that would have resulted had I limited my scope or lengthened my stay. I was often too controlling in interviewing the women and didn't always allow them to create their own pace and structure. At times, it was difficult to strike the proper balance between listening and encouraging open discourse. I was fortunate that all the women I worked with were extremely kind and patient.

My age, class, and cultural background had an immeasurable impact on my work. I was twenty-five at the time of our original fieldwork, but could easily have passed as eighteen. Some people, especially men, did not take me seriously. As a white woman from an American middle-class background, there was never a moment when I was not perceived by Belizeans as a cultural outsider. I spent a good deal of time acquainting myself with what was common knowledge to the women of Belize. I also lacked the understanding and sensitivity that an insider would have had. One difficulty was the language barrier. All of the interviews were conducted in English because it is the only language that I speak. All the women spoke English well, but most were more comfortable conversing in Garifuna, Spanish, or Creole.

My age and background did offer some unanticipated benefits. My youth enabled me to interact with people without intimidating them. Because the women felt more at ease, they exerted a greater influence on the research process. Younger women could see me as a peer. Older women took me under their wing and treated me like a daughter who had much to learn. My youth and recent episodes of indecision and change had left me with an acute desire to understand how people form a sense of identity and determine the course of their lives. My questions and the tone of the interviews reflect this concern with personal identity as it is expressed in work and relationships.

The difference in perspective and skills that Peta and I brought to the project enhanced it. We engaged in constant dialogue over substance and method that constantly expanded my notion of what it was we were engaged in. The project was not static but continued to develop as it progressed. I am sure that this is not unique to research and may be what makes any work of this kind valuable and exciting. Nevertheless, our differences in perspective stirred the brew and helped us to maintain critical self-awareness.

I was in Belize for four months in 1988. For the first month, I lived with a family that I met through one of Peta's friends. For the remainder of my stay, I lived alone in a house rented from a woman whom I interviewed.

The women I interviewed do not reflect the diversity of women in Orange Walk. Like Peta, I deliberately sought out women of different ages, backgrounds, cultures, occupations, marital status and political views. Because Peta was primarily interviewing women in San Miguel with low incomes who worked chiefly in the home, I interviewed a disproportionate number of women who were economically better off and worked outside the home, either at paid jobs or doing volunteer work. Many "types" of women are not represented in this collection, such as prostitutes, refugees, lesbians, and women who have political views that differ widely from the norms set by the two political parties. Often the language barrier and the fear of disclosure prevented their involvement.

I met most of the women I interviewed through referrals or at meetings and social affairs. If the woman expressed an interest in becoming involved in the project, we would meet for an initial interview. During that first session, we usually talked off-tape and got to know each other. I described the project and answered any questions she had. After we reached an agreement to work together, we met several times for taping sessions that lasted anywhere from ten minutes to three hours. I did between one and six hours of taping with each woman. Between interviews, I tried to spend as much time with each woman as possible, visiting them in their homes, attending birthday and graduation parties and accompanying them to work, meetings or church. I was unable to spend much time with some women, like Bianca, because they were either too busy, or I met them late in my stay.

The interviews took place in the women's homes, within the normal context of their lives. Because the interview was a collaborative effort between myself and the women, each interview was unique. Some women were very comfortable telling their stories and I needed only to ask for an occasional clarification. Others were less comfortable and so we used a more structured question-and-answer format. In a few cases, I established a close friendship with the woman and those interviews had the give-and-take of conversations between friends.

22

In April 1991, I returned to Belize to share the edited stories with the women I had interviewed so they could make any changes they considered appropriate. I talked with seven of the nine women whose stories are included in this collection and gave each a copy of her transcript and asked her to read it at her leisure. When I visited her a few days later, we went over the transcript together. They all made changes and corrections. Some of the corrections were of minor mistakes I had made in the transcription while others were changes in content. Several women re-worded certain passages to make them clearer or to more fully express their meaning. A few of the women cut passages that were too personal, or were about other people, or contained confidential information about work or politics. Most of the women agreed with Lotty's sentiment when she said, "When you are just rambling on, sometimes you forget that other people will be reading it. There are some things in here that I want to be just between you and me – they aren't for other people to know."

Most of the women felt that the informal nature of our conversations had made them careless in their use of words and they would be "shamed" if people thought they talked that way. They made some grammatical changes to the manuscript and asked me to make their stories more "grammatically correct." Lastly, most of the women thought that it made more sense to follow a strict chronological format in retelling their stories. I complied with their requests.

Revisiting the women made the project, albeit in a limited way, more participatory. In addition, I reaffirmed that we had permission to publish their stories.

This project has increased my respect for oral history as an invaluable tool for uncovering and documenting our lives. It offers a glimpse of the day-to-day life of the narrator: her relationships, her work, her hopes, her pain. Individually, each narrative is a story of one person's life and perceptions. Collectively, the stories can be read as a community ethnography.

Oral history is often a valuable experience for the participants. Several of the women I worked with said that telling their stories was interesting and useful because it provided a forum for self-reflection. The lessons I've learned about myself and others have benefited me immeasurably.

Because of this work my notion of how best to do oral history research has changed. The women we worked with contributed the original material and had a limited editorial role: I regret that they weren't more intimately involved in the other stages. I also regret that the interviews were often one-sided: I asked the questions and the women gave the answers. In retrospect, I think that the interviews were most honest and powerful when there was an equal sharing of experiences and ideas. The one-sided nature of the process increased the power imbalance already inherent in the project due to the class and cultural differences between ourselves and the narrators.

I now think that oral history research can be more effective and accurate when all parties can participate equally from inception to interpretation. I have also come to appreciate the changes that can occur when women actively organise their own history-gathering for collective action. I am privileged to have participated in an oral history project coordinated by the Belize Rural Women's Association in August of 1988. The participants were mostly Belizean, but women from other Central American and Caribbean countries as well as the United States attended. We came from an astounding variety of backgrounds. For four days we shared stories about our lives, focusing mostly on work, relationships and health issues. The stories provided a way to discover and reflect upon the similarities and differences in our lives.

Many of the workshop participants used the information generated as a basis for individual and collective action. For example, several Belizean craftswomen discovered they shared the common experience of being underpaid by markets that sold their crafts. They decided to form a crafts collective through which they could market their own crafts. Such action is an example of what happens when there is more grassroots discussion, not merely recording, of the participants' histories.

24

The stories as they are presented in this book provide a bare outline of the rich texture of the lives of the women interviewed. The very processes that we use to research and record a culture or a person's life serve also to change and obscure that reality. The narratives in this collection are another step removed because we present them in a form that belies their origin in the interaction between two people. This presentation does not let the reader see the give-and-take of the conversation and keeps the interviewer hidden.

Nor can the reader know what surrounded the conversation: the rain dripping from the eaves, the phone ringing, or the chicken sizzling on the stove. At least the tapes were one step closer to the actual interview. You can hear the laughter, the pause when a woman tried to recollect a lost moment, or the tears when talking about a particularly painful memory. Compared to the actual lives of the women, the written transcripts sometimes seem dry and lifeless.

Despite the limitations of the format, the voice of each woman comes through with clarity and strength. I am honoured to have known some of the women whose stories are in this collection. I offer their narratives with a gladness of heart that springs from the power of shared stories.

I am exceedingly grateful to Peta Henderson for giving me the opportunity to work with her on this project. Many people have influenced and encouraged my work; in particular, I'd like to thank Kate Miller, Stephanie Coontz, Kwadwo, Kristen Onno, Arturo Aldema, Elizabeth Coe, Beth Myhr, Naomi Morris, Randy Tillery, Maggie and Peggy Hasbrouck-Lay, and Sallie Mykel. Jennifer Lewis was involved in the fieldwork in Belize and helped us with the original groundwork for the book. Steve Foote at Emory University provided much appreciated computer support. My friends and colleagues Bryan Willis, Marcia Macomber, Joanne Brown, Mary MacArthur, Christine Sarkisian, Elizabeth Rice, Shana Sniffen, Julie Seder and Harry Thomas all read sections of the book and gave me helpful feedback. I'd also like to thank the folks at the Atlanta Friends Meeting and the Beacon Hill Friends House for their support.

My family has been wonderfully supportive of me during this endeavour, and I thank them from the bottom of my heart. Vincent

Houghton-Brown has given me an immeasurable amount of editing assistance, guidance and encouragement. My parents, Pete and Gay Houghton, never lost faith in me and helped me every step of the way. My mother, who taught me to listen to and appreciate the stories that people tell about themselves, died in the spring of 1992. I would like to dedicate my portion of this book to her memory.

I'd like to thank the Paredes family and "Ana," who opened their homes to me while I was in Belize; "Lotty," who offered me her friendship and support; and the Marquis Welsh and "Charles Gordon," who helped me to get to know Belize.

Introduction
Peta Henderson

This collection of life stories of women living in the Orange Walk District of Belize is meant as a cultural text, not as a work of scientific analysis. Its goal is to aid in the recovery of the Belizean woman's past and the awareness of her present, to help in her struggles to "rise up."

Insofar as was possible, we wanted the women to tell their own stories and so we decided to use an oral history approach. This was a conscious choice on our part because we are acutely aware of the tendency in Western social science to name The Other – to objectify one group by imposing on it our category of "undeveloped," setting ourselves in opposition to it as "developed" (Minh-ha 1989:54). Not only do we impose our own categories on the people we study, but we deny their role as subjects who can generate knowledge and reflect on its importance. By focusing on women's life stories, I don't think that we have overcome this tendency. To do so would require the elimination of the distinction between U.S. interviewer and Belizean interviewee, between our role as editors and interpreters and theirs as respondents and narrators.[1] We would have to employ a more interactive model than the interview, one which incorporates ourselves as subjects into the research.

There are nonetheless several reasons for employing oral history as a tool in critical and feminist research. It is by now a truism that Western social science has limited its range of vision to the more easily objectifiable and public arenas of human social action and discourse, arenas that more often than not have excluded women. It is not just women who have been excluded but the whole spectrum of gendered social relations in which all social beings, both male and

27

female, are involved. Such relations involve areas of life often ignored by traditional research, particularly the exercise of informal power in such non-public settings as the family and the formation of gender identity. At least two reasons exist for this absence of a focus on gender: 1) the exercise of informal power and domination is less amenable to "scientific" investigation than institutionalized power; 2) the dynamics of these relations seem to be more clearly revealed in the stories of women than of men, but women's stories have, until quite recently, been ignored (Personal Narratives Group 1989:4).

Oral history can illuminate the effects of relations between the individual and the larger socio-cultural context. Life stories may be viewed as valuable information about the dynamics of relations of power and domination seen from the bottom up. With the tape-recorded life history as our primary data, we can gain an understanding of women's situation, of their cultural categories for grasping that situation and of their responses to it. Whether these responses are adaptive or resistant, they represent important information about how the system operates on the individual within particular social and cultural contexts.

Furthermore, the act of telling their life stories can help to empower women by making them conscious of themselves as historical actors who make decisions, set strategies, cope, and sometimes resist the dominant cultural rules. In this respect, oral history may be seen as an agency for change as well as a research tool (Gluck and Patai 1991). The Belize Rural Women's Association has used the oral history method successfully in training women to become community leaders. Women in the villages where the BRWA is active find solidarity in collective storytelling.

But the oral history method is necessarily limited. It gives clues to the lives and world views of individuals who live within a particular cultural setting. As editors, we see a need to provide a wider context for situating the individual stories. Therefore, the balance of this introduction is devoted first to an analysis of the cultural rules which guide the behaviour of men and women – what I call the "gender context" – and then to an account of the historical context of economic and political changes affecting families living in the

Orange Walk District. In the conclusion that follows the stories, we offer our interpretation of some of the patterns that emerge from the stories.

In providing a context for editing and interpreting these stories we had four goals. First, by publishing this book in a form that is readily accessible to a general Belizean audience, we want to acknowledge Belizean women's contribution to their families and society and to support the personal and political struggles described in these testimonies. With humour and pain, women told us of the lengths they were forced to go to feed their children, please their husbands and achieve their personal goals. Many of those we interviewed do not have the benefit yet of the collective energy and support offered by such groups as the Belize Rural Women's Association. They tend to individualize their experiences and problems. But each in her own way has done what was necessary to survive and to oppose gender-based oppression. Although these stories represent only a small sample of Belizean women's experience, we think that the histories of these "heroes of their own lives" will help others to remember that they are not alone.

Second, we wanted to present a coherent story of each woman's life, emphasizing the key events and aspects that animated her most. Each life is unique, even while framed by a common socio-cultural system. By choosing to edit the texts as whole life stories rather than fragmenting them into themes or topics, we assert the integrity and importance of each woman's experience and of her account of that experience.

But individuals do not exist in a vacuum: they are constrained by cultural rules, symbols and customs, by their history and by their material environment. It is often more difficult for women than for men to transgress cultural values that dictate appropriate behaviour. Therefore, as our third goal we wanted to understand how Belizean women have experienced and responded to the cultural rules that dictate what men and women should do, and how they should relate to each other. We wanted to see to what extent these women's lives do or do not conform to accepted customs and norms governing gender behaviour, and to understand their strategies for accommodating and resisting such rules.

In addition to the cultural context, there is a broader framework of institutions and power relations extending from the local community outwards to the international political economy. As our fourth goal, we wanted to understand how the development of the Belizean sugar industry and related changes in the global political economy have affected women's lives and how women view these influences from the outside world. In his book *Sweetness and Power,* Sidney Mintz points out how dependent the industrial world became on agricultural products of the New World and "the significance of a colonial product like sugar in the growth of capitalism" (Mintz 1985:xxix). But it was precisely the industrializing world's dependence on the contributions of the colonies that brought on a whole set of power relations between social classes – between wealthy slaveholders and slaves, between absentee corporations with huge landholdings and factories and small farmers or wage labourers. These power relations continue in the present even though Belize is no longer formally a colony.

In the process of interviewing and editing, we have become acutely aware of the extent of our own intervention in the production of the stories. In the prefaces, we have each said something about our personal biases and motivations and our relationships with the women. We acknowledge that all interviews involve an interaction between the interviewer and the respondent and that the very questions we asked tilted the balance in certain directions. Differences of culture, class, education, age and a host of other factors influenced what they told us. The research design reinforced those differences. A power differential is inherent in a project in which the product belongs to the researchers and not to the producers of knowledge. This is a dilemma that feminist researchers are beginning to discuss and to confront in a variety of ways (Gluck and Patai 1991; Personal Narratives Group 1989).

We have come to believe that oral history can best serve the purpose of personal and political organization when women are encouraged to talk to each other, rather than to an outside researcher or trained professional. They can help each other link such private concerns as domestic abuse and poor access to health care or employment with such public purposes as political education and legislative action. The recognition of shared experience is a powerful impetus to solidarity between women across ethnic, racial and class barriers and is essential for a class-based feminist action.

We were not looking for particular information. Instead, we wanted the women to tell their stories freely and in their own ways and hoped that common themes and experiences would emerge later. The format of the book follows this process – we have left our interpretation of what we found to the end, rather than trying to direct the reader's attention to specific aspects of the women's stories. We used a broad topical and chronological guide to help frame the interviews (Jacobs et al. 1988:22-24), but as time went on we increasingly diverged from it, preferring to let the woman determine content and chronology. The tape-recorder and the camera were our only equipment.

In the process of editing these histories, we used the same non-directive format. We did not try to analyze themes before editing, nor to edit the stories around a predetermined set of topics. First we made a full word-for-word transcription of each taped interview, providing as literal a rendering as possible.

The need for translating most of my interviews presented other difficulties. Financial and time constraints made it impossible to translate the entire texts, so I did a preliminary edit of the Spanish texts before translation. I also got help from "Celia" in "San Miguel" when local idioms were in question. Inevitably, much of the rhythm and pattern of local speech was lost in the translation. Although we decided to publish the book in English because the larger Belizean and North American audience is English-speaking, I would like to think that some day a Spanish version might be possible.

We edited the narratives keeping in mind our goal to produce a coherent life story for each woman. Within the broad framework of the project goals, we selected those ideas and experiences that interested the narrator or illustrated aspects of historical and contemporary trends as we understood them. In the process of editing, we re-ordered portions of the texts to clarify chronology or to eliminate duplication. We also cut repetitive phrases and words which inevitably appear in oral speech but interfere with the flow of a written text. Where necessary, we added qualifying words or phrases in parentheses, as transitions or clarifications. Since we had assured each woman of confidentiality, we assigned pseudonyms and altered place names, except for Orange Walk Town.

Finally, we read and discussed the edited texts to elicit common ideas and themes for an interpretive conclusion. We agreed on the need for comments from as many of the women as possible. Therefore, in January 1991, Bryn returned to Belize to seek reactions to her edited texts from the women she had interviewed in English. She successfully contacted most of them and after her return she re-edited the narratives to include their suggestions. Since all but one of my interviews had been translated, it was not possible for me to do the same.

We cannot assert that the stories are in any sense "representative" of the range of female experience in Belize or even of the region where we worked. We did not try for a scientific sample. What is striking, however, is the evidence that women are undergoing very similar contradictions and continuities in their daily lives.

The Gender Context

Most of the women whose stories are told here are descendants of Maya and Mestizo peoples who moved into what was British Honduras from the Yucatan in the mid 19th century. They are therefore influenced by the cultural model of gender relationships which resulted from this blending of indigenous Maya and Spanish traditions. Other cultural traditions are also represented: two of the women, Miss Bird and Lotty, are Garifuna, the descendants of Afro-Amerindians from the island of St. Vincent; two, Sister Grace and Amelia, are Creoles, the descendants of African slaves brought to the colony to work in the lumber industry.

All cultures have rules for ensuring the survival of the population and society. This means that they must regulate production to ensure an adequate subsistence and also regulate reproduction to ensure biological survival and the perpetuation of the society. In all cultures, this involves some kind of division of labour by sex, dictating that men and women should play different, complementary roles, at least in some areas of life. Social and biological reproduction are also accomplished through customs surrounding marriage or other types of union and through moral prescriptions regulating sexuality. Since women are the child-bearers, they are often the sex that is regulated most strictly by these cultural rules.

There is, in other words, an ideal model of how the woman (and to a lesser extent the man) should behave. This is not to say that most people's experience conforms in all respects to the ideal gender model. Nor does it imply that, because they grow up within a cultural system of shared meanings, people accept the system without question. One of the interesting aspects of the women's stories is the evidence that women find ingenious and appropriate ways to resist the cultural expectations placed on them as daughters, wives and mothers.

Traditional gender rules, then, lay down a model of the ideal relationship between men and women with respect to work, household management, marriage, sexuality, childbearing and rearing, and personal behaviour. In the rural Belizean household which I have observed since 1968, the fundamental dynamic of the household is the division of labour between a woman and a man in marital or common-law union, supplemented by the contributions of children and adults of both sexes who live there. Marriage involves the notion of a contract between the man and the woman by which he is ideally responsible for maintaining her and their children, in return for which she owes him personal services: washing his clothes, serving his meals and taking care of their children. Sexual fidelity is enjoined on the woman more than on the man, at least in practice, if not in theory.

In the northern villages, under the traditional rural household system based on *milpa* – now almost destroyed by the dominance of sugar cane production – the economic relationship between men and women was basically cooperative and interdependent. Men produced the crops and were primarily responsible for harvesting and transporting them to the home. Then the woman took over, converting them into food for people and animals, or for local sale so she could purchase other things she needed. Most women in the traditional household, just as most men, were involved in some way in the cash economy, as reflected in many of the stories of village women (Magdalena, Cristina, Amelia, Clara, Estella, Susanna). Women would sell cooked food, or provide services to other households, including washing clothes, cleaning, grinding corn or making tortillas. Some would run small stores. Although the division of labour was clear-cut, some tasks were shared by both sexes: both men and women, for example, gathered firewood and shelled corn.

In this traditional household, both men and women made decisions affecting their own spheres of authority. The man made the decisions about the *milpa*, although women participated in discussions and were intimately acquainted with the details of *milpa* location and activity (Stavrakis 1979:163). In the household, the woman had authority with respect to food and animals, often making crucial decisions about how to spend the money since she was the one who knew what was needed in the household. Each sex had a high degree of autonomy in his or her own sphere of production.

Since sugar cane production replaced the *milpa* as the dominant means of making a living, men's work roles have changed quite radically. They have had to participate in new forms of partnership and cooperation beyond the immediate kin group, and the pattern of their work life has been adapted to the alternation of *zafra* and "dead season." But the changes have affected women's roles less than we might expect, although some women also own cane licenses and fields. In the household, the traditional clear-cut division of labour has remained virtually intact, except where store-bought food has replaced the products of the *milpa*. More important, the advent of sugar cane has in some respects served to reinforce male dominance in the household, since in most cases it is the males who generally control the income from sugar cane.

In the northern villages, the culture ascribes a dominant role to the man *(el hombre manda)*: the woman is viewed as dependent on her father or husband, the man as having authority *(poder)* over her. In general, the man is believed to have a proprietary right over his wife's or partner's sexuality and over that of his daughters until marriage. Great importance is still attached to the woman's virginity at marriage. Once she reaches puberty, her activities are carefully chaperoned to ensure that she has no opportunity to be alone with young men. Although, of course, the reality is that young women "fall," as Gloria puts it, and as Susanna found with her daughter, the cultural ideal is still in force.

At marriage the woman is passed from the "power" of her father to that of her husband, who is interested in ensuring that the children she bears are his. Therefore, following marriage, the woman is obliged to ask her husband's permission to leave the home or, at a minimum, to inform him of her plans. The man accepts no reciprocal restrictions on his activity, however, and "outside" liaisons, including children, are not uncommon (Magdalena, Estella, Juanita). Great importance is also attached to the husband's recognition of the children, for if he denies paternity of a child, it is taken as rejection of his obligation to support the mother and child with provisions, clothes, etc. Therefore, the woman dare not risk even the suspicion of an affair by disobeying her husband, unless she is willing to risk losing his material support. Refusal to admit paternity appeared among some of the women I interviewed (Juanita, Magdalena) and may be associated with the difficulties some men have in supporting their families adequately under changed conditions.

Today, many women, especially those living in the towns, no longer live in traditional households on the model described above. Increasingly, urban women and some younger women living in the villages (Gloria, Gabriela) are taking jobs outside the home and sometimes they bring home more money than their husbands. But even where they have outside employment, this does not necessarily result in a change in the fundamental cultural rule of male dominance within the marriage and the household (Ana, Rachel). It is also true that many women live at some time in female-headed households (Susanna, Miss Bird), although this is more common among the Creole in Belize City and the Garifuna in Dangriga than among the Maya-Mestizo of Orange Walk.[2] Even so, according to a survey conducted in 1986, the ideal type of union in Dangriga and Belize City is still marriage (Government of Belize, Ministry of Health 1986:12,20).

Thus, it seems that two apparently contradictory cultural models co-exist in gender relationships. In her productive life under the traditional *milpa* system, or in "modern" households where she is employed outside the home, the woman has a relatively equal role and considerable practical autonomy. However, in her reproductive life, her sexuality is carefully controlled and she is viewed less as partner than as dependent. In practice, as we will see, there is great variability in male-female relationships, depending on many factors, including the age of the woman, the personality of the husband and, above all, his ability to provide for the family. Despite the Roman Catholic emphasis on marriage and the Church's prohibition of divorce, many men and women engage in more than one union.

Childbearing and childrearing play a central role in a woman's life after marriage, especially in the villages. The cultural expectation (at least among the Catholic population, which is sixty-two percent of the total population of Belize) is that a woman will bear as many children as God gives her; if she does not, she is considered to be impoverished. Artificial birth control has played little part until recently in women's reproductive strategies. In the villages, families of ten or more children are not unusual; two of the women I interviewed had given birth to seventeen children each (Amelia and Cristina), although not all were living. Obviously this places a tremendous physical burden on the mother over many years.

Statistical data suggests that these patterns are changing especially among younger, more educated and urban couples. In the 1986 Government survey, the number of children per mother/guardian was 9.9 in rural Orange Walk (Government of Belize, Ministry of Health 1986:12a). The same survey revealed that only just over a quarter of the women in rural Orange Walk were using some method of contraception (Government of Belize, Ministry of Health 1986:24d). However, among younger couples, especially the more educated and better-off couples in the town where the woman is employed outside the home (Lotty, Bianca and Ana), fewer children are being born. The total national fertility rate for women with secondary education or higher was 3.5, compared to 5.6 for women with a primary school education or less (Caricom 1985:48). Fertility rates in Belize have been relatively high, although declining in recent years. In 1960, the crude birth rate was 44.3 per 1,000 population; between 1980 and 1985, it fell sharply from 43.1 to 36.0 (Roberts 1987:1). Thus, there is some reason to believe that Belizean women are slowly gaining control of their fertility and this is likely to have far-reaching implications for the gender balance of power.

Historical Context

In the Orange Walk District where we worked, most people are the descendants of Yucatecan Maya-Mestizo people and of earlier Maya populations, indigenous to the region.[3] There are also smaller populations of Creole, Garifuna and Asians, mostly living in the towns.[4] The Creoles first came to the area as slaves or contracted labourers in the mahogany and logwood industry. After the decline of this industry in the early 20th century, some Creole families settled in the area to work the sugar cane. For example, Amelia's husband first came to the village with his uncle as a boy; when he grew up he worked alongside his uncle as a member of a logging crew. He later stayed, first cutting cane on the sugar company's plantations and then acquiring his own cane smallholding when he decided the Company was taking advantage of him. They are one of only two Creole families living in "San Miguel." The Garifuna are more recent arrivals from the south. Many, like Miss Bird, were attracted to Orange Walk by the opportunities created by the sugar industry in the sixties and seventies.

Unlike the Creoles and Garifuna, the Maya were not initially a regular part of the territory's labour force. They were considered unsuitable for hard labour in the lumber camps because they were less easily controlled than the Creoles and Garifuna, being well-adapted to subsistence living in the dense forests of the west. Only in the twentieth century have Indian men been incorporated in large numbers into the labour force, first, like Don Gaspar and Ana's father, as contracted labour in the chicle and caoba camps, then as cane cutters on the sugar plantations.

For most rural Mayan women, colonialism was mediated by the economic and cultural system based on *milpa* farming which kept them close to home. This is not to say that they did not undergo the racism and exploitation characteristic of British colonialism, but they were less directly exposed than Creole and Garifuna women to the effects of slavery and indentured labour.

For centuries women had participated actively in the dominant cultural system based on *milpa*. As Allan Burns notes, for the Yucatecan Maya the *milpa* is "a symbol of Mayan identity. Corn farming is not a mere commercial activity for Mayan people but is a way of life based on a sacred and fulfilling tradition" (1983:8). Besides providing the staple dietary item, corn is central to the language, religious symbolism and gender relationships of *milpa*-based societies. The making of tortillas is still the quintessential female activity. In addition, as Burns notes, "corn unites men and women" in a clear-cut and complementary division of labour.

In a brief ethnological introduction to Thomas Gann's archaeological survey of Maya sites in what was then Northern British Honduras, published in 1918, he provides a first-hand description of women's work at the turn of the century:

> The women are very industrious, rising usually at 3 or 4 o'clock in the morning to prepare the day's supply of tortillas or corn cake. During the day they prepare tobacco (kutz) and make cigarettes; gather cotton (taman), which they spin (kuch), weave (sakal), and embroider for garments; weave mats of palm leaf and baskets (kush) of a variety of liana (ak); make pottery (ul), and cotton and henequen cord, of which they construct hammocks (kan).
>
> In addition to these tasks they do the family cooking and washing, look after the children, and help their husbands to attend to the animals. Till late at night the women may be seen spinning, embroidering, and hammock-making by the light of a native candle or a small earthenware cuhoon-nut oil lamp, meanwhile laughing and chatting gaily over the latest village scandal, the

older ones smoking cigarettes, while the men squat about on the low wooden stools outside the house gravely discussing the weather, the *milpas*, the hunting, or the iniquities of the Alcalde. (Gann 1918:17)

The way of life described by Gann in 1918 would persist to some degree for another half-century, but the roots of its destruction had already been planted in the fertile soil of the northern region. The Yucatecan Mestizos who entered the territory began to rent land, producing sugar cane and more traditional crops. Although sugar cane production was very small-scale and inefficient, it nonetheless quickly showed promise as a profitable cash crop. The success of these plantations, together with the decline of the forest products industry after mid-century, led to a reorganization and consolidation of landholdings. Large, often foreign and absentee-owned, sugar plantations began to supplant the Mestizo family-owned ranches and depended on the Indians as a labour force, drawing on the populations of settled villages on a seasonal basis (Bolland and Shoman 1977).

One of such was the village I am calling "San Miguel" (Ayuso 1987:3). Since Indians were denied the legal right to own land in the colony, they gradually came to depend on the plantations for wage labour to supplement the product of their *milpas*.

By the 1950s, sugar had replaced forestry products as the major export. The event that most directly affected the lives of the people in the Orange Walk District was the construction in 1967 – one year before my first stay in the village – of the modern Tower Hill cane-processing factory near Orange Walk Town by the English multinational, Tate and Lyle (Belize Sugar Industries, Ltd.). In conjunction with the construction of Tower Hill, the Government provided incentives for families in the local villages to plant cane through a programme of loans and the distribution of blocks of land, on the condition that the latter were planted in permanent crops and not used for shifting agriculture. At first the Company relied on its own plantations for fifty percent of the cane processed at the factory, but in 1974, as its cane became old and uneconomical to harvest, it sold the plantations to private cane farmers. Since that year, BSI has relied on local farmers for all of the cane it milled, including families in "San Miguel" and Orange Walk Town with whom we worked.

These changes in land-use struck at the very heart of the cultural system based on the *milpa* and hence at traditional gender roles and relations. They signalled the transformation of the Maya into commercial farmers dependent on the international market and vulnerable to its fluctuations (Henderson 1990).

The women whose stories are presented here have all been affected in one way or another by the changes thus set in motion. In the villages, although in many ways the rhythm of daily life continued to centre on washing, cooking and childrearing, new opportunities presented themselves. During the *zafra* some women began to supplement the household income by providing assistance to migrant cane workers in the village, cooking their meals and washing their clothes. Without corn and other *milpa* crops, they were forced to depend less on livestock and more on store-bought food.

In the towns, new opportunities arose for employment outside the home, upsetting traditional gender arrangements. In Orange Walk Town, a middle class of entrepreneurs (Marta, Bianca), service employees (Ana) and educators (Sister Grace, Lotty) emerged from the former colonial two-class system of propertied and non-propertied. All were responding to the opportunities created by the sugar industry and the opening of the factory. Some families experienced considerable upward mobility with the high cane prices of the seventies, sending their children to high school (Marta, Ana, Lotty, Gloria) and even to college in the United States (Ana, Lotty). In some cases, families of the larger cane farmers moved from local villages into town to take advantage of new services and resources (Rachel; see also Stavrakis 1979:144).

Socio-economic differences also began to emerge in the villages as some wealthy cane farmers built large houses or invested in expensive cane loaders, tractor-trailers and trucks. In this realignment of living patterns by class, the industry also attracted Garifuna and Creole families from Belize City and southern Belize to the town, and an underclass of migrant seasonal labourers from Guatemala and El Salvador to the villages.

In the 1980s, two new factors came into play. First was recession in the sugar industry, referred to in several of the women's stories. Just as people had begun to expect that sugar prices would continue indefinitely to increase, the world market price for sugar plummeted. Between 1980 and 1981, the price per ton of cane dropped from $65 to around $35 BZ. Families which were already indebted found themselves in worse straits as prices fell. Production levels began to decline. Cane fields were left untended for lack of money to pay the necessary labour. In 1986, BSI closed the Libertad factory in the Corozal District, laying off most of its workforce there. There was an across-the-board reduction in the number of tons each individual was licensed to deliver to Tower Hill, and those who had been unable to meet their license quotas in previous years had further reductions (Cristina, Amelia). Migrant farm labourers ceased to come to the area, causing hardship to local families who were accustomed to earning a little extra by cooking meals for them or washing their clothes (Susanna, Estella). The loss of this business, combined with the inability of village residents to pay their accounts, caused Susanna to close her shop for several years. Farmers, who in the halcyon days had purchased tractors and pick-ups and built houses, found themselves scrambling for a piece of land on which to plant corn. Competition and conflict replaced the former cooperative division of land for *milpa*.

The effects of the recession spread to the town, where most businesses were dependent in some way on the sugar industry. Many young people found migration to the U.S. their only recourse; many made the journey without papers and were forced to take jobs at the minimum wage or below. Some went to study and have remained there because jobs for high school and college graduates in Belize are scarce. There are few families who do not have at least one member living in the U.S. and, like many other families in the Third World, many Belizean families are dependent on remittances from relatives in the U.S.

Even when cane prices recovered after 1987, families have been reluctant to return to their former total dependence on sugar cane. Efforts are being made to diversify. But even where families have been able to find a piece of land for planting corn, the ancient system of cultural and ecological relationships surrounding the *milpa* has been destroyed. How women have experienced these changes will become apparent through their own stories.

The women's stories should also be understood in the context of the politics of the post-independence era and the growing influence of the United States. Belize achieved political independence from Britain in 1981. The British legacy of two-party politics divides regions, communities, social classes and ethnic groups and inhibits effective coalitions based on class or other common interest. The two major parties, the People's United Party (PUP) and the United Democratic Party (UDP) have perpetuated the patronage system that existed in the colonial era. Villages or districts that elect a council which supports the party in power are rewarded with electricity, water pipes, parks, or other perks. Party affiliation in the local communities, such as "San Miguel," may determine access to land for growing subsistence crops. Although many women abstain from party politics, others are becoming actively involved in public life. Susanna is treasurer of the local branch of the UDP in "San Miguel" and Felicia is the deputy mayor of Orange Walk Town.

It is not the British, but the Americans who have become the real power in Belize since Independence, despite the continued presence of the British Army. Given the turmoil in the rest of Central America, Belize offers an attractive opportunity for a U.S. presence. The U.S. Agency for International Development (USAID) established itself in the country in 1983 and maintains an elaborate and well-guarded embassy in Belize City; the more modest Peace Corps office is adjacent to it. Between 1983 and 1987, Belize received $62.7 million US from USAID, second only to El Salvador in the per capita amount of aid received. A growing proportion of this is military aid (Barnett and Shoman, 1988).

Unfortunately, Belize has also become a trans-shipment point for the U.S. drug market, causing an increase in drug-related violence and deaths in Orange Walk and the surrounding areas.

The U.S. influence is most directly felt by local families in the pocket book. The U.S. participates in a quota system, by which it agrees to purchase a certain amount of Belizean sugar at a price above the world market rate. Through its effect on price and demand for cane, its ability to manipulate the Belizean sugar quota has immediate economic implications for all who are involved in the industry. This has ripple effects throughout the non-agricultural service sector, especially in Orange Walk Town. In 1984, Belize's share in the global U.S. market was reduced by 5,000 tons over the previous year, despite the pleadings of a delegation of cane farmers who travelled to Washington, D.C. in August (Cane Farmers' Association, December 16, 1984). The U.S. again reduced its sugar quota for the year 1985-86 (Cane Farmers' Association 1985-86). In short, the U.S. economic policy of price supports for agricultural commodities has a major and immediate impact on the families we interviewed.

The U.S. influence in Belize is not simply economic: it is also more subtly felt, penetrating the society and culture at multiple levels, provoking complex and ambivalent responses. On the one hand, there are direct benefits from U.S.-funded community development programmes. Such projects as a village latrine construction programme, an infant immunization programme and health education for mothers are funded by USAID and administered by CARE. Gabriela is employed as a community health organiser by CARE and Cristina's daughter is a health volunteer in the village.

On the other hand, there is also awareness of a humiliating and unsettling cultural dependence. North American evangelical Protestant ideologies compete with media-generated sexual imagery to undermine traditional cultural understanding. Even in the villages that are not yet electrified, many families have acquired a TV set which they operate on their truck or pick-up batteries. Although Mexican soaps tend to be more popular than U.S. programming among Spanish-speaking villagers, in the town the daily network news is filtered through the Turner Cable Network. Commercials exhort the people to buy everything from cars to recliner chairs (800 numbers are included for convenience and you are welcome to use your credit card). My family's favourite entertainment is the hype and drama of professional wrestling.

The system of education in particular promotes ideological identification with the U.S. on the part of grass-roots community leaders, women as well as men. USAID offers summer seminars in the U.S. to high school and primary school principals. Scholarship programmes bring hundreds of Belizeans to the U.S. for study. Both Lotty and her husband received scholarships to go to the States to work on their degrees, although they were married with a child. Lotty now teaches at an Orange Walk high school. Much of the primary and secondary school education in Belize is delivered through a system of government subsidies to the churches. Many church leaders have been educated or trained in the U.S. Sister Grace studied for her novitiate in Rhode Island and is now the manager of a high school as well as a teacher. The humiliation of U.S. cultural dominance was perhaps most keenly felt when, in 1986, a relatively obscure college in Michigan, Ferris State College, was made the degree-granting institution for University College of Belize. The controversial restructuring of the system of higher education reinforced the awareness of national dependence on Big Brother to the north, although the association with Ferris College has been terminated.

Much is in flux now in Belize. Women, as well as men, face a plethora of contradictions and choices in their daily lives. Images of women on TV, of peroxide blonds in illicit sexual relationships, are so much at variance with both the cultural expectations and experiences of the average young Belizean woman that we wonder how she can assimilate them. Women opting for education, careers and birth control face conflicting cultural demands and expectations. For some, the irony is that in the midst of so much change, so little has changed.

The Stories
There are many ways to think about the interconnections between the stories. Life histories are inherently difficult to categorize because they touch on most areas of human experience and overlap at many points. Not unexpectedly, gender roles and relations are central to all the stories, cross-cutting other aspects of the women's

lives. Our arrangement is somewhat arbitrary and means to provide structure without predetermining the reader's response to each woman.

The stories are divided into two sections, Women's Work and Continuity and Change. All women work hard in their lives: the primary distinction is between those who work primarily in the home and those who work outside the home in various capacities – as volunteers, politicians, teachers, health workers and business-women. The second section is organized differently. Since we interviewed three generations of one rural Maya family and a Garifuna mother and daughter living in the town, we have juxtaposed their stories to illustrate continuity and change in experiences and attitudes between the generations. This arrangement also highlights class and ethnic differences.

And now it's time for the women to tell their stories.

---

1. For recent in-depth discussions of these issues of narrative and interpretive authority, see Gluck and Patai (1991:59-106) and Personal Narratives Group (1989:201-258).

2. In Orange Walk, ninety-seven percent of household types were classified as male-headed, compared to just over sixty-three percent in Belize and sixty-nine percent in Dangriga (Government of Belize, Ministry of Health 1986:12a, Table 2.3).

3. Although the contemporary residents of this region trace their ancestry to the Yucatecan Maya-Mestizo migrants who moved southwards during the War of the Castes in 1847, the original inhabitants were descended from more ancient Maya groups. The site of Nohmul, about ten miles from Orange Walk, shows evidence of continuous settlement from around 200 A.D. to 1100 A.D. (Hammond 1982:104,143). However, there are gaps in the record both before and after the Spanish Conquest of the New World. By the 18th century, they were probably much decimated by disease, but "those Maya who remained in Belize by the 18th century probably lived in small politically independent villages in the west of what are now Cayo and Orange Walk Districts" (Bolland 1988:14). For as long as possible, they kept out of the way of the English, retreating to the west. But as loggers encroached further they resisted, attacking white settlements with some success (Bolland 1988:93).

4. Creole and Garifuna represented approximately 11% of the population of the Orange Walk District in the 1980 Census (Caricom 1985, Volume 2, Table 7.2.1:350).

REFERENCES

Ayuso, Mateo

1987   "The Role of the Maya-Mestizo in the Development of 'Belize,' 200 B.C. to 1984". Society for the Promotion of Education and Research (SPEAR), *Belize, Ethnicity and Development,* Papers presented at the First Annual Studies on Belize Conference, University Centre, May 25-26, 1987, Belize City, Belize, Central America.

Barnett, Carla, and Assad Shoman

1988   "Belize In Central America and the Caribbean: Peace, Development and Integration. Where Does Belize Fit In?" Paper presented at Conference: *Belize in the Caribbean and Central America - Peace, Development and Integration*, Society for the Promotion of Education and Research, (SPEAR), June 24-26, 1988, Belize City.

Bolland, O. Nigel

1984   *Belize: A New Nation in Central America,* Boulder, Colorado: Westview.

1988   *Colonialism and Resistance in Belize: Essays in Historical Sociology.* Benque Viejo del Carmen, Belize: Cubola Productions.

Bolland, O. Nigel, and Assad Shoman

1977   *Land in Belize: 1765-1871: The Origins of Land Tenure, Use and Distribution in a Dependent Economy.* Mona: Institute of Social and Economic Research, University of the West Indies.

Burns, Allan F.,

1983   *An Epoch of Miracles: Oral Literature of the Yucatec Maya,* translated with commentaries by Allan F. Burns. Foreword by Dennis Tedlock, Austin, University of Texas Press.

Cane Farmers' Association
1984   Report of the Annual General Meeting, December 16, 1984.
1985   Chairman's Report, Belize Cane Farmers' Association, Or-
-86   ange Walk District Division, for the year 1985-1986.

Caricom
1985   *1980-1981 Population Census of the Commonwealth Caribbean. Belize.* Volumes 2 and 3.

Gann, Thomas William Francis
1918   *The Maya Indians of Southern Yucatan and Northern British Honduras.* Washington, D.C., Government Printing Office.

Gluck, Sherna Berger and Daphne Patai *(eds.)*
1991   *Women's Words; The Feminist Practice of Oral History.* New York: Routledge, Chapman and Hall, Inc.

Government of Belize, Ministry of Health in Collaboration with UNFPA
1986   *Knowledge, Attitudes and Practices: Survey on Family Life and Fertility in Belize.* University of the West Indies, Department of Extra Mural Studies, Belize.

Hammond, Norman
1982   *Ancient Maya Civilization.* New Brunswick: Rutgers University Press.

Henderson, Peta
1990   "Development and Dependency in a Belizean Village". Society for the Promotion of Education and Research (SPEAR), *Slavery and Freedom in Belize: Yesterday and Today,* Papers Presented at the Second Annual Studies on Belize Conference, University Centre, October 14-16, 1988, Belize City, Belize, Central America.

1972　"A Sugar *Usina* in British Honduras. In H. Russell Bernard and Pertti Pelto, (eds), *Technology and Social Change*. New York: Macmillan.

1969　"The Context of Economic Choice in the Rural Sugar-Growing Area of British Honduras". McGill University, unpublished Master's Thesis.

Jacobs, Sue-Ellen et al. (eds.)
1982　*A Handbook for Life History research.* Seattle: Washington Women's Heritage Project at the University of Washington.

Jones, Grant D.
1969　*Los Caneros: Sociopolitical Aspects of the History of Agriculture in the Corozal Region of British Honduras.* Brandeis University, unpublished Ph.D. dissertation.
1971　*The Politics of Agricultural Development in Northern British Honduras,* Winston-Salem: Wake Forest University.

Mintz, Sidney
1985　*Sweetness and Power: the Place of Sugar in Modern History.* New York: Penguin.

Personal Narratives Group
1989　*Interpreting Women's Lives: Feminist Theory and Personal Narratives.* Bloomington: Indiana University Press.

Roberts, S.A.
1987　"Recent Demographic Trends in Belize". Society for the Promotion of Education and Research (SPEAR), *Belize, Ethnicity and Development,* Papers presented at the First Annual Studies on Belize Conference, University Centre, May 25-26, 1987, Belize City, Belize, Central America.

Romney, D.H. ed.

1959   *Land In British Honduras: Report of the British Honduras Land Use Survey Team.* London, H.M. Stationery Office. Colonial Research Publications, No. 24.

Shoman, Assad

1987   *Party Politics in Belize.* Benque Viejo del Carmen, Belize: Cubola Productions.

Stavrakis, Olga

1979   *The Effect of Agricultural Change Upon Social Relations and Diet in A Village in Northern Belize, Central America.* University of Minnesota, unpublished Ph.D. dissertation.

Topsey, Harriot

1980   "The Role of Women in Maya Society". *Network: the Journal of Belizean Women,* Vol. 1, No. 1:14-17.

Part I

WOMEN'S WORK

HOME WORKERS

Cristina

Cristina was born in 1946. She is the mother of fourteen children and lives with her husband and younger children.

I was born in Alvaro Obregon (Mexico). When I was born I was the only one because my parents had more children, but they died and I was the only one left. And so they loved me a lot because I was the only one. They say that food was scarce and so the people had to go work elsewhere. Now, my grandfather left and went to Obregon with his wife and my father went over there – that is where he found my mother, in Obregon.

They got married there. That is where I was born, I believe, because there was work. They worked there. There was work cutting caoba for a Company called Mengel – they say it was an American company. The place wasn't called Obregon. It was called Mengel because the company that was working there was called Mengel. Well, they worked, cutting caoba. They say that the Company was robbing a lot of high Mexican bush. The fields were Mexican. And so the government didn't like it and went to move the Company – they didn't like it because it wasn't benefiting Mexico. They would cut it and take it mostly for export. And so the government kicked that Company out.

They say that all the Belizeans that came to Mengel – when they saw that the company had left – decided to stay because they were only workers. But they saw there was a place to live – even land. To this day there is land. They began to work and some who became nationalized Mexicans stayed. My father didn't like it because he also wanted them to give him some land, but he couldn't get any. That is why he brought us here. (I was) nine years old.

I grew up very poor. When we came here it was hard. And so my father began to work so he could support us because there was myself and my sister, Marta. Since he didn't have his own land he had to work for others. Well, at that time they say that cane was beginning. They were cutting cane. There was the factory at Libertad. In those days they used to cut cane by the ton. One ton, two tons, five tons. The truck could only carry five tons, but they would cut like that by the ton. Sometimes the poor man could only cut one ton and they would only pay one dollar per ton. And when he had to cut that ton, there were times when he wouldn't arrive home until two o'clock. But no matter, the poor man – perhaps he would earn a dollar or sometimes not – but he would be there all day working.

I and my sister and my mother would stay home. My poor mother had to work for other people, washing clothes and making tortillas. It was worse when Hurricane Janet came in 1955. I was nine when it came. Well, we were left without a house. The house fell down and my poor father had to struggle to build another house. And we didn't have any money. My father was alone; he had no help. There was nobody to help him work, just him. My grandparents were poor. They couldn't help him.

My mother had her animals, but who knows why. The poor woman always had to sell them. Sometimes she'd sell them to buy sugar, lard, milk for the baby; and that's how the money went. Out of the little that my poor father earned, sometimes we would get beans, lard, and maybe once a week we would eat rice on Sunday. Or flour. But all week long we ground corn. We had to grind in that (hand) mill because there was no (mechanical) mill like there is today. None. Nothing but grinding. Every day from the time you woke up early in the morning you would wash the *nixtamal* and begin grinding. As soon as you finished, you would begin making tortillas and then eat. If you didn't have corn, you didn't eat because you were not going to say, "Go get the money and go buy flour." There was no money.

And that's the way it was. But now there isn't poverty. Before there was. That was how my poor mother and father managed. That's how I grew up: without the necessities. We would buy one egg for all of us. We would divide it in little pieces—one egg—and an egg only cost five cents. But we couldn't buy very much because there was no money.

My mother would have a baby every year. Every year. She only breast-fed me for five months. After that she didn't give me any because she was pregnant again. After a year, another baby was already crying, another child. Well, that child didn't survive and died, and again she became pregnant. And the same every year, every year she had a child. There are ten living children. Three dead and three miscarriages.

My mother would remain pregnant by God's grace. She didn't know what tonic was; she didn't know what a doctor was; she didn't know what it was to go to someone who could cure her when she had a pain. Nothing. With God's blessing she remained pregnant. When the day came, they would go look for a midwife. Once finished with that, there she was. The poor woman stayed as she was. She didn't know anything.

I had to work. I had to wash, cook, grind, make tortillas. I used to have to clean my mother's kitchen before I went to school. I had to do the dishes. There were times that I had to prepare my *nixtamal;* if I could do a little, I would grind at least one-fourth to leave for her. When I returned I would grind the rest, but I had to do my work before going to school.

I never failed to go to school even though I had to get up early so I could get my work done. When the bell rang – at the last stroke – because they rang bells so you would know that it was eight o'clock – at the last bell I would enter. At that last moment I would go running and reach the line just in time. I would have to take two of my little sisters with me when I was about twelve. Marta and Constanza. I had to comb their hair and get them ready, take their clothes off, clean them well, their feet, hands, nails so I could take them too. All that was my work because my mother sometimes had to feed her baby and she didn't have time.

When I got home at noon, I had to finish grinding the corn and sometimes I was still doing that when one o'clock struck. I would go and eat something, like two tortillas, and with these I would return to school. When I came home in the afternoon, my work was ready: wash dishes, sweep, put the water on for my mother's drink and bathe my little sisters. Otherwise I would go to carry water, I would go to shell the corn for the *nixtamal*. Sometimes it was already night-time when I was finishing. As soon as I had eaten supper, I would go to sleep or to study. Sometimes I would study until nine o'clock – my dictation. If it was spelling they gave me, I would have to study. And then early, at three or four in the morning, I would be up again. Yes, that's how it was.

I didn't go to school for more than five years here. When I entered the school, I didn't know how to speak English. They would give me work; I would look at it to see if I could do it, but I couldn't say the numbers in English. When I learned my ABCs, then I began to learn to read. Well, from there I continued step by step – to Standard 6, but by then I was fourteen years old and so they took me out because I was going to continue studying, but my mother said, "If you keep studying you won't be able to help me." And she needed me in the house.

I needed my studies and so I cried because they took me out of the school – I wanted to continue studying. The teacher was interested. She wanted to continue giving instruction, but my father and mother didn't want it and they took me out.

I'm going to tell you the truth: we were poor. We were poor. I hardly played. So I tell my children now that I see that they have a lot of opportunity to run and play and amuse themselves because it was not like now. I see my children – even though there are a lot of us we always get something to eat. Before, even to get a pound of beans was hard – we could only get it with hard work. Yes. Now I see that it is different for them even though their father has to fight to get it. But it was very hard for my father. It took a lot to maintain us. My father punished me a lot. I'm going to tell you the truth: I suffered at the hands of my father when he was drunk because, as I am going to tell you, my father didn't like my fiance. He absolutely didn't like him. My father drank, and my fiance, too, when he was young, drank a lot. He drank a lot when he was young because I saw him when he was single, and every Saturday, he was drunk. There was no Saturday that he was not drunk because even when he came to visit at my house, sometimes he would come drunk. And my father, the more drunk he was, the angrier he got. You know how when they are drunk they don't have all their senses? The alcohol goes to their head and they begin to say things and to get angry. And for that reason my father told him that he didn't want a drunk son-in-law. Well, I didn't say anything because my parents didn't like us to talk to boys in front of them. When a young man came to visit, they would go and talk with the boy. And we girls, young people, we would go and find something to do. We worked. I didn't talk with the boy, not at all.

Then one day came – I think he waited for the day when my mother and father weren't there – and he came again to chat. He always said the same thing – that he wanted to marry me. I told him, "Señor, I'm not thinking of getting married. I'm still young. I would rather stay with my father and mother," because I still thought that I was young. I was hardly fifteen. And I said, "My God, this boy won't stop bothering me."

And I said, "I have noticed that my papa treats me badly, you know. I notice that sometimes he tells me that I do wrong, and I don't see that I am doing wrong. I don't know if perhaps there is gossip that I am a bad woman, or that I am not being obedient, or perhaps that I behave badly. I don't know why."

(Mama) said, "No, child, you know something?" "What, mama?" "It's because when you were young, since you were a little girl, your father didn't like you."

"Mother, why did my father not like me?" I asked. "Ay, child, it's because I became pregnant before we got married. When you were born, he said that you are not his daughter."

I said, "But, Mama, could it be that is why my father treats me like that?" "Yes, child, that is why. But it is not true. He is your father. But he scolded me before I got married to him. Because I had bad boyfriends before him, he claimed that you are the child of so and so, of somebody else."

I said, "Well, that is fine, mother. But I notice that my father doesn't treat me very well. He is angry. Better if I get married."

I didn't give thought to how, when he got drunk, my husband might hit me or mistreat me. I didn't think of that. I think that I still had the mentality of a child, because it never occurred to me to say to him, "Señor, I hope that when I marry you are not going to hit me, or not going to hurt me, or that some day you are not going (not) to want to give food, or money, or something like that." I didn't tell him anything like that. I believe I had the mind of a child, because I didn't say any of that. Nothing. I said to myself that I would give him my consent. I decided to get married.

Well, it is no lie, after I married I suffered a bit. I got married the 26th of January—and in March they took me to the other side (Mexico). He found some land and a little house and we moved there.

Then we experienced need. We didn't have any money. There was nothing to eat. There was no money – there was work but it was too far. And they were working, but there was no money. They were cutting *milpa*. He would leave around four in the morning and would not return until eight at night. He was working all day. I didn't know what he was doing; he said it was far away. He had to walk three leagues to reach the workplace. They were cutting bush to make *milpa*.

Well, I don't know if I was sick or was in the beginning stages of my first child. I felt bad: I didn't want to eat beans; I didn't want to eat anything. Even the water had a bad taste. I was always feeling like throwing up and throwing up. I felt that I didn't have any strength to work, nor desire to get up. I wanted to lie down, to do nothing but sleep. And my husband was not there. And he would leave in the morning and it would be night before he returned again.

One day I packed my stuff, and I said to myself, "I'm leaving. I know where I came from and where I'm going back to." Well, I didn't tell my husband anything. When he woke up, he went to work. When I heard the bus coming, it stopped and I got in. I had little animals which I left with my sister-in-law. I told her, "I'm leaving. When your brother comes tell him that I went to my mother's."

Well, when I returned to Obregon to the place where my grand-mother lived, I arrived at my aunt's house. And she said, "What's wrong?" I said, "Nothing."

"What do you mean nothing? You are sick. Girl, you are pale, pale and very, very thin. You were fat and now you are thin," she told me.

I said, "I am not going back. I'm going to my mother's. When my grandfather goes there, I will go with him."

And my aunt began to laugh. Well, I am not going to lie to you. I arrived at noon (and) at three o'clock my husband was there. I don't know how he did it, but he arrived in Obregon. I stayed with my grandfather. We found a house and we lived over there. There things got better because I got better. They cured me – a doctor. He gave me an injection of vitamins. I was pregnant with my first child. When I got better again, and when the time came, the baby was born but it was dead. It was a little girl.

It was very sad. Before she was born—maybe three months before—I fell and this knee hit my stomach. I slipped on the stones of the hill and then when I turned around I struck my stomach. So I think that perhaps she received a blow. But I didn't abort; her time came but she was hurt. I was left very sad because I was awaiting my first baby, dreaming of how I was going to take care of him, and of how I was going to touch him, to love him. And when the day came, nothing. It was finished.

I nearly died from that delivery because when she was about to be born, the midwife said that she didn't know what was being born; she didn't know if it was a baby. She didn't know what it was because it didn't have any hair; it was smooth, smooth. She was useless. She had two balls here behind the nape of her neck. When she was born she was crying, and I believe that she wanted to breathe, but when those balls broke, pure water came out, and that was when she died. The two balls that came – they all got scared and I don't know why, but they scared me too and they said that it was not a baby. That is what the woman said, "It is something else." So when I heard what they said, I, too, became alarmed. And I said, "What have I got?" And in a jiffy the pain left me. I didn't have any pain giving birth to the baby. No. Nothing, nothing. It had stopped.

Thank God and my poor aunt – the one who lived there – she said to my husband to go and get the man (traditional healer) who cured me (as a child). My husband went to talk to him and he came. And when he entered, he said, "What's happening?"

She said, "Nothing, señor. It's that the señora doesn't feel any pain. She can't give birth." "Why does she not have pain," he asked? "Now," he said. He approached me and he made the sign of the Cross on my stomach. Then he took hold of me and began to massage, to massage my whole stomach. Then he told me to sit down and he began to rub my whole back. And when he was done rubbing my back he said, "Lie down."

It's no lie: when I lay down I felt a pain come. The moment that the pain came is when the baby was born, and then they saw that it was useless. That man saved my life. Yes, that man. That was my first childbirth.

I nearly died. How can I explain? In my five senses I could see how I was going away little by little. I was dying. I felt like I was asphyxiating, like something was coming and covering my nose so I couldn't breathe. I don't know, I think it was the heartbeats of the child that were dying, or who knows? Like I was drowning. It's an ugly feeling when one is dying.

Raoul told me that he didn't want to stay in Obregon any more. "Why?" I asked. "Because nobody wants me here in this place. They don't want to give me land so I can make my own house," he said. "You are in a bind because I don't want to go back to Belize," I said.

He replied, "Can it be that you don't want to go? Your mother is there. What are you going to do? Better we go. We know how to live in our own land. What are we going to do here in a foreign land?" "I think you're right," I said. "Well, let's go!" So we got ready. In eight days we came here.

We hadn't lived here for a year. He worked for other people. He would go work for the Company. In the afternoon he would do a little for himself. He didn't have cane. There was no cane. I think they were going to begin ploughing – the ploughing of this land that the Company took. So he went there to work. They were going to cut down trees and to plant cane and other types of work. That's how he worked.

As soon as he came here, he went to see if he could get a little piece of land. Thank God, there was a person who began to advise him to get his little piece of cane and that way he would see a bit of money coming in. There was a man here called Don Ernesto Mascal. That man said to him, "You know something? If you want, I can give you a bit of cane for you to sell. Go and apply so they will give you a quota. If you get the quota, I am going to give you cane so you can put it in your name, but you will give the money to me."

He (Raoul) said, "That's fine. If you help me, I won't cheat you. I will bring you your money." "Good," the man said. "Go and get your quota and I am going to give you cane." So that is how he did it the first year: he went to see if he could get the quota, to see if luck was with him. And he went at the right time. They said that, yes, they were going to give him his quota. It was only twenty-five tons. He got it and the man advised him when it was time to sell the cane. He said, "The cane is ready, so cut it and put it in your name." That's what he did.

Then, since he now had a quota, he began to struggle to plant for himself. So the next year, he didn't borrow from the other man – it was his own cane. The land was his godfather's – the godfather that took me to be married. He had a piece of land over there where his block is now. He said, "Son, if you want, I can give you a piece of land and you can make your *milpa* there and in another you can plant your cane. I am tired and old and I don't believe I can work those lands."

He sold his quota. I would help him to plant cane, to plant the seed. It wasn't very hard work. I didn't cut. When the time would come to cut, he would look for people to help him. Well, we would borrow a little money to help ourselves plant another little bit. Yes, little by little. Now he has 240 tons. It was 343 before. But we had a terrible thing happen. Since I had a quota of 70 tons, he preferred to give me the cane (to deliver the cane on my quota). So we suffered a setback because he didn't fill his quota. And the poor man, they took it away from him. They only left him what he delivered that year. And they didn't give me – who had delivered (my quota) – more. They only gave me a little.

Cane is money here in this country. Nothing else. Because even though we have a little corn and a few other things, we are always waiting for money so when we get it, we can go and buy clothes and other things we need. For example, say we want to do a little job. We begin thus, little by little. You have to get money, and if you want to continue working – for example, you want to plant another piece of cane, or to make another piece of *milpa* – well, the same money from that same cane is what we use. Even when the price goes down you still get a little. But when the price his high, you get more. Yes. I tell him that it's better to have enough so one can distribute it. So when we get some money our sons will have some too. Yes, we share it among them, the sons, the big boys. We only give a little to the girls so they can buy their clothes.

There were times that we would only make a little *milpa* and then when the time would come when we needed some corn, we would have to buy with the money from the cane. And that is why I tell you that cane does bring us some benefits because almost everything comes from it. From it almost everything comes: if we want to build a little house, or something like that, we go to the bank; they lend us money to be paid back the next year. That way you can go ahead and build what you want. That's why I'm telling you that cane has helped this country a lot. Poor people, like us. Now the people who have a job, they don't have such a hard time because they are working with the government and they are paying them. But we, no.

We had hard times because in the days when my kids were small, we could only depend on their father. What I did was to raise animals. I began to raise my hens, my turkeys, my pigs, and that helped us a lot. I would sell eggs, chicken, turkeys, pigs. We got in the habit of killing three times a week – Saturday, Monday, and Wednesday. We had meat for sale. We didn't kill big pigs but of a size that we knew wouldn't leave waste. My only hope was my animals because I liked to raise them – it was a help. Sometimes when we didn't have milk, somebody would come and buy a chicken or a hen. I would go and get it and sell it. There were times when we needed a lot of money to go to the doctor because they were sick. That's how we managed during the hard times when there was no money. Only my animals help me. Even for food, if there's nothing to eat, I kill a chicken, I kill a hen, and we have meat. There's food to eat. That's how we used to manage when the cane season was over. Just with the animals.

I like to sell – I used to. Now I'm lazy. Before I used to like to make tamales, to make bread, to make pudding – that *jamote* pudding, plantain pudding – I made it for sale. With the money I bought sugar, lard, sometimes beans. Up to three times weekly I would make *tamales* and I would sell them all. Now no. Now I don't sell.

Whenever he would say to me "I need so much to pay such and such," we were always in agreement, the two of us. Always. Since we began living together until now. When he is thinking of doing something, he tells me. And then I tell him if it's okay. We make an agreement. He tells me, "I need so much for work, or I want you to help with such and such a thing; if you have money, help me." I say, "Fine." When he has some little problem, or I have a problem, well, I tell him, and he, too. Up to this day, we hardly have any problems – only sometimes when he drinks – for a little while.

Three months after the birth of the baby who died, I got pregnant with that little one over there, Felipa. I had eight babies in my house and nine in the hospital. When I began to have babies, I was innocent. I didn't know anything. Whatever people would tell me, whatever the woman would tell me, I would do. So at first I gave birth kneeling, like that. But when, after I had finished having the first eight, I went to the hospital, then no more. In the hospital they don't let you kneel or stand up, nothing. There they put you on a bed. That is how I bore the rest. But at first, no, only kneeling.

Only one midwife looked after me from the beginning until the eight were born. She only helps at the moment of birth. That's all. You have to do the things that you know that you have to do because when they come, they only rub you to see if the child is ready to come, if it is time or not. And they tell you that your baby has arrived.

After the baby is born, we get into bed. They wash us, they fix us up in bed, and they wash the baby, they bathe it. After they finish washing it, they put powder on it. They warm its navel and then they clothe him well and then they put the baby next to you. But first you have to wait because they have to wash the baby's chest with hot water, or maybe with a leaf from the orange tree. After washing it two or three times, then the baby can begin to suckle. But before that the baby has to drink grains of anise. They give him that to suckle so he will pass all the dirt in his stomach.

After the eighth day, I get up. They bring everything I need: my food, my bath – everything. After eight days, I can get up. Before, I used to take a lot of care of my children. So the insects wouldn't bite them, I would handle them under the mosquito net, a very fine mosquito net so nothing would bother them. That's what we used to do.

Afterwards they passed a law that you have to give birth in the hospital because, after having had a lot of children, the woman's body is tired, and there in your house you don't have medicine like they have there. They can give you a little more help because if things are going badly, if you have a lot of pain, they have the intravenous. They put it on and it helps. It helps you a lot. And if you lack blood, too, they give blood. For that reason, my husband told me, "Better you go to the hospital because I see that you're tired. And you should rest a little. Here at home, certainly we can take care of you, but we don't give you the kind of attention that you should get in the hospital." So I decided to go to the hospital.

But now you can take the big babies out after three days because on the third day you go home from the hospital. You bring them out. Before, no. Sometimes you wouldn't begin to take them out for two months – because I was afraid of the wind that comes with rain – sometimes they were born during the rainy season, sometimes they were born in the season when there were a lot of mosquitoes, a lot of insects. One had to take care of them because before was not like now: we didn't take the children to doctors and nurses much. We weren't constantly at the clinic so they could examine them, attend to them. With those first kids that I brought to life no, but now yes.

Sometimes the wind that comes with rain eyes the infant. Sometimes the sun – the reflection of the sun – eyes the baby too. It harms them. The sun falls on it and harms it. Or a wind blows on it, like now when we have rain. Sometimes it loosens his stomach; it gives him a stomachache. He begins to dirty every minute. Well, that's when we say that the wind of the rain did it. Then there are herbs for that and there are herbs for the sun's reflection. And there are herbs for when someone eyes the baby. They harm the baby.

One time my son was dying of a stomachache caused by the wind of the rain. We took him to the doctor and he didn't get better. Meanwhile, he kept having diarrhoea. He was six months old. My baby kept on dirtying. I didn't know what was wrong with him. I was taking him to the doctor, I was giving him medicine the doctor had given me and I didn't see any improvement. In the end, my husband said, "Let's go to my family. Let's go to my cousin because she knows herbal medicines. It could be that my child has something – perhaps someone eyed him."

So we took him to the woman. The woman told us the minute she saw the child – his feces – that it was not the eye from a person but the eye from the wind of the rain. Immediately, she went off and gathered some herbs. After she picked them, she mashed them well and then she took it out and put it in the sun in a bucket. Having put it in the sun, she told me, "You are going to bathe the baby this afternoon." I said, "Fine."

Well, when the afternoon came the bath was already hot from the sun. Then she got a stone and put it in the fire so it would heat. Then she heated the water more with the stone so the herbs would cook, I think. She threw it in the water – a coloured stone. She threw it into the bucket of bathwater, and then when she estimated that it was right for the bath, she told me to bathe the baby. Then she got the water and put it in the room, and I began to bathe the child. Having bathed him all over, I dried him well, and I laid him down, I rocked him well and I left him. All that night he didn't have diarrhoea. The stomach problem had gone away. For almost a month my baby had been having diarrhoea. He was dirtying and it went away. When I returned to my house, my baby was well.

Well, that woman began to teach (me) the herbs, their names and how to use them. But the woman died. Up to this point, they (my children) don't know much. They know that I pick them because when I need something for a little brother I go picking. Sometimes I take them along, but they are stubborn. They are scarcely interested enough to ask, "What's this called, mami?" Or, "What is that? What is that herb?" No. They are not interested.

Thank God, with the other births I had no problems. They all came fine. I had a miscarriage. I had been pregnant for only three months. I only went to cut a little firewood because I was always in the habit of collecting firewood. And I said to my husband, "Let's go and look for a little wood." He said, "Let's go." So I went with him. We had just cut the wood and all, and he told me to put it in the sack. "Aha," I said. I began to put the wood in the sack. When I finished I said, "Let's go."

I got my little sack of wood, I lifted it and put it on my head. Then we came back chatting. But he was angry because he said, "Why did you lift that sack? It weighs a lot."

I said, "It's not heavy. I lifted it." Then I brought it home and threw it down, and that was done. We went inside in the evening and had supper. We ate supper and went to sleep. I awoke fine. There was no problem. I got up in the early morning, made his breakfast and he went off to work. It was not more than a quarter of an hour after he had gone when a pain began in my stomach. A pain. I had felt some tension for three months. I said to myself, "I have never suffered any discomfort. I was always pregnant, but it never caused pains like that," I said. "What's wrong with me?"

I said, "My God, could it be that I'm pregnant again?" because I felt that pain again. I didn't know yet that I was pregnant. I didn't pay attention to the blood that was coming out. It wasn't just a little – it was a lot. Then I said, "What can this be. This pain?" Afterwards, I felt that my back was paining me too, so I went to lie down in the hammock for a minute. It passed. I got up again. The same thing happened. Then I said, "My God. How soon will this pain go away?" Then I took off the cloth that was dirty and went to wash it so they

66

didn't pile up on me because I was taking one off and putting the other on, on and off.

I told myself that it was going to pass and I realized that I was scared – I didn't know what was wrong, I didn't feel well and I was alone. My God, I was thinking. I was praying to God to help me, that he would take this pain away. It was coming up to noon when I said, "My God, they are going to come home and when they come what am I going to give them to eat if I haven't made anything?"

Then when the twelve o'clock bell rang, I said to myself, "Ay, but I feel awful." I went and lay down in the hammock. When I lay down I felt as if something had come out of me. "My God, what can it be?" But I was lying down because the hammock felt delicious. When I lay down I felt the pain leave my back and my stomach. Then I said, "My God, thank God, I believe that the pain has gone away. Now I am going to do my jobs, because my children are arriving, coming to eat."

Well, when I got up, I went to move because I felt that something substantial was coming out and when I moved I saw something ugly. "Dear God," I said, "What is that thing? It's ugly." So I picked it up and wrapped it up. I said, "When my children have gone to school, I'm going to go and throw it out." So I wrapped it well and put it in the closet. "I'm not going to show that to anybody," I said. "Thank God, the pain has gone."

Well, when they arrived, I was in the kitchen. They said, "Mama, we want to eat something." I told them, "In a minute you will eat. You are going to eat hard tortillas, because I haven't made tortillas." I prepared their meal and they all ate. Then I was getting their father's lunch ready when I heard him come. When he entered he asked, "What's wrong?"

"Nothing," I said. "What do you mean, nothing? Do you have a fever?" "No," I said. "Yes, it's something. I can see that something is not right. You are pale, like you don't have any blood." I said, "No, I don't have a fever. There's nothing wrong".

He said, "You're lying to me. Something happened to you." I said, "I don't know what happened to me. I had a pain but it has gone away." And truly it had gone away. "Hm. You have had a miscarriage." "That could be," I said. "Yes, that's what happened." He knew from the time he saw me because he saw that I was very pale. I didn't know anything. I had raised eight children and they arrived on time. That had never happened before. Then he said, "Well, I am going to see it at once. Where is it?"

Well, thank God that I hadn't thrown it away. He came in and saw it and said, "Hm, it looks like it was two babies and both are girls." They were twins. So he said, "Never mind. There's nothing to be done. It wasn't time for them to be born." Well, thanks be to God, I was all right. And I didn't delay. By the end of three months I was once again pregnant.

There was a time when my kids were getting sick all the time and I was going to the doctor a lot with them. Now, the doctor said to me that I shouldn't have any more babies because a woman can only take so much and children, for the most part, are a lot of work. Sometimes the parent has to sacrifice a lot, to work to raise her children. My mother, little by little stopped because she didn't have the strength to have more children, to give birth to more children.

Well, he (the doctor) said what I should do was to have an operation so I wouldn't have more. So I came and I told my husband. He didn't agree. He didn't want it. He never wanted them to operate on me. He never wanted me to use suppositories, nor drugs. Never. Even up to today. I tell my children, "If your father had been a person who listened to me, perhaps we would not have had so many children." I had agreed, but he didn't. He didn't like it. He asked why they were going to operate, that he felt like a father. He supported them and was not sorry.

Sometimes I got angry because he never did what I said. He said it was better we have the children that God gave us, and when it was finished, well, it was finished. I said to him, "If it is my fate, I will live. And if I die, you should marry again and have more children." That's what I told him.

"You're not going to die. God will arrange it so you stop having children," he said.

I said, "That's fine. You're the father. But I'm the mother who suffers. Aha. I'm the one who suffers. I'm the sufferer."

He replied, "But never mind, it's God's will: we have to accept it because it's God's will." I said, "You can say `never mind.' But what am I going to do? It's my destiny, I think, to be mother of my children. I have to bear whatever comes."

With this last baby – I'm not lying – thank God, I didn't suffer. I didn't suffer at all. When the time came to have the baby, on a day like today, when I got up I felt pain. I had pains, but not strong ones, so I went into my room and I said, "My God, if God is great and powerful, he sent us to be mothers in this life, no? Blessed Virgin," I said, "Help me. Don't make me suffer much and bring my baby safely." And then I sat down and began to say my rosary. I said the whole rosary. Then I finished everything and I said, "My God, if it is my destiny that I am going to die, I will die," because I had three births before this one and they nearly killed me. And the pain was not from the baby but rather was due to – how can I explain – my uterus that was tired. It gave me a lot of pain and I felt that it was going to kill me. Then I begged God to help me with this baby, that it be the last.

Then the afternoon arrived. I said to my husband, "I'm feeling worse. You'd better go and look for the vehicle to take me." He said, "Fine." He had to hire Don Arcadio's van. When he came, he asked me, "How do you feel, the van just arrived?"

I said, "I feel bad, but it's a pity because you're going to throw me in the hospital. You know how I suffer. Only God knows if I'm going to live or not." He said, "Don't say that. You're going to get better. You will live." Then I left. We left together. When I got in, my God, I felt an unbearable pain. I said to my husband, "I don't know if I'm going to get to the hospital. I feel like I can't bear it. I want to scream." He said, "Be calm. Have patience." Well, we went and, thanks be to God, we arrived in Orange Walk.

When I arrived, the nurse began to ask me my name. I said, "Nurse, I don't want to hear anything. I want to go to maternity. Take me." They took me quickly. She said, "Get in and lie down." Well, I got up on the bed, and I lay down and the baby was being born. It was arriving. The nurse said, "Why didn't you stay in your house, girl?

Don't you see your baby has already been born?" My God, I nearly had it in the street.

"Dear God," I said, "God is powerful. He helped me a lot." When I arrived at eight o'clock, my baby was born. That was the last one. Without any labour. No doctor, nothing. She came easily, even the afterbirth. Everything went well.

I don't understand, nor do I think about how I came to have so many children because at the beginning my midwife told me that I was only going to have eight little ones. The first woman who helped me. She knew. She said that under the afterbirth there is a little chain that has little balls, like rosaries. They say that they can count on it how many children one is going to have, that when she counted, she only saw eight. Well, for that reason I dreamed that it was the truth – that I was only going to have eight children. It's not for sure. It wasn't certain because I had more children than she predicted. The eight passed – passed on to seventeen!

All my life has been sad. With the children there are times when they are sick, or crying. There were times when their father said of them, "Why do you think so much about the children? The children are not going to die, they will get better." But I don't like to hear them crying. I want to cry along with them. I love them a lot. But, no. I don't want more. No.

For my part, I'm not afraid to die. I pray to God that when the time comes for Him to take me, that I will be prepared, that I will be ready for that hour.

I would prefer to be alone. Alone. Without husband. To deliver myself only to God, to dedicate myself to religion, to make my offerings to Him. That's what I think. Even if my husband is living, I would prefer to transfer the love I have for him to God. That's what I'm thinking – yes, to God because I want everything I do to be with God.

So at times he tells me I've changed a lot. He says that it's not like it was before. Before I didn't, let's say, take the time or opportunity or leisure to say my devotions. I would rather lie down, or do other things and I didn't prefer to be praying, or doing things that might make me feel good. I tell him he should get married again. He tells me I'm mad. I say, "No, but I see that you're getting tired of me. Look for another woman and get married."

"I can't get married again," he says to me. That's what he says. I tell him, "When I die, you're going to get married again." He says, "What? Are you going to die?"

He doesn't like it because sometimes I say to him, "Let's go to church to listen. Wait, you will see that you are going to change a lot." But he doesn't like to go to church.

In truth, God is great because if one begs like that, He listens. Yes, He listens to you. Yes, I believe that it's perhaps my time to stop having children. The doctor said that I am ready for the change of life. I hope so. I already have a lot and I think perhaps that it is enough that God isn't going to give me any more gifts.

Amelia

Amelia was born in 1940. Married and the mother of thirteen children, she lives with her husband, her younger children and two grandchildren, whom she has cared for since her daughter's death. She narrated her story in Creole.

I have forty-eight years. I born 1940, the 16th of March.

I born Nago Creek, down the river: "Where you gwine?" "Where you gwine?" "I see you yonder." "Where you did they?" Pure Creole, they talk. There were no Spanish people there. Pure Creole. Well, only a small place because plenty people never lived there. The biggest family be we.

My grandfather is used to farming. My daddy too. My mammy, she stay at home and she do his work. She stay home and she cook, you know. She wash. My mummy was a nice person, only she couldn't walk me a'tall. She can't walk for the sake of the children – she's minding them. Eleven of us. She got sixty-five years. December, she will have sixty-six.

And myself, like when I go to school, when I come out I go to the riverside and I help my daddy with his work. My daddy, he does cut firewood –the hardest job, cut firewood, yes mam. I saw firewood, I chop it and I tie it. When I get tired then I go home, back in time for dinner. When I finish eat, I go back again. I was about fifteen years because I cut wood for myself. We go out in the dory, and we cut our wood, and then I go to the waterside and then we bring it up. To saw the wood, we have to use a saw. When we don't saw the wood, we take the axe and chop the wood. And when we done chop it, we get the leaves and tie it into a bundle.

He take it in the leaves in the boat and he go sell it many days at a dollar twenty-five a hundred – cheap, cheap, cheap, man. Sometimes they have to sell one or two thousand bundles for making a little money – two thousand, sometimes one thousand five hundred. Sometimes in the evening he send it to the (middle-) man because he know he don't get nothin'. He sell it to the man, and from there he take the wood to Belize and the man sell it, and when he come he give him his money. I had to work because the things stand bad, you know. Got no money: me have to work.

My grandfather, he does his farming in the bush. He plant plantains, cassava, potato, coco, everything. My granny, she stay at home and she cooks, washes dishes, scrub table and everything. I go every day. Every morning and every evening, we visited our granny because they close, because they just about the coconut tree. She was all right and my grandfather too.

My father does make *milpa* but not plenty. But he make a little, and you know, with them lean *milpa* and with so much children we had it hard. In those days we eat the plantain, the fish, with the coconut. With the coconut sometimes we eat rice, beans –because in they days you can't get beans every day. There be days when there were no beans. During the week we eat them plantains, fish. I go fishing.

We lived in our trash house. We sleep in the same room because most naturally there was no money for door and that kind of thing –only for the little dinner. There were eleven of we. Eleven. I was the oldest one of them. Well, I take care of them but I had to go to the riverside to cut wood, so after my mummy stay with them.

I does go to school. When we does go to school, we learn the lesson, but most natural if in the evening we don't know something we can't help ourself. I tell the children they all right because sometimes they get their book. But we –nothin'. Nothin'. You couldn't get no book. But the government put book to the school – the only way we could get. But my mummy can't buy. Sometimes I no want to go. But I started go, I never lose school. We study geography, English, arithmetic.

We does have friends, small girlfriends and boyfriends. Sometimes we does fight up with the little boys then. Sometimes when we come for school, because some of the little boy – they upstart, you know – and we begin to fight. Sometimes we fight and like that and we no talk, till afterwards we get pleased again, and we talk. Well, we talk, but when we fight and things we cuss up one another. After when that pass, we are friends again.

After when I left school, I begin to help my daddy. I may have one li'l boy, you know. You know when you have your first child? Most natural when one boy come to you and he tells you like that: "I want you" and like how you are young, you did believe everything. But when you (mother) lash your head, that day you see the trouble, yes mam, because after when they give you dat, they give the pregnancy right now. They left you right there and you have to say, "Well, what I'm gwine to do?"

My (future) husband he do the work. He made the work in the mahogany. He worked for a man named Mr. Charles Brown. They call the place San Juan. He see me and I see him and we talk and I come here with him. He there nearly for a year at San Juan. When them children father come and talk with me, I'm 'fraid because I say, well, he gwine do me the same thing. Because I'm 'fraid now I said, "Suppose now I going to go to him and then when I see him he fool me?" From there I said I gwine to wait wee bit until two years' time I come for him.

Well, he see me and I see him and we talk and I come here (to San Miguel) with him. When I first come here I saw no street. You no ever have no street and when you see rain you can't walk on the road – you slip off. You have to put your foot in a rubber boots. And you have mostly like a trash house. But right now, plenty change a lot because the people they have their little road right now and everything.

From there I come here with him and from there we live and we have a little children and the children they done grow and everything. They go to school. Sometimes they come and tell me, "Mama, they call me Black." I tell them, "Study then, man." I tell them that God made everybody same. From there they come and tell me, "Ma, this one they tell me this." I tell them, "I no want to hear nothin', because I no like for enemy or like that." I like for friendly with everybody. If I see you and I do talk with you, you show me a bad way, still I no vexed and so I go because I tell the children we must learn to live with the people. Even if they show you bad way, left them to God because He loves each other. He make everybody: no care how you stand. Most natural I tell them like that because God make everybody. He love everybody. He put everybody into this world.

That was when they first begin to go to school. Right now, I don't have no trouble with them. They go to school quite nice right now. I don't hear nothin'. Before, yes, mam.

When I first came, it be hard – hard because from there the children come down. Like you not know what to do because at that time he never got no cane farm. When I first here, I does make bread, potato pong, wongla sweet – I does do that because he never have no cane. My big boy does sell bread. Then after, when he get big, my little girl that is sitting there right now. After when she get big, Dalia does sell bread. Now after Dalia, now she, Clarissa, and she no wants to sell bread. Ashamed.

I had to help him, you see, and all the time he go to work. Every Saturday he can't get the pay, man. They does cheat him. And, you know that when you work out for people, you have to satisfy with anything they give you because afterward you need the money, because nobody else never does they. And in them days, you find the one have the money, they take advantage of you. They give you a miserly pay. Then from there they do you all kind of thing because they have their money and you listen to that because you need it.

Then from there he tell me one day, "Girl, you know, this one a fool." He say, "Girl, they advantage you, like you can't see your headway and the best thing I want to do is I want to plant one little piece of cane and see what it could do for my life." "Because," he said, "working they advantage you too much." That's what he done do till now. Like we said, it no a lot, but it help us plenty for us. In them days, when he not got the cane, he does got the corn, but that no help, you know, with the lot of children, so he decide his mind that he would plant a little bit of cane.

Praise God, out of the fifteen children, I no have no difficult time. Three were gone. I say like this: God gave it to me and He clear the way for I may have it, yes, so that when he go call the midwife I lay in on my bed and I say, "Trust in the Lord and He will help." That's how I got all of them, trusting in the Lord. There no help, nothin', because the lady (midwife) does done watch you. You have the pain – till when that time come, she just save the baby and when they done, they cut the baby navel, then bathe them and everything. They no help you nothin', a person like that. That's why plenty people tell me that I have – *como dice en español* – *valor* (like you say in Spanish – courage) because I have them children on my bed, because he went call the midwife. When the midwife come me done got the baby. The only one I have where the *partera* may be there, that was the oldest daughter. I tell him the only thing I no learn is cut the navel string, but if I could cut that, I no need no granny (midwife).

Right now, I have my daughter die and I have two little children die. She gone over the Mexican side and she get one (man). The first time I see, the man may look good and everything, but I see that he have the fault that he done married already – and why he never tell the gal that may done have a wife? But he left the wife when he take my daughter. My daughter never know. I hear them say that the wife hurt my daughter because when she sick, she vomit a worm. Then that day she stool one black, hairy worm. Like how the Spanish people say, *"La esposa del señor es media bruja"* (the man's wife is half witch).

After she come (home), I no believe in them things. She sick the 4th October. October, November, the 6th of December she die. She say it belly, something like you want to tear out of her belly. But I tell she like that, that she should trust in the Lord. She say, "Yes, Mammy, I will." I never have the mind that she will dead and when I see she get worse, she pure vomit, vomit, vomit. Stool, vomit and stool, vomit and stool. Her daddy say, "Well, I carry she home." The bush doctor looked like he couldn't do nothin' to her. Nothin'.

So I does take she to the hospital. No one in the hospital could find the sickness, man. They only say it AIDS and all kind of thing, but they couldn't find the sickness. And I carried she to the hospital and she said she want some blood. I say at least that maybe should help, but they never gave her. She went to Orange Walk, but the blood they never gave. Gone to Belize, they fight and fight. They could have gave the blood and they never gave her, man. Never gave. So I do tell the daddy: I say, "Lord, the doctor be hard." I say, "At least they should have satisfy her with the blood." But like I say: three time to the hospital.

They may treat her bad because they no want to go close up. They would (reach) across the table for give it to her because they say she have AIDS. And she never have that sickness because that no exist in we family. After, when they take out the paper that say that she have the sickness, when they test the blood again, and they send it to Tobago, and when the blood come back, the blood no have no sickness. I may worry bad, man. When she do come (home), they bring them and they carry she straight to the burying ground.

I got one died at the born and one got sick – when she got one year and five months when she dead. I don't know why she got dead because the li'l baby from the born is sick. Sometimes she have fever. I think (it was) the eye because the last time I took her to the hospital, I done sit down in the place where I usually wait for passage and she stool (had diarrhoea). And two Spanish lady took me inside and the two Spanish lady say like that: *"Se parece que es ojo esa niña"* It looks like that baby has the eye. He no believe till when he see the baby dead.

Till now he believe in the eye –that when he see the little baby sick now because he boil medicine for them, he anoint them, he do everything they say. And "Gal," he say, "if you see the baby no feel good – the eye." Yes, now he believe. When he see that the baby get sick so he began to stool and vomit, "Gal," he say, "you'd better see what you can do with the baby. Look like the eye have."

That's why I say nothin' like God: because when my children get sick, he tell me like that. He say, "Sometime we no have the money for care." So he tell me like that, "Well, girl, we will try. Now," he say, "we will try. By the blessing of God, they will feel good." He will massage them and he will give them the medicine and God help the little baby then that they give me no trouble when they are sick.

But after, sometime when he sees them sick: "Gal, he needs to see the doctor." So we send care them, but most of the time we try with the children because you have some people say that when you have a lot of children you can't mind all of them. Make we say that is true. But God give you them. What you gwine do?

You know, them days gone by, the older generation they never does do nothin' with theirself. No. They have all them children, and when you say you have your children like that, your body left good. The younger generation, they done got two baby and they done look weak already. That's why I say, right now, that younger generation, them weak, but they're wise, yes, because especially the younger generation, you can't hide nothin' from them because they know everything. Right now, if you see one girl, one something happen to (she got pregnant), she will because she want, because she did see what they happen. I have my daughter, Patti. She says she no want have one lot.

When I was at home, the same thing catch me with my boy(friend). My first boy because when we be at home my ma would never tell a gal, "Mind yourself because you got something for loss." My man (father) never tell me that, but now that I have them children I do make them know everything – what they could loss and what could happen. My man never teach me that because when I asked my mummy, "Mummy how old me?" "What you want to know that for," she said. "You done see yourself a big woman?" she tell me. After, when I gone and do the things, now, my mummy lash me and I did bawl. I said she have the fault because she never tell me one day what I could loss. I 'fraid because she beats me.

I never know nothin'. Nothin', man. Those days, I do hear them say that you could do this, you could do that. But them days like nothin'. I never know – only one day when I get sick. I may have pregnancy with one li'l baby and I go to the doctor and the doctor tell me like that: "Too much children you have." I tell him, "Well, doctor, I have ten children."

The doctor say, "Ay, what a lot of children. But," he say, "you could come to me when you done have that baby and I will give you coil." But when he show me one, I 'fraid for that thing because I hear some people say the pill is good, but I 'fraid to because plenty people drink that pills and from here they say sometimes it could hurt their stomach. And I hear it could give up to cancer.

He (my husband) said, "Well, if you want to have no children, then you have to sleep alone." Well, he no want to sleep alone. It hard for true, man!

Right now, I say maybe I finish, you know, because sometimes three months, I no see nothin' (her period). Sometimes when I see it come, sometimes one month it stop. I glad for true because you left like a little girl, because you don't have to wash, because you have a lot of children, you don't enjoy life because you just mind your baby. You just be minding baby, you can't go nowhere. You can't go no way. I say that no life because sometimes I say I want to go walk, sometimes one little dance. You want to go to little dance and like that so because sometimes – again I say when I was young I never does like that and thing – but sometimes I would like to go to Orange Walk and dance. You know, sometimes the older you get, you do change too: sometimes you want to come out to go and dance. Sometimes you want to come out to a little theatre. Because sometimes when I realize when you do sit down in your house you no see nothin'.

When we does be at home my man (father) never send me to dance. Sometimes I does cry for to make go to dance. He no send me. She (her mother) say, "Well, if he want send you to dance, he will send you." When I come here I worse because them children daddy no like when I go to dance.

I listen. I don't get for understand. If he no like one thing, I no do it because when you want one living, you have to listen what the man say, yes man. If you want one good life, you listen. I listen, because like I tell, I a person that scarcely come out. Sometime again, like the mind say, "Come out." The mind would say, "You no goin' nowhere. Sit down, man." Them (the daughters) does go. He never does want them go, but sake of me make them go because I tell him

79

like that: "These gal, make them go dance." I tell him, but he does vex. He never does like that because he the boss of the house. And he does the work, you know, but you know the woman does work too. When you want sit down, well, you will listen, because you want sit down. But if you no want to sit down, you listen, you going to do what you want.

He have to go chop bush, he have to chop harder because they in the sun and we be in the house. That true because, when the man work yonder, the lady work too. I see he go to the bush to chop. When he come, that the time when I will knead my bread. Sometimes I will wash up or grate some coconut and things like that so. He done come from bush. He bring in more. But sometimes, when you understand again, you listen, to get a life, yes man.

Now these days, it no make sense that you walking about like when you got your own little house because right now you have a poor lady (in San Miguel) who suffer with the husband. That true because after when they (he, the husband) get their little money, then from there they (he) go in them canteen with the other lady. I say that the rum would a' flying to the head – and they right there with them – and when they get to the wife's house they lashing the wife. When they come they beat the lady. That poor lady, I tell you! The (other) lady go right up to the house, yes man.

Sometimes the things come so difficult, sometimes you do have to left because that woman she want to come in your house, take you out from there with all your children. But you got some ladies, they no wanna come out with all the bad life, all the thing. But it hard because you have your husband. Now you suffer with your husband from women that are young, or that have a little piece of land, or a house, everything. When you get old, that the time they make the things come in bad because the man, he want one next (another) woman. Then he will left you. I say maybe he must done tired of the lady. Then he want one next one again (laughs). He there with a next woman.

I say one thing like this: you there with your husband, you wouldn't wanna left him because you together so long and then perhaps too much children, so you wouldn't wanna left him. But sometimes again you do have to try to do something.

I feel happy: I eat and no one is sick like that so. He no beat me. Like when you have your husband like that, you have to love him. Sometimes you hug him up a little, sometimes you kiss him like that for make him for feel good. When you have your husband like that, and you no do that, he may say you no want them. So you have to hold them a little, make them feel good, kiss him a little, and talk to him nice because sometimes when we do talk together. If I want him to do something for me, I will tell him, "Go move that plate for me, darling," just like that so. Sometimes again, when I tell him I want nice my body, you know, I tell him, "Well, darling, I feel bad. I would want you tonight," (laughs) just like that sometimes.

The cane good, you know, because that is the only l'il money there is. But still, it still be hardish because right now only the sugar cane he have. That why I do tell him that you have to try and see what we may do to make one next budget. Alone, cane it no give because he license is small. You get a little bonus, but this year we no will get nothin', or only just a little, because them days he went and borrow a little and he have to pay that back. I say that the cane would help if you have a lot of license because you have some people that have one thousand tons of license, one thousand five hundred. But with two hundred ton, it no give – because he may have three hundred and twenty-six, but they take it off (they reduced his license). They come to a time that they take one license from the people.

Right now, he can't work hard. He's not so young anymore. You can't do that work, climbing up on top of the truck. One time he was trying to cut cane, but he can't make it because he get with a pain to his side and he have to sleep in the hospital one day. He no have nothin' but just a pain. So I tell him like that: you better forget about that because he got twelve years in the work. You got some poor people when they young they cut the cane, but they look old. The sun hot, hot, hot, and as you see them come to eat their little dinner – they done, out again they go. He get people to help. When you see they cut cane and so on, the truck haul it, you no make nothin'. Now, if you have a truck and the truck is very good, well, you are left with something. But too if the truck is not good, the minute you have to fix, you left with nothin'.

Suppose now the people done work their cane – because after you see them done work the cane field, they no have nothin' more for do because you can't even get one l'il job for help yourself. Nothin'. Right now, I have my two boys in the work, but they work with they daddy. They can't say, "Well, I'm gwine next week. I'm gwine do a l'il work in yonder." It's true people have the choppin', but they don't have money.

The time is very hardish right now because sometimes when you make the things, they no sell. Like yesterday, one man come buy bread and he said, "No bread, brother, no way." But when I put myself bake bread – everybody they make bread – and now that I stop – right now, isn't anybody doing bread. Nobody. It very hard right now. In them two months, October and November, it be hard, man, because you can't go back, you can't go front. And it rain for true, so that you can't do nothin' because first I does make my little oil. Right now, I can't go peel the coconut 'cause it's full of mud. But it nasty. It very nasty. Work the coconut into the mud. Them days, I do tell him: this day I come in I have to try and see where I want to do. I grate my little coconut. I still have to make my sweet and my bread, for make a little budget.

And I feel happy. I feel happy because no mind that things is poorly, but every day we eat. We used to eat the corn tortilla with beans and he was making *milpa* still. I do help him because I say: well, he not lazy. Most natural when you have your husband and you see he try, you help out too because you see that he do try. Most natural too when he no have, I no angry with that. I satisfy because I say: well, when he have I see we have. When you see him go get a little money, he put every change into my hand.

I can find no fault when I come to him because no one day he beat me. We have we little fights and things about the children – when they do the rudeness, you know. Going for thirty years now – no one day I can say, "Ay, me back hurt me because he beat me." No. From the luck, I say, we be poor. And sometimes for I say, "God no love vanity." So I do tell it like that: if we live the way that God love now, make we no hate one another, live good with people, do everything that what God love.

Magdalena

Magdalena was born in 1945. She is the mother of ten children and lives with her partner and younger children. A married son, his wife and baby also live in the household.

My father used to make charcoal. He burned the wood, we put it in sacks; then, around seven, we picked the charcoal up. We would leave early in the morning and come back the next day. We slept in the mountain. We did this until we finished. I used to cry when they took us because we were so sleepy – if we didn't go, my father would get angry with us; he would scold us. My mother also went. Everyone went. It was very far. We used to walk for about two miles. We slept under bushes. Then we picked up the charcoal. We had to fill the sacks before dawn, otherwise the sacks would burn because we couldn't see the fire in daylight. We did this around three, before daylight. In the darkness you can see the fire and put it out with water.

At times, he used to drink a lot – that's why we were so poor. He worked a lot, but all the money would go toward buying alcohol. He mistreated my mother a great deal when they lived together. He beat my mother a lot. When we were small we couldn't do anything – we couldn't defend her. Once we grew up, we wouldn't let him beat her. Once when he beat my mother she was really bloodied – there was a lot of blood running from her nose. They were married when my mother was fourteen years old. He left my mother when I was fourteen – he moved in with another woman. All of us were older then. There were four of us (girls). I was the youngest. All the others were married when my father left my mother. My mother was better off because the beatings stopped. She never left him when they were together. She cried a lot. Even when she was sick my father would get angry and make her get up to work.

At the time the boys died, my mother was being mistreated by my father. I think that's one of the reasons they died. He beat my mother a lot. First, a boy died. The second boy died. Then she had a girl, then another girl and they lived. Then she had another boy and he died. Next she had another boy and he died. Then she had another girl and she lived. My father was upset, "Why is it that the girls live and the boys die?" he would say. Some died of whooping cough, others had a bad stomach, vomiting.

I was the last one. My father was far away cutting cane. Every fifteen days my mother would send his food rations. A truck would come by and pick up his food. She couldn't send it one day because I had been born. When the truck arrived at the place he was working, he came running looking for his food. They told him it hadn't been sent because I had been born, to go see his family because his wife was sick.

They say that when he returned, my grandmother, who has since died, was in the kitchen helping my mother. My mother was inside. He asked what the child was. They told him it was a girl. "You should have held her nose and killed her," he told my grandmother.

"How could I kill her? How could I do such a thing? She's an innocent," my grandmother told him. He went inside and kicked the door where my mother was and told her to get up and to get the water for his bath. My mother got up and got him the water for his bath. He wanted my mother to get up because it hadn't been a boy. If it had been a boy she could have stayed inside, but it had been a girl, so she should get up to work. My mother went out. My poor mother had a very hard life with my father.

He beat my mother because he had another woman. He had three children with the other woman. My mother knew but she never did anything. My father would come and say that a girl had been born again, that he was going to look for a woman who would give him sons. Like they say, "God punishes, He doesn't beat you with a stick,

He punishes you slowly." He looked for another woman to give him sons. Nothing! He had three girls! God punished him.

The saddest memories are when there was no food. Sometimes I wanted earrings, or a necklace or shoes and there weren't any. That's when we were children. I would wear string around my neck then – I would make a necklace out of thread. My doll would be made out of the corn cob. We would make dresses for the doll – we never had toys – or a rock would be the doll. That's the saddest part because you want a real doll but you can't have one. Later, when we were older and started working there was a little more.

I wanted to be happy, not like my mother. Her life was so sad because she was beaten. That's not what we wanted, but we wanted to get married. Even when we see how someone is suffering – even your mother – you don't think about it. You think your life will be better than theirs, that it will be different. But it wasn't possible. My first husband also mistreated me the way my mother was mistreated.

I was fourteen when I had my first husband. He started coming over to my house. We were friends for about a year and a half. We used to go to dances, to the movies, for a walk. We went with my mother. When we returned my mother would go inside. We stayed at the door. Another boy used to come to see my sister. When one is a young girl one is kind of foolish or one loves the boy. I can't figure it out, but he asked me to have sex with him – we would marry later. I told him,"No, what if I get pregnant? Then you won't marry me." He said he wasn't lying to me, that we would get married. So I had sex with him.

I didn't tell my mother anything. I didn't want to say anything. But I realized I wasn't feeling well. I was working in a house then. I did laundry. They saw what was happening because I couldn't eat, I would throw up. My mother said, "You must be sick. You must have caught something." I said, "Probably." My mother gave me some-thing so I would stop throwing up. She didn't know I was pregnant. I would cry because I knew I was pregnant. I cried and cried. You couldn't tell. I got fat. I was with my sister then – my mother was working. My father had already left us. So I started ironing, working.

One day there was a dance and my sister asked if I was going to buy shoes. I told her I was and she said that when I was ready we would leave. Then I felt a pain, but I didn't know what it was supposed be like – it was time. They didn't know. I asked myself, "How will it come out? Through my mouth?" I didn't know. Through one's buttocks? How? I started feeling a lot of pain in my abdomen. I told my sister I was in pain. She asked what was wrong and I said I didn't know. They went to buy mineral water for the pain.

The dance was out in the street. I felt as if I wanted to go to the bathroom but there were no bathrooms there. One has to squat. So I went out there and squatted. When I pushed the baby came out. I was in the house but out in back. The baby started screaming and my sister heard it out in the street. The baby was a girl. "What happened?" she asked. "What is going on? Whose child is this?"

"He's Raoul's," I said.

"Why didn't you tell me? Look at the baby and it's raining!"

They ran to get my mother from her job. When she came she held the baby. She was covered with mud. That was the first child. The first and second died. My mother picked her up and said, "It's only that I don't want to, but otherwise I would break her over your head. I won't go out on the street with you any more. Even if you throw yourself in the well when you go out. You are a woman now. You are no longer a virgin. You are a woman now. And whose child is this?"

I told her it was Raoul's. Then they took me inside. My mother told my sister not to let me go lay down – go out and make tortillas, that would be my punishment. I started to make tortillas. The baby had just been born.

When the baby was three days old they took me to his house. When I arrived they set up my hammock, my room, everything. She (her mother-in-law) was happy. That day there was a dance. He got dressed up. "Now you're happy; now you're with me. Well, I'm going to the dance."

What could I do? I couldn't say anything. I had already let him have his way. What could I do? He went to dance. It was dawn when he returned. I said something.

"What do you expect?" he said. "When we were young we went to dances, to the movies, I bought you what you wanted, we ate, we drank. Now, it's over. Now you stay in your home. I'm going to continue having fun."

So there we were. He would beat me, he mistreated me, I would have no food – because he had other women. He liked other girls. If I said he shouldn't go to a dance he would insult me, beat me. He didn't go to work; he didn't like to work and didn't give me any money.

He didn't want to work. When his stepfather – he had a stepfather who didn't like this – started telling me not to serve him any food because he wasn't giving any money, Raoul would force me to give him food. I served him his food. As soon as he ate he went out again. I started ironing. I treated him the way I should. In the morning, he changed his clothes. His clothes were well-ironed. When he came home at noon he took a bath and changed clothes again. He lived in the street. I put up with everything. I guess – well, I loved him. Sometimes there was no food. Sometimes we only ate beans without tortillas. Sometimes in the morning there were no tortillas for breakfast and we would go buy hard tortillas from a neighbour to roast them and eat them. My mother-in-law had many children. We made *atole* out of flour and that's what we had for breakfast.

A year later I had another child, but my first girl had already died – she got sick from whooping cough. When the other one died she was already pulling herself up on the table, she wanted to walk. Her father left us. He went away to work. I stayed with my in-laws. He didn't send me any money. My little girl got sick – she was about a year old when she got sick. We couldn't save her either. She had a blood transfusion, that's when she died. She was getting blood from her grandmother at the hospital. She died at the hospital. Raoulito had already been born – the third one – he was really tiny. We went to the hospital to take my little girl so she could get a transfusion. They wouldn't let me in. I had to wait in the waiting room. I heard my girl screaming, screaming, then she stopped. I said, maybe they've stopped, maybe the blood is gone. After a little while my mother-in-law came out and said, "She's resting now. She has died." We started to cry.

I went to my mother and stepfather – she already lived with him. Raoulito was already crawling, he was big then. Then he got a fever. I took him to the doctor. On my way from the doctor's, I ran into Raoul again. He had returned. He told me to bring him the child so he could hold him. Then he asked me if I would do his laundry the next day. I said how could I do it? My mother wouldn't allow it. He said, "Come on, come and wash my clothes. Remember we were young when we got together. We have a son together." I kept thinking: what will I tell my mother? Should I tell her I'm going to wash Raoul's clothes? She won't allow it, she won't permit me to go to his house to do his laundry.

So I went back. I realized then that Raoulito was sick and he told me to take him to the doctor and I did. When I went to the doctor he examined Raoulito and he examined me and told me I was pregnant again – yes – for the fourth time. I was happy because I knew the child was his. When I returned he asked about my visit with the doctor and I told him the doctor had said I was pregnant. "Whose child is it?" he asked.

I said "It's your child. The child is yours."

"No," he said, "not mine. The child you're carrying isn't mine." I said yes, he said no.

He said, "It cannot be. Is it another man's child?"

I told him no. He said he was going to look for the midwife so she would tell him how many months pregnant I was. I agreed. I wasn't afraid because I knew I had done absolutely nothing with any other man. It was fine with me. I didn't mind. She came over and told me she would check me immediately.

She checked me. "You're two months pregnant," she said.

"Fine, leave it at that," he said. "But that child isn't mine."

"That's your problem," they told him. "You know she hasn't been with another man."

That's how things were left. He started mistreating me even worse. He went out and found another woman. He ate with her, he slept with her, he spent his time with her. I was with my child at home. I was making tortillas de panuchos. I made six kilos every day.

I started making tortillas at eight and finished at six. I would eat nothing all day long. Nine months I suffered like this and I was pregnant.

One day when he came he was really dressed up – his bicycle, his sparkling shoes. And I? My torn clothes, my hair. Well, he didn't want me. On the other hand, the woman he lives with gets all made up – she uses lipstick, has a necklace, her hair is fixed up. He didn't want me. That day I was washing clothes. I told him the boy had no milk.

"I don't have any money," he said.

"So how do you manage where you live?"

"My woman gives me my food, my clothing, everything," he said.

I told him, "The child has no milk. I don't have money." I had stopped breast-feeding him because I was pregnant again.

He went looking for a small container of milk. When he came back he threw it at me and kicked me. I started crying and went across where the saints and the Virgin are and, crying, I begged our Lord that the next time he came he wouldn't come in the same manner. It was because of the things he had that he mocked me. He dressed well, he had a new bike, a gold tooth – and I was poor.

"So, you're accusing me before God," he said.

"Yes, because you mistreat me, you don't love me."

"Well, that child you're having isn't mine."

"So that's why you're mistreating me?"

When he returned fifteen days later his clothes were rumpled; the bicycle had been taken from him. He had nothing. Like I say, God listened because He could see that what he was doing to me was wrong. He was still with the woman, but she wasn't ironing his clothes. He was poor. She had another man.

Like I say, God is omnipotent: if you aren't guilty of anything, He will help you anytime. In nine months, to the day, the child would be born. When the child was dressed they wrapped him up in his diaper and handed him to Raoul. "Here's your son, Raoul."

"My son? He is not my son. Who knows whose son he is because I'm not light skinned."

He left to be with the other woman. I was left crying. He still didn't believe it was his child.

Then, there was a festival. My son was eight days old when he came one morning and kicked the door. He told me to get up and get water so he could wash up to go to the festival. I got up and gave him the water and he left for the festival. I told myself: if he's going to the festival, I'm going too. My son was eight days old. I went to the festival with the little one. We came back together – he found me at the festival. "Who said you could come?" he asked.

"I came to see you," I told him.

He was drinking. We came back together. When we got home he said, "Now I'm leaving. I'm going for a walk." He went to the other woman's.

When my child was fifteen days old he came to say good-bye. "Good-bye, now you will never see me again."

"What about your children?"

"I only have one son with you. Leave him with my mother and I want you to leave with that man you've got now."

I grabbed him and said, "That child is yours," and he pulled. I wasn't letting go, but he's stronger so he pulled away and left.

My son met his father when he was thirteen. Let me tell you, he even cried, he said, when he met his son. He cried. He asked forgiveness of his children because he had denied he was his child and when he saw his features, just like his father, then he cried. They say he told him, "Forgive me, my son. Forgive me. Your mother was never at fault. It was I who abandoned you. You have every right to speak to me or not because I left you." That's what he told my children. They were already big. But he had left me. The father looked exactly like that boy.

To support her children after she was abandoned, Magdalena worked in a tomato nursery and then as a waitress. She had two more children, a boy and a girl, by a man whom she met while working at the nursery. She never washed his clothes. Shortly after she began waitressing, she met an older man and decided to accompany him to San Miguel, taking her children with her.

90

When I arrived here, the village seemed pretty to me. It wasn't noisy. There wasn't music. Where I lived, there was music, dances, everything. Here they didn't have dances.

Since I wasn't used to going out, it didn't make a difference to me. It was quieter here. I liked it here. Don Luis was better. He knew his responsibilities: he didn't beat me; he didn't leave me for other women. He was with me. When nighttime came we were together; here he awoke. He went to work and I stayed. When he got home from work his dinner was ready.

It was so nice for me because I had never had a husband where we were together – always we were separated. In this case, I knew he was at work, I knew that he would come home and when he did we would have dinner. It made me happy. He looked after me.

Later, children started coming. Nine months later, Marina was here, the first girl. A year later I had another one. We started struggling for them. I went to the ranch, to the sugar cane field. We would go and burn the brush, clear where the sugar cane was to be planted. The kids would be there, sitting next to us while we burned the brush. When we finished clearing up where we were going to plant the cane, then we would plant it. Right there – where we were going to plant – was a mountain. We cut down everything, then we cleared all the brush so we could plant the cane. We worked together, he and I: he cleared the land; so did I. When we finished, we would come back to make dinner.

We had a store. We sold a little bit of everything. We worked together: we sold ice, cold drinks, but we didn't know how to manage it. When I came here, I didn't know how to read, how to add. I learned here at the store. Don Luis taught me. I started doing it – this is so much – I would add it and learned it.

(After a while) he had a woman in Orange Walk. He wouldn't give me any money – he gave it all to the other woman. When I found out, I went to talk to her. They had told me her name, where she lived, where she worked. I went so she could see my children. I told her, "Maybe you don't know him and don't know me and don't even know that he has a wife. I came so you would know me. I have children by him. He isn't giving me a cent."

I already had four children. I took a blade with me, a knife – just in case she wanted to hit me. She didn't say a word. She left Luis.

Life went on. We were fighting. It happened that he violated my daughter (by Magdalena's previous partner). My daughter had his son – Lupita has a son by Luis. We started fighting. I suffered a lot. I took her to Merida. Twelve years old. She had him in Merida. He's big now, the same age as Alfredo (Magdalena's youngest son). I was this big and so was she. I thought of leaving him, but I thought about the other kids. I couldn't leave him.

When I knew that she was pregnant, I didn't know who it was. She knew, but she didn't tell me. So I took her to the Adventist (the Seventh Day Adventist doctor). When I arrived there at the Adventist's, I explained to the doctor what she had, that she wasn't getting her period and that I didn't know what she had. Then the doctor told me to come in. They put her in a bed and examined her and they saw that she was pregnant. So the doctor said to me, "She's pregnant."

"Doctor, is she really?" I asked. "

Yes," she said. "You didn't know?"

"No." "For how many months has she not had her period?"

"Three months."

She's three months pregnant.

"But doctor, I don't believe it."

"Yes," she said. "She didn't tell you anything?"

"No, she didn't."

Then I asked her, "Lupita did you hear what the doctor said? That you are pregnant. Whose child is it?"

She said, "I'm not pregnant, Mami."

"But the doctor said you are."

"But I'm not."

So then – when we arrived at the market – we drank a soda. I said to her, "Lupita, tell me the truth." And I kept thinking who it could be. Who?

When we returned we arrived in a truck and he asked, "What happened? What did the doctor say?"

I told him, "Lupita is pregnant."

"But how?" he asked. "I don't know."

I thought he was going to scold me, because he kept me in all the time, to the point where I couldn't even go out visiting anywhere. I was afraid of him.

I said, "I think I'm going to take her to Don Crispo so he can see her."

"I'll take you."

Then he took me. When I came out he was waiting for me in the pickup. I was thinking: what's he going to say to me? He's going to throw me out.

I said, "Your father is going to throw us out."

He said, "I'm going to stop in to ask Don Bacab if he can get me a truck."

"All right," I said.

Then he got down. When he had left I asked her, "Whose child is this that you are going to have?" And she made a sign.

"Whose is it, Lupita?"

She said, "Papa."

"What?"

"It's my father's."

I thought: it's bad; people are going to see. No! What I'm going to do – I'm going to grab the steering wheel of the pickup so we die.

That's what I was thinking. I was angry. But then it was as if God told me not to do it because I was also pregnant. Both of us. I said (to myself): I'm going to kill three innocents; I'm not going to do it. So I stopped. I didn't do it. Then he came back and got in.

At the bus stop I asked him, "Listen, Luis, is it true that this child that Lupita is going to have is your child? Wretch! Dog! You're a goat. Traitor."

He said to me, "Why did you leave me with her?"

"If I leave you with her, I'm not leaving her with a young man. I'm not leaving my daughter with an animal. I'm leaving my daughter with an old man," I said.

"That's my revenge," he said. "Yes. Because when I had a woman in Orange Walk, you took her away from me."

Then he began to say things that made me angry, made my blood boil to the point where I couldn't even see. When we arrived here, before he had stopped the pickup, I got down and him behind me. I went to tell his mother, "Come and see your son because he defiled my daughter."

"But it can't be," she said.

"Well, come and see her," I said.

So she came. "Is it true, Luis? That you did that?"

He said, "Yes, Mama."

"Why did you do it?" she asked.

"I'm an animal," he said.

"Well, what you should do," the señora said, "Lupita should stay and take care of her little brothers and she, Magdalena, should go away." That's what she said.

"No. If I go, she goes with me. I'm not going to leave her to him. I have to take her."

So the same night we gathered up our things and went to a woman here to sleep. Then when the next day dawned we took our things. He didn't let me.

He said, "You're not going anywhere."

I was going to leave him with the children. There were five of them. Then I asked the girl, "Lupita, how did this thing happen?"

She said, "Mami, while you were sleeping, he came to my side."

So then I asked her, "Lupita, why didn't you tell me? You see, you don't tell the truth."

She said, "Yes, you're right."

"He hurt you, didn't he?" "Yes," she said.

So then she began to tell me what he did to her. Then I asked Luis, "Do you see what you did to Lupita?"

"Lupita was already a woman when I got her," he told me.

"Even if she were a señora, even so, you still should not have touched her. And how could she be a señora?"

He apologized because when I was going to leave he cried bitterly that I not go, that I should kill him, that I take him and kill him. I told him no. I mustn't do that because I didn't bring him into the world and I can't take his life away. Only God can punish him, not I.

94

I left him for three months. Before the child was born, I was there (Merida) for three months and then I came (back) here. My child wasn't born yet. He was born here. Fifteen days after my son was born they called me and they told me that her child had also been born. I went to see her. A boy.

Although Magdalena returned to Don Luis for some years, her struggles continued, often over control of money.

When they gave the cane bonuses – before they gave it – he was angry. He didn't want to talk and then when he went to get his bonus he told me to go with him, but I didn't want to go because I knew that he wasn't going to give me a single cent. So I didn't go with him.

Then on Monday when we were doing the laundry, I said, "Marina, we're not going to wash his clothes."

She said, "Fine."

We left his clothes in the bathroom and only took our own. Then when he saw that I didn't gather up his clothes to wash them, he put them in the washtub – his own clothes, thus. Then I got his clothes and returned them to the bathroom. I didn't wash them for him.

When he saw that I had taken them to the bathroom, he said, "Why did you not take my clothes to be washed?" He said, "All right, leave my clothes there. I'm going to go to my mother's house so she will wash them for me."

Then he said, "Well, you know the road, if you don't want to."

And I said, "Yes, I know. Do you think that I'm going to stay with you? I'm not going to stay with you. I'm tired," I said.

Then, yes, I told him that I was leaving. One Saturday, I went to Merida and spent two months.

He asked me to forgive him, that he wasn't going to do it any more. He was sorry for what he had said to me.

"I don't care, but I'm not going to forgive you," I said. "I'm not going to stay with you. I'm going to go away again."

Then he said, "You're going to leave me with the children? What am I going to do? You know that they want you to take care of them," he said to me.

And I said, "Well then, why did you throw me out? You do that every time. You don't want to give me money. It would be less bad if I knew that you didn't have money, but you have money. But you don't want to give me any," I said. "I don't have clothes, I don't have shoes. And when they gave you money, you didn't want to buy," I said. "I'm not going to go on like this. I'm better off with my sons."

And he bought clothes for the children and for me. The condition was that if he continued thus, if he didn't want to give me money, I would leave again – and he would work; I wouldn't work. I wasn't going to make coconut oil. I wasn't going to go out selling. He should do it. He should maintain me and his children. And I in the kitchen: washing, making tortillas and sewing. Then if he asked me to help with something – well, I would always help. We make oil, but I'm not going to sell.

At first, he took all the money. He didn't give any to me. When I wanted sugar, I had to ask. If I wanted salt, I had to ask for it.

Then afterwards I told him, "I'm not going to continue this way. I have to ask. If I want an egg, I have to ask. If I want a piece of chicle, a candy, I have to ask." Better I go with my comadre – to work there so I may have money.

Then he gave to me – when he has finished selling, he gives me the money. Now the money is in my hands. If I want a pound of beans, if I want an egg, I don't have to ask. But I don't want to continue living with him. Right now, I can't do anything because I'm living in adultery. I'm not married. I don't feel right. When I go to church, I see people going to confession, to communion. They can take the Sacred Host and I can't. I feel bad because I'm not married. I'm living in adultery. I'm living my life wrong. I've been asking him for a separation, but he doesn't want one. I don't know what to do because I'm not going to continue this way. He's a married man. I'm not a married woman. I like going to church. When I see others going to confession it makes me cry. When I see them in line to take the Sacred Host, I cry. I don't know what to do. I need to make a sacrifice so we can live like brother and sister, not as a couple. But he doesn't want this. He says it isn't possible. I tell him to let me go then. He says no, that he's going to ask for a divorce. I tell him I don't know, I can't make him do this.

When I was child I went to church, but when you are a child or a young woman you don't think much about religion. You think about dances, about having fun. You don't think of these things. But now – it's been about eight years that I've thought differently about going to church.

When I joined the Legion of Mary, I got even closer. It's a group of women – even young women if they wish – who become apostles. We visit the sick, we visit those who are in jail. You give advice to those who aren't married or those who don't come to church. We can go and help the elderly who can't work, clean their house and so on. That's the kind of work we do: apostolic work they call it.

And the Brother says I can't go make visits or give advice because I'm not married because if I go visit those who aren't married – I tell them they should marry because they are not living right – the first thing they'll tell me is, "How about you, you aren't married?" My biggest problem is that I'm living this way, that I'm not married.

Don Luis was telling me last night, "If you leave, when I get here the house will be dirty. There will be no food for the kids. Who will do the laundry?"

He says, "That's why I don't want you to leave, or to separate, or to have to find another woman – to start my life anew. I don't know what kind of woman I'll find. That's why I don't want you to leave."

Because he wants someone to make his meals, because he's a man who – between you and me – who I think cannot give his love to only one woman, so he doesn't want a woman – he wants someone that he just has in his house and when he needs it. That's all he wants.

In a marriage or partnership, the man must respect the woman and the woman also must respect the man. Respect is like – like he did to me, he didn't respect me. He betrayed me with my daughter. He didn't respect me, that's what I told him. I'm not going to betray him; on the contrary, he betrayed me. It was as if I was nothing to him because the man is well off: the man can do whatever is profitable for him. But he should respect. He didn't show respect here in the house. Why does he say that he can do whatever he wants because he's in his house? I agree that he should give the orders, but also he must realize that he has obligations. He must meet his obligations – not leave us without eating, not leave us without money and everything.

COMMUNITY WORKERS

Felicia

*Felicia, a community activist and politician, was born in
1944. The mother of a daughter and two sons, she lives in
Orange Walk with her husband and sons.*

When I was a kid, I wanted to be somebody in the community that
helped people. From when I was eight, nine years, I was interested in
helping others clean up the town and helping people out. At that
time, people had more civic pride, more concern about the town.
There were more rules. Each month they would go around inspecting
your yard.

I wanted to help the community, but my parents believed that
girls should stay at home and learn about cooking and cleaning.
They wanted me to get married and have children. I didn't like
housework. I founded the first group of Pioneer Girls in town because
I wanted to do something else than stay at home. At that time, we
could only get six girls, but then it increased. I was fifteen when it
started. We did community work, like visiting the old people. The
group is still active.

I went to school through the Sixth Form. My favourite thing
about school was being involved with my other schoolmates. We
would go to other villages, like Pine Ridge. I was adventurous –
sometimes my mother didn't know where I was. I was usually home
at the right time, so she didn't find out. I played with both girls and
boys. We all played together.

From the early age of nine I was interested in politics. Politics
was just starting in this country. The ex-prime minister (George

Price), he is the one who started politics. The first time he came to Orange Walk, I cannot forget. I was in the front lines listening to him. I remember that he said that he came to save Belize and I told him loudly, and the crowd too, that he didn't come to save Belize, he came to take it to Hell. Some fellows came to tell me to leave the park. I told them to leave me alone because I had the right to be there and from that time I knew I had to beat him. Even though I couldn't vote, I talked against him. It was a long fight. I struggled for many years, but I didn't give up.

When I was young, people didn't always respond favourably to me. They said that I should not be active (in politics), that I should be home doing the cooking and washing. Some men would say that is not a job for a woman and I would say, "It is a job for both men and women, because our country needs it." But still there were many people who said it was not a woman's right to be in politics.

When I was coming up, I also wanted to be a nurse, but my parents didn't believe in giving a girl an education. And at that time they didn't have a college here, so you had to go to Belize and we didn't have no relatives there. So I did practical work at the hospital, at the age of fourteen. We had a pre-natal clinic. That is where I worked mostly. So I knew all about birth and birth control. All the nurses and doctors wanted me to become a nurse. They said that I had the intelligence and the patience. I used to help there a lot. Sometimes I would be the only one there. I was just sixteen, seventeen. Sometimes the ladies thought I was too young and they'd want the doctor. I used to tell them, "Well okay, if that is your will. I could help you, but if you want the doctor, that's better for me, less work." But then, they would begin to trust me. Many women got confidence in me. I would examine them and I would give them a date for their birth. Probably, I have some sort of gift for this because I was usually right or at least within a few days. I was right more than the doctor! Even if the baby was going to be born very early, I would know. So they would get confidence in me.

When I got married, my husband did not want me to continue working at the hospital, so I stopped. But on days when they had a lot of work I would help. I wasn't angry at my husband for not letting me work at the hospital. I was angry at my parents for not letting me go to nursing school. I could have received a scholarship.

I wasn't a girl that could stay at home. I was twenty-one when I got married. I didn't want to get married young. I saw my friends getting married young and they didn't have any time for themselves because they had to take care of their husbands. I marry in 1965. I thought twenty-one was a good age. I still continued my active way of life. I had other boyfriends before my husband, but they said that I was too active and they wanted someone who would stay at home. I used to be on a softball team and I did voluntary work and I was a clerk. I was used to coming and going on my own, so I was active in many things. If I had a boyfriend who didn't like me to be active, then I told him that I would never marry him because I like to do many things. And I was always around boys and girls, even though girls weren't supposed to always be talking to other boys. But they were my friends. My husband, I told him that I didn't think I would ever change my ways, so he should leave if he wanted me to and I told him that he knew what kind of girl I am, so he should not get jealous.

I was going out with my husband for three years before we got married. I liked being married. Being with my parents, I didn't have the opportunity to go out of town very much. When I got married, we would go to Belize City, Chetumal, Merida.

When I got married, I went to live with my mother-in-law. Being there, I did not want to have kids until we moved out. I used to pray that we would not have children until we had our own home. I thought that having kids with your mother-in-law is hard because the kid will be confused. The mother will tell him one thing and the grandmother another. So I asked God to wait. And he gave that to me. I thank the good Lord for that. We moved into this house in March and I got pregnant in April!

After having my first two children, I started taking birth control because I did not want to get pregnant again. I waited for seven years to have the next one. And then, because of complications, I had the tie-up, so I can't have any more children.

My two oldest children, they are grown now. My daughter is in Los Angeles, going to school. She is studying computers. My oldest son, he works with my husband at the gas station. My youngest son is in school.

Me and my husband, we have good relations. He understands my way and I understand his. What I dislike about him is that he is very reserved. He does not get involved in nothing. I am the only one that is involved. People who know him at first will say he is a bad husband because he is the opposite side of me. But we have had always good relations. I had a lot of men friends before I got married. After I got married they would come around to say "hi" to me. I would talk to them because they are my friends. My in-laws, they are very reserved; probably that is why my husband is that way. They would hardly talk to me. My husband wouldn't talk to the men who came to say hi to me. One of them told me that he stopped coming around because he thought my husband would probably beat me if I talked to another man. But it was not that way. He knows that I am friendly. It is just his character to be quiet. He is not friendly, but he loves me to be. Everybody laughs that we are so different. You have to know him to know his character. He works hard. He owns and runs a gas station out at BSI.

My husband has never stopped me from my work. We understand each other. Whenever he needs my help at the gas station, I will go and do it. If I have something else to do, I will leave it and go help him. He loves fishing and he will go fishing and I will work at the gas station. So we have never had a fight because of politics.

One thing that is a pity is that my husband will not let me buy a car because then I could go around to the villages and meet the people and do community work, not political work but work with a clean mind. My husband will not buy me a car because he knows I will be gone all the time! He will allow me to have one, but he will not buy one. I don't have enough money to buy a car. But I think if I wait, he will. I do not want to put so much pressure on him.

When it comes to the housework, my husband doesn't help. You see, what happened to the men of Belize, the few that help the wives in the kitchen are the ones who have been out of the country and have seen that. They will help for a while, but then they will stop.

Here the belief is that woman is for the kitchen, man is for the bread earning. It is very rare you will find a man doing housework. I always think that he should know how to help himself because it is not always that they will have a woman. Our first people came from Mexico and you know the Mexicans have the *machismo*. I notice that a lot.

The older son, he takes care of himself. He will cook for himself sometimes. The youngest one, no. The biggest help I will get is from my daughter. She is the only one who helps.

I have a maid; she comes in every day. When I am at home, I will do the cooking. She does the cleaning, the washing and the cooking sometimes. She has been here for thirteen years. Sometimes you have problems with maids and you have to change and change. But with her, she knows me and I have told her the way I want it. The problem I think people have with maids is that they will take advantage of them. For instance, two of my friends came over this morning. I was cooking. One asked, "But don't you have a maid?" I said, "Yes, I do," and they wanted to know why I was cooking. I said, "Well, I have time." They said, "You are paying her to do it." I said, "But I have time to do it now and I am not paying her to be a slave." Sometimes people will come around and I will be working and Cynthia will be sitting. I say she needs to rest. When I am here I do everything. I think why she has stayed for a long time is that I don't expect her to do everything.

For me, the most important work I do is hospital work and community work. I help out at the hospital visiting people. I first started getting involved in politics officially when I was twenty-one. When I was twenty-three, I ran for Town Board. I lost. I continued to fight, and in '81 I was elected finally. In '85 I ran again and won. I was deputy mayor. I served for three years. There was also a woman deputy mayor in Corozal at that time. I wasn't the first woman elected in Orange Walk. In '62 there was a woman on the Board. She won under the NIP (the NIP is the precursor to the UDP), but the people persuaded her to become PUP – she betrayed her party and became PUP so they would have majority. So when I was nominated I believe many people did not vote for me because they believed that, because I am a woman, I would betray the party just like she did. But I won the next time. When I won then, the PUP had a majority and I did not betray the party.

When I was first on the Town Board, it was PUP. They were in the majority. Our voice was never heard. Whenever we suggested doing something for the town, we were outvoted. Those three years to me, it was wasted. We wanted to educate people to keep their yards clean, to have civic pride and sanitation. I would suggest that letters be sent to people about that and the mayor would always say to me, "We are not in a communist country, so we don't have to have laws like that." My answer was, "Well, we are going to be communist with your government." He would not enforce laws because he was trying to win votes.

When we (the UDP) took over in '85, the first thing we did is send out letters to those people, advising them about what would happen to them if they didn't keep their yards better. The laws were already there – we just enacted them. Many people got vexed about that. For example, we had a neighbour here who had a lot of pigs and at night the pigs would run around. I went to see him myself to talk to him and he did build a pen. The law says that at first we impound the pigs and the Board sells them if they are not claimed – that is for pigs who are running around. I think in three years we did much more than the other government did in the fourteen years they were in power. We paved many streets, put up lights – all the streets in town has lights now. The new streets that have just opened don't have lights. We put lights up at the park and put tables there.

Being on the Town Board pays very little – a hundred and thirty-five dollars a month for being on the Board and three hundred and fifty a month for being the deputy mayor. Mayor pays the most, but it is still little. It is a full-time job and it pays only seven hundred and fifty a month. The mayor cannot have another job because being mayor takes so much time, so he usually has money saved.

I was the only woman on the Board. My ideas were different than theirs. Sometimes we would not agree. Many times they would say, "We are blessed that we have a woman on the Board because if it wasn't for her, we wouldn't hear such ideas." They said that I have more patience than them when it comes to dealing with people. I would always be the one to come between them in fights. I would sometimes have the courage to do things before them. For example, we would send letters to people in the market telling them sanitation rules and they would ignore them. I always had the courage to go down and talk to them face-to-face. I would always be that person. They would avoid doing it.

Many times I have officials in for tea, like the ones who are visiting here with no family. People criticize me for that, like I am trying to bribe them or something like that.

One thing I do is I try to get rid of prostitution. Just a few days ago I was talking to the inspector of police, telling him we need to do something about that. There are many prostitutes. I don't like it. When I was on the Town Board, I used to go to the bars and I would talk with them. They are mostly all foreigners, from Guatemala, El Salvador, Honduras, a few of them Mexican. I talk to them and have meetings with them. It is true that they have it hard in their country. Some of them say to me that they do it because they don't have any other job. But I ask them, "But have you tried any other job?" They say no, they do not know how to do anything else. I have pity on them. I try to get them to see to doing some other kind of job. I know it is a very tough job. It is hard. I think that there are other options for them.

I would like to see my town have a good hospital. I would like to see the prison and the poor house improved. I would like to see more playgrounds and recreation centres for the kids.

Everything in Belize is politics, even the Church. The party that was in power then (the PUP), everybody was afraid to be in opposition. And I was in the opposition. And being around, it was hard for me. I was very brave. I was not afraid, but sometimes people would ignore me or say bad things to me. But I never did change. Many people changed over. My cousin changed over to the opposition because he said our party kept losing and losing. He wanted me to change, but I said no, not as long as you have that person (George Price) as the leader of your party. I never gave up.

There have been many changes in Belize since Independence. I was against Independence. Our party did not want Independence because we did not think we were ready to be independent. We didn't have the hospitals, schools that you need and we needed the protection and the help that England gave us. We didn't have the factories and things we needed.

(When we were a British colony) we were dependent. It was good and it was bad. I say it was bad because they had us tied up; we had to do everything their way. One thing I respect about the British is they taught civic pride. They trained us to respect and take pride in our country and people. But since we have had self-government, with the PUP, everything went down the drain. We didn't have that civic pride, everything was careless. That makes me sad. The PUP gave the people too much freedom; they let the people do whatever they want because they wanted to be in power. They were afraid that the people wouldn't vote for them if they didn't let them do what they wanted. Now the people are used to too many freedoms. For example, we have a law in Belize that no one under eighteen can drink alcohol. But that law is never, never enforced. And look how many kids there are that start drinking when they are so young and they grow up not knowing better.

People thought that the country would flourish with Independence. That is what the PUP told them. Finally, in '84, the people voted for a change in government because they saw it was getting worse. People expected that with a change in government that things would get better a few months after the election, but it takes a long time, especially since it was so bad.

I would have wanted Independence much later. When we got Independence, I did not celebrate. I told my friends that it was not what I wanted. I would not even sing the national anthem. I don't think it is right: that anthem is a political anthem, not for all the people. People scold me for not singing it. One time I remember I was sitting next to a minister at an event and I didn't sing it when everybody else did. That man asked me why. I said I don't sing that anthem because it is a party anthem, not a national anthem. He said I was right, but I should still sing it.

I believe that we should accept any aid that people want to give to Belize. My belief is that we should help one another, no matter what race, or colour or country, so I do believe that it is good for American companies and people to come in and help us because I do not want to see Russia come in. I know for a fact that the past government did want to lead us to communism. They didn't want development. They didn't even want for us to have TV. They say that our party is the rich man's party because we want development.

When Assad Shoman and Said Musa came back to Belize (in 1968), I think they came back with communist belief. Even the past prime minister accused them of being communist. They started to say, "Americans are no good, Americans are this, Americans are that." Price made Shoman the minister of health. But Price got help from the Americans – how could he criticize them (the United States)?

When Shoman was minister of health, he wanted health care to be free. He wanted everything to be free and I think that is the worst thing to do, to teach our people that everything should be free. I always say that they wanted our people to get used to everything being free, so the country will be poor, so when Russia will come the people will welcome them.

I think Cuba and Russia are definite threats to Belize; they want to take us over. Part of the PUP invited that. Shoman and Musa, they used to offer scholarships to Russia and Cuba, never to the U.S. If the PUP ever came back in power, I think the country will be in danger. They don't want us to be protected, so anyone could come in. We need the aid of other countries, but not Russia and Cuba.

The sugar cane has been good, it has brought more development into Orange Walk. Its quota is controlled from outside. Unfortunately, in '85, just after the elections, the quota went down, the cane prices went down and people suffered.

I don't ever feel like I have too much to do. I think whenever you want to do something you plan and do it and it works. My family has learned to be independent. They know that the work I do in politics and the community is not out of self-interest. Many people are in politics because they want the power. My family helps me. When I was deputy mayor, or a counsellor for the six years before that, I never did take advantage of that for me or my kids. My kids would boast that I would have the position, but not that I took advantage of it.

I always wanted to get other people involved. I got many other ladies involved in community work and politics. Whenever I am in a group of ladies, like with the BRWA, the first thing I advise them is that the country needs them to be involved. We grew up with the tradition of our grandmothers that you should care deeply about what other people say about you, that you shouldn't do anything that would get people talking about you. But I tell them that for our country we should not think about that so much. I tell them that they should just do things for the community and not listen to what people say about them. I say if you do not do something, then people will talk about you, and if you do something good, people will talk about you, so you might as well do something good because then they will talk something good about you.

I always say what I think. Many people say I do it too much, but whenever I say something, I respect what I have to say. Some people will say things or grumble, but they will not stand for what they say – they will not show their strength. I have taught my daughter this. When she was growing up, I taught her what it is to have the public relations because you have to be involved to help the community. I taught her to respect the leaders in the community and the country, even when she does not agree with them, not to be afraid of anyone. And my daughter grew up that way. She is like me. She can go anywhere and talk to anyone.

What I like about myself is that I have a lot of patience. No matter what people do to me, or say about me, I don't get too mad. I get angry for a while and then I forget it. I wish others would have the patience I have. I do not gossip; I do not talk bad about people. Even when I was young, I did not gossip. When someone would come to me and say something that the other person said about me, I would never say anything bad about her. Even when I got married, if a woman came and told me that my husband was with another woman, I would say, "Well, he is lucky to have someone to hug him up when I am not around." Then when my husband would come, I would say to him, "This is what I heard about you," instead of getting all fighting and jealous. And I would tell him, "If you are doing it, the day will come when I will see it for myself. If you are doing, it, I will see you." But I will never fight my husband because of what somebody says about him. I see many people doing that. I always advise people to wait to see for themselves and then fight.

In some couples you will find that the woman is so jealous or the man is so jealous. I sometimes invite ladies to join things and the husband will get angry. I will go to the husbands to talk to them. I tell them, "You cannot have your wife on a string. It is not like if she goes out there she will be having sex with any man she meets. We are human beings. God made man, and God made woman. If He did not want us to talk to each other, then we would be dumb." I try to break the ice in that way.

Between a man and a woman, the weakest is the man. A woman is weak, that is what the men say. But I say no. They ask me why and I say, "I will prove it to you." I say, "If a girl comes and sits in front of you and she just lifts up her dress and shows her leg, then what do you think?" The men, they say, "Well, my mind is to get to her." I say "Well, that's it. You don't notice what she says, what she looks like. You just want to get her because of her leg. But a woman, she has to like the man – many things about him – before she will choose him. So the weaker is the man – he is easier to get. A woman is hard to get." That is why there are prostitutes – because the man is the weaker.

I always tell persons who worry that the only thing that worries me in life is age because my age is right there. Other things, if it happens, it happens. I don't worry. With my children, I don't worry. If they are out doing something, then they are enjoying themselves and I don't get restless in my bed worrying. I just pray to God that nothing bad happens and I go to sleep. I am that way with my husband too. I am a person who does not worry, like some women, about the lack of money to spend. I make whatever I have enough. But I wish I had more to give more. I do worry about getting old. I will be forty-four this month, but even that does not worry me much.

I am not afraid much of dying. When I was a kid, I was never afraid of death or of a dead person. I would touch the dead and want to see the dead, to make sure. Then, when the town was much smaller, when someone would die, I would be there. And with sick people, I am the same. It does not bother me. I notice when I was young that I would feel something funny when that person was going to die. But I did not study it. Sometimes I would tell the doctor that a patient was going to die and he would say, "You are crazy. This patient is well already." But you know, that person would die. And sometimes they would say, "A person is dying," and I would say, "No, that patient will not die." The patient wouldn't die. And the doctor would say, "You are trying to take over my job."

Sometimes I would see a healthy person and I would get that feeling. So I studied it and I saw that it was three days after that feeling comes that the person dies. I don't know how to explain it. I have proved it to others. Immediately when I feel it, I tell the person that is with me.

My husband thought I was crazy, but he realized that it was right. There was a man – he came to the gas station on a motorcycle. I saw him and I had that feeling. I told my husband that he would die. And three days later he had a heart attack. Another time, I have a niece that I warned not to go to a party. She wanted to go to a party in another village with her boyfriend. I had a bad feeling and I told her she should not go. I had a feeling that she would die if she went. Her mother made her stay at home, and her boyfriend, he died in an automobile accident on the way back from the party.

Sometimes people will have problems and it will so happen that I will drop by at the moment and I will help them solve their problem. They say there is something in me that does that.

For myself, I would like to travel more. And I would like to go to nursing school and become a nurse. I still regret not being stubborn with my parents about going to school to be a nurse. I wanted to be certified nurse – that was my wish from when I was small. Still I am wishing for it. I will do this if I can get the finances.

Rachel

*Rachel was born in 1940. The mother of six children, she
lives with her husband in Orange Walk, where she is active
in community affairs.*

I was born in San Roman in 1940. We were very poor at that time,
though we were not one of the poorest in the village. We had a big
house with a zinc roof. Most of the houses then were thatched roof.
In those days, very few houses had zinc.

My parents were very involved in the Church. In fact, my
mommy used to go to the houses to lead the prayers for people in San
Roman. My grandmother, every night she would kneel us in front of
the candles – everybody had an altar at home – she would kneel us
around the altar and we had to say the rosary every night. I would be
so sleepy. I always remember that. We didn't want to pray – you can't
force small children to pray; it doesn't go in. I wouldn't do it. That
was their custom, to pray every night and every morning. That sort
of custom is dying out of our culture.

In church, we had the Holy Week then, the celebration. It was
something great. From all the towns people would come to San
Roman. On Holy Thursday, the priest would celebrate the washing of
the feet with the twelve apostles. He would find twelve men in the
village to be those men. The whole day, people would eat tortillas
with beans and meat. There was a big feast in the school. Then, on
Good Friday, the women would go very early in the morning, at
about five when it was still dark, on a procession with the Blessed
Mother. The men would take Jesus the other way and they would

meet in the middle of town. It was something very beautiful. They had big huge trees that they would bring in from the bush and they would tie the trees like the Cross of Jesus. They would have everything like Calvary. They called it Calvary. It's is something I remember from when I was small, but they do not do it any more.

When I was six, my mommy came to live here in Orange Walk and she brought us. My daddy was worried because at that time in the villages the schools were not so good. The teaching was slow. He was worried that if we stayed there we would not have been able to go to high school. So we came here. At first we rented a house and then we bought it. We had a big yard.

We went to school here. My daddy wanted both boys and girls to study. He say that girls needed it because they should be able to work and be free, because you never know if you will get a good husband. He said that marriage is like the lottery: you never know what you will get and if you do not get a good husband, then you can leave him and work. He wanted us to do good in high school because we did not have the money to pay for college and needed scholarships.

My parents worked very hard, but I never saw them fighting or doing the thing where the men have other ladies, like they do now. One thing I remember my mommy used to tell me was never to even answer if a married man calls you on the street. She always said, "Don't accept a married man." My parents were like that. They were poor and worked together and were loving. They didn't lash us – my daddy, he didn't believe in that. All he wanted is that his children have a little education and not live like he had. He didn't like the way we were growing up in San Roman.

And though I was a bit older than the other kids, I started school here. My sister, she was older: she was thirteen years old, so she didn't have that opportunity to start school here. After she finished school, she went to my aunts in Chetumal and there she worked doing sewing and housework. She would send money to us or sometimes buy material for clothes for us. That helped.

My second brother, he went to college. My father sent him to Belize to finish. My youngest brother, it was better for him because my sister was already working. My other sister got a scholarship to Guatemala.

When I came out of Standard Six, my parents didn't have the money to send me to college. We didn't have much money. My mommy used to do bread. She used to sell it all around here. My daddy was just a small farmer and he did catch-and-kill (temporary) jobs at the Public Works and the Town Board and places like that. But the Sisters sent me to PG, to the Palatine Novitiate, and I studied there. I was fourteen when I went. That's where I studied for a few years as a teacher. I passed my second class teacher exam there. I stayed there for three years in the convent. I wanted to be a nun. I respected the nuns. They were very good teachers and they cared about the job they did.

After the three years as a candidate, I told my mommy that I wanted to be a nun. She said "No, because when I die you will not be able to come and see me." In those days, '57, nuns were not able to go out as freely as they are now. They would go out, but they wouldn't stay in your house or eat there. But now it is modern; it is not like that. So she didn't want me to be a nun and it was not my vocation because if it was I would have fought. I would have told her, "No, I am going." But now if my daughter wanted to become a nun, if it was her vocation, then I would not discourage her. But it isn't her vocation – she likes dancing and that sort of thing. I didn't when I was young and I don't now.

I came back and I told my mommy that I was going to teach so I could finish my studies. So I went to the priest at the school and he said that I would have to teach for one year without pay before they could employ me as a teacher. And I told him, "No, I am a second class teacher already and I need to earn money because I don't want to be a burden on my parents." The priest said, "Then no, we cannot employ you." I think they were a little bit vexed because I didn't do it. So then I started working with a lady in a saloon for three years before I got married. In those days, they called it a saloon, but it wasn't like selling rum and things like that. We sold soft-drinks, sandwiches, biscuits and sweets. The pay was not much, but it helped.

It was a hard life then because I used to work at the saloon and I used to help my mommy. At that time, she was having boarders from the villages who were going to school. She had two of my cousins and three other boys. She used to charge twenty dollars a month for each of them. She would do the washing and I would do the ironing. I used to start work there at the saloon at eight in the morning and come home at noon and then work until nine or ten at night. And then I would iron. She also did the cooking for the boarders. It was hard, heavy work. That was my life then. I would go to church as usual.

It was in '59 that I met Artemio, right there in the saloon. We were going together for one year before we got married. I think he was the right person for me. He has been very good and very helpful for me. When I was growing up, I don't think I wanted to get married. I never had it in mind. I wanted to be a nun, but I think that God was preparing me for that marriage, even though I didn't see it that way before.

Artemio came from a poor family too. He lived in a house right next to our house then. His parents were separated. Artemio lived with his daddy and his mother lived with her mother, but after a while she found a man, a nice man. Artemio's daddy was an alcoholic. He used to treat his wife very badly: he would beat her and he wouldn't give her money to buy food and things for the kids. She worked very hard doing the washing and making things to sell so that she could grow her children. Artemio got his education because he was smart and he got a government scholarship.

So I got married. When we got married, Artemio asked if I wanted to stay at his father's house. It was right in the centre of town. I said, okay, that we could try it to see if it worked. We got married in 1960 and moved there. But then I got pregnant and I did not like the way his father would come home drunk every Friday and Saturday. And he would talk the whole night. So we said, "No, we cannot have our baby here." So we moved out and rented a house.

I had my babies at home. There still are midwives working here in Orange Walk who still go to houses. The one who attended to me is in the hospital now. She is very old and sick. She was with me for all my births. I never changed: I started with her, I finished with her. She worked hard: she attended me before the baby was born and during the labour. After the baby was born, she would come every day, sometimes three times a day, and bathe the baby. And she took the diapers home and washed them, boiled them. When they boil it, they put the leaves from the orange tree in it. It gives it a nice scent. So they bring it back and then you only need to iron it to use it. Now that everything is modern, you don't use the ones you wash. You buy the pack. It is better.

The midwife used to do a lot of work. They came every day (after the baby was born), for nine days. On the seventh day, they come with a lot of leaves. They boil them and then you take a bath in it. And afterwards, you are in your bed and you won't get up that day. And not on the other days, either. The following day, they massage your body – they say that it closes your joints. They massage all your body like that. I think it's good. They have strength, you know, those midwives. And they only used to charge fifteen dollars for all those days. Recently, when I had Patty twelve years ago, it was twenty-five dollars, but you usually give them more.

In the villages, usually there was the *partera* to take care of the mothers who are having babies. In 1965 or 1966, the government asked all the midwives to come into town to get some kind of training for hygiene and health. They would come once a month for a day and after a few months they would get their certificate. They had to have that or they said they couldn't be a midwife. I think that was good, although they already knew what to do. Few people died. They used to use a lot of leaves. I think it is good, the leaves they used to use. The old people, they took good care of themselves and they were very healthy. Some of the women would have twelve or thirteen children, with only the midwives. Now, with your first child, they say you should come to the hospital, even if you are from the village. After your fifth or sixth child, then they say you should come again because you are weak. But I had my six children at home.

Whenever I would give birth, my husband would be there. He would be holding my hand and maybe that's why he knows what a woman goes through. He knows that it's no joke. That's why I would

116

not go to a hospital because you can't have your husband there. But he would go for the midwife and he would stay right there with me.

After I had my first baby, I didn't work out of the house any more. I wanted to be a teacher, but I didn't want to leave the baby in somebody else's care. I couldn't. I don't think it's good to do that. My mommy didn't much like children, but she would help with them when I went out. I would never leave my children alone and I would never have somebody paid to help me. My work was hard, but I enjoyed doing it. I would get the kids up and prepare them for school and make the breakfast. When everybody went to school, I would do the cleaning, the washing, the cooking. This house is too close to the street and all the dust comes inside from the road. It is paved now, but still it is dusty. It was very hard to clean. At noon, I would have to have food ready for them and then they go back to school. And I clean again. Then I made dinner. Then I did the ironing.

Not until last year did I get someone to work for me – and then only because I got sick – and now I don't want to let her go! I find I can do much more work out, like visiting the sick. I enjoy that kind of work.

Artemio encourages me to work out if I want, to do some kind of voluntary work. But he doesn't want me to work for pay: he says that he is the man and he should bring the money in and I should stay with the kids, but once they were old, I could do any volunteer work I wanted. Since 1964, I have been working. All of my work is voluntary. I am in almost every group in town: I am in Red Cross, Women Against Violence, political groups, women's groups, St. Vincent de Paul – this is a group for poor people. We give clothes and provisions. And I am the coordinator for Help-Age. We help the older people. I try to do my best to do as much as I can.

I think the most important work I do is for my church, for my sodality. There are so many people in our community who are sick and poor. It is in the Maya-Mestizo culture to take care of the old people. They have very close ties. I grew up very close to my grandparents in San Roman. My mommy and my daddy, I would take them in for as long as they wanted. Once they got tired of us, they would go to another son or daughter. I was the only one who didn't work out, so I could take care of them and we had a room for them. They would go stay with the others, but I used to be the nurse very often for them before they died. I was very close to them. My parents were always at home when we were young, they were so very kind to us. My daddy, he came to visit us every day after we got married. Only when he was bedridden he wouldn't come. He helped with the kids. Now we don't have any old people in our family. I am happy that I was able to take care of them. I love that and feel good. I hope that when I am old, someone will take care of me.

I am happy that I am able to do my work. My husband, he is not the type of person who would say no to what I want to do. I wish I could do more; I wish I can reach out to more people. But I try. What little I have, I want to share with others. It's not much. I am always ready to help others. I enjoy working for poor people. Maybe because I was brought up like that. We were never rich, so we would share anything with anybody – like last week, Sister Grace told me that a girl needed a place to stay because she was having very bad problems at home, so we let her stay with us for a few days.

Another thing I do is Marriage Encounter. In 1964, we joined Marriage Encounter. Artemio and I are team leaders. Marriage Encounter is all over the world. We travel to all the districts and do that. It is an experience: it works to help you and your husband find out who you are and who you want to be. You can't really talk about it, you have to experience it. It's not really active in Belize any more. We haven't given a weekend in a year – before we would do one every three months or so. But all the couples who have done it have something from it in them that they can keep. It has helped us a lot in our communication. We communicate a lot. Artemio knows me very well. I tell him everything and he tells me. I never keep anything from him, even if it is going to hurt him. We have worked very hard on our communication. In our family, we have good communication. We trust each other, so whatever happens, we know where the other is. And Artemio always supports me. He would never tell the boys something different than me. Working with the women, I see that this is not always the case. Many times the mother will say no and the kids with go to the father and he will say yes. I am lucky. I am the one who

118

has the say. With our children's education, we leave it to them. We let them choose what they want to study. They know that they have to go to high school. My husband – he feels like my father – that women and men need education. We always try to encourage the young girls to study. I have a lot of *comadres* and *compadres* in the village and I encourage them to send their daughters to high school. I believe that education is for both and I will try to get my daughter everything she can get.

My daughter is going to go to high school. She is in Standard Six. She hasn't told me what she wants to do. She is twelve. From when she started in school, she has been going to "A" groups, but when she started Standard Four they put her in a "B" group. "A" is the highest, the smartest kids. I think it kept her back a lot. In Standard Six, they brought her back to "A" group. I asked her teacher this year how is she doing. She said that Patty is above average but not in the fast group. She does not do well in English. We speak Spanish here at home, so she doesn't get the practice. She took the entrance exam this year and any time now we should get the results. I have told her that if she passes high, she is going to high school, but if she passes low, she will repeat Standard Six. She can do that because she is so young. I want her to go to Muffles College. They won't accept her if she has less than eighty percent on the test. Technical (College) accepts people if they get fifty percent. I have also promised her that if she passes high, I will take her on a trip to Mexico City. I don't know how well she is going to do.

From when our children were small, we tell them they have to go to high school. We try to give them as much education as possible because we can't afford to send them out unless they get a scholarship. If we had family in the States, we could afford to send them there. Only one is living out. He is a chartered accountant in England. He was a great student and, as the oldest, always took care of the rest. The other boys studied either physics or math.

One son, he wanted to teach, like his daddy. He applied to several high schools to teach physics, but they had teachers from the Peace Corps, so he couldn't get hired to do what he is trained for. So he works for the Coke distributor, doing paperwork, but that is not what he wants. I don't think they should take the jobs from the Belizeans. I believe that if a local can do the job, then they should let him. With this government now, they don't have the money to pay for the teachers, so they want the Peace Corps to come in and then our people don't have jobs. And there are many less scholarships: it used to be that if you passed high in your exams, you would get a scholarship. But not now. It is very hard.

I hope my son can teach because in teaching you will have more responsibility. Now he is so free. He lives at home. He doesn't have to do any preparing, like a teacher. He likes to drink too much. I have to fight with him about that. I don't exactly fight, but I try to encourage him to leave that. It is no good, the alcohol. It doesn't lead him anywhere. But thank God that my five boys studied, finished high school, finished Sixth Form in Belize and that three of them have studied out. I have only the young one, Patty, to go now.

The most important thing to teach my kids is to try to live the life we have given them. We never quarrel or fight. We do have some misunderstandings but not in front of my children. We try to keep this unity. I hope they have seen this and that they will live like this. I have seen my son with his wife. He helps her in whatever way he can. She works out and he works. I took care of the baby until he was one year and then they found somebody. But my son, he helps her with the baby, helps with cleaning the dishes and the house, just like my husband used to do. When we had our children, Artemio would help with them. He would say that they were our children, not just mine to take care of, so at night, he would make bottles and like that we would share work. I am glad that my son is that way with his wife. I encourage that. When they married, she was in a different religion and in the other political party. But she changed churches. We didn't pressure her; she wanted to change. And with politics, we don't talk about it: as long as they are happy, then it doesn't matter. They are happy.

The women of Belize, I would tell them to get involved, to come out of their house because when you are in your house every day, all the time, you get sick. You need to come out. You need other people, to hear what they say. I would advise them to get involved in community work – everyone needs to come out of their house, to learn something, to be educated about their rights because most of our women don't know about their rights. They think they have to accept all the beatings that their husband gives them.

When I was going to get married, I told my friends I would not accept a man who would beat me. They say that a man is always strong and he can always keep a woman down because of his strength, but I would say, you have sticks, you have brooms – I wouldn't allow a man to beat me. I would take something and beat him back. Artemio and I, we used to talk jokingly about it before we got married. But he is a very religious person: he wouldn't do that. And he tells our sons, "No, never beat a woman." Because if he beats me, or if he hurts me, he has to pay for it.

I am upset about the government (the UDP) now. Everything was going neatly, gradually, slowly but surely. With the type of government we had (the PUP), things were going well. Our biggest change was to get self-government, Independence. We had seen many countries have to go through war and blood-shedding to get Independence, but we did it very calmly. Mr. Price (Prime Minister George Price), he loved everybody. He didn't want the poor to suffer and if we had a war, it would have been the poor that would have suffered the most. They would have been the ones to have to do the fighting and so he did it gradually and peacefully.

Price started fighting for change in the 1950s. He wanted the poor to get a better living. During colonialism, many more people were poor. Only the rich people owned land. Belize Estates practically owned all of the Orange Walk District. Price started negotiations so the people could start buying the land back. Now many people own the land. Even some of the smallest farmers can own their own piece of land.

Price improved Belize in many ways. Many of the older people here, those of us who remember how things used to be, appreciate him. It is some of the young people and the rich people who support the UDP. Those people who say that Price didn't achieve what he said he would don't understand that change is gradual, that you have to take it slowly. Sometimes they criticize Price for not being married

121

and not having a family. He doesn't have a family because he has dedicated his whole life to helping Belize.

I am glad that Price was in government, but since this government (the UDP) took over, I have seen that our country is going backwards, not developing as it should. Like in the shops: you will go there and find Mexican things – some American things, but mostly Mexican. The American things are more expensive, but they are better quality. But we find that they are selling Mexican things for very high prices and making much money off of people. So the poor have to go to Mexico, to Chetumal to buy things. They pay to go there because they charge entrance fees, so the poor really have it hard. This government is not seeing things through the eyes of the poor. The PUP had different laws regarding sales of foreign objects and border laws. The UDP cares more about the rich people. I see a lot of disadvantages for the poor with this government.

When the PUP was in power, I think that people had more say in decisions then than they do with this government. The UDP doesn't want to be challenged. I have seen that we are going backwards. For example, right now we should have had our University of the West Indies, but the UDP decided not to open it. Everything was ready to start the building. They had the funds and everything they needed, but the UDP didn't want anything to do with anything the PUP had started. So the UDP started things up with this college in Michigan, called Ferris College. I was investigating it when I was there. It is a small school and it wasn't even a university until recently. So why didn't they at least link us with a big university? Ferris is not a great college. We needed more links with the Caribbean. And the standard of education is much higher with the University of the West Indies than with Ferris. That was one thing that took us backwards.

There have been a lot of changes in Orange Walk. Most of the houses used to be thatched houses. You scarcely saw a wooden house – wooden houses were mostly for the very rich or for the government. Gradually the houses began to change. Everybody changed because of the sugar cane; they starting getting involved. The company sold a lot of sugar cane fields to the farmers. A lot of people started getting money and getting houses, so there have been many changes.

Orange Walk is pretty new. We were very poor. In Corozal and Orange Walk, sugar cane has made a big difference and brought many changes. More people have work. Many customs have died out, like the carnivals. There used to be a carnival every year before Ash Wednesday – it used to go on for a week. For three days before Ash Wednesday, they would have the dances. The different groups would dance – every village would have a group and the town would have several groups. The groups would all come to town and all day they would go around and dance and the people would give you some money if you would dance for them. One day they would go to Orange Walk, one day they would go to Corozal and one day they would go to Belize. They dressed in costume. That custom is dying. Only in Corozal do they do that, I think. There are only three groups now. That is a custom I would really like to come back. It was very good. The Mexicans still do it and I think they do it in Jamaica.

I do not know why we don't do it now. I think it might be that they are too busy to do it because of the cane. They don't have time to practice. It might be because of that. With the cane, the people work hard. When they come to town, they have to spend the night sometimes. They have to wait in lines to take care of their trucks. It is really hard for the poor cane farmer. And they are the ones that do it: you will not find the rich people doing it. It is too hard.

The people are the same, I feel. Now we have a lot of new people here. To the back of town there, I have noticed there are a lot of poor people. Many of the poor people are from El Salvador, Guatemala. They are renting the houses. When you go to the houses, you see that many of them don't even have beds. They come here without bringing anything. They have things there, but they come here running and hiding so they can't bring anything. They just barely bring themselves. We have to go out and visit. Yesterday, I was talking about this with a friend. I was saying that we need to go visit, to visit the sick and the poor and to get to know the people here.

It is a pity that everybody went into the sugar and few stayed in the corn and beans and vegetables. But since that is the thing that brings in the money, people grew sugar cane. I think that people should have planted food too because then if you don't have the money to buy food for that week, then you can eat your own.

When I was young, everything like sugar and flour was so cheap. At that time, my aunt used to work for three dollars a week and that was enough. Things have started to get so expensive now. It is hard to live on fifty dollars a week. I remember when my grandfather had a big house full of beans and corn and we would use it when we needed it. We didn't have the money, but we had the food. We had everything: plantains, coconut, yam, all kinds of vegetables. He did not grow cane because at that time there was no factory. And there were the pigs, the chickens and fish. To buy books, I think they sold corn. We had a lot of corn to sell to the towns. I believe that we should have kept a few of those things and have not only cane but vegetables and beans and rice. So everything considered, we were poor before the factory, but we had everything we needed.

ENTREPRENEURS

Susanna

Susanna, born in 1942, works at home where she also owns and operates a village store. She lives with her mother and two of her three children.

When I was little, I remember that my mother worked. She used to sell things and would send me to sell them – she would sell bread, tamales and sometimes a kind of coconut sweet. When I returned from school, my basket was already ready and my mother would send me to sell. I would go to everybody's house selling the bread. As I didn't have a little brother, I liked the little kids. I used to stay hugging them. So when I returned home my mother would lash me because I was late. Also, sometimes on Sundays, my father would send me to find out who was playing the lottery. So I would go to ask, but as I had a friend called Lupita, I would go to see her and would begin to play with her. They came to find me and I was playing with Lupita. So when we were on our way back home my father lashed me. We had a guava tree. My father grabbed the rope, hung me with my two hands tied up and belted me – only because I was late.

When we were growing up, parents were awful. Nowadays we are different with our children. We don't like to lash them all the time – that's probably why they do things to us sometimes. My parents used the lash quite often. I never said anything because it was okay the way they brought me up. I still live with my mother. I punish my children once in a while but not all the time as they used to do before when I was little.

Susanna

The first house my father had was thatch. It was on this plot – over there where the kitchen is. We were poor before – poorer than we are now. We could hear the frogs making noise at night. Sometimes we had to get up because they were under the bed. They were noisy, but they didn't bother us. We slept in beds made of palm leaves that my father cut. We slept on rags and sacks that my mother put on the bed. We had a whole room and a half. In those days, a room was made of sticks and rags together. This is the life we had with our father and mother. I slept with my sisters and brothers in one room and my parents in another one.

I was eight (actually thirteen if she was born in 1942) years old in 1955 when we had a hurricane that destroyed the house and my father had to build another one made of wood. I remember that he sent me to look for stones. I also remember that he placed them to reinforce the poles. This is where we slept when my father built the house. Half of the house was used by us to sleep and the other half was for the little shop that my father owned.

When I was little and was going to school I had to grind corn. I would leave for school, but at twelve o'clock, when I came back, my mother used to tell me, "Go and grind." I had to do it because it was my share of the work. I liked to play with the children at school a lot. I liked to play baseball among other things. I was very lazy with my studies. I decided that school didn't do me any good and I didn't like it. English and counting were difficult. They didn't allow us to speak Spanish at school, only English. I didn't like to study very much, so when I was thirteen, I decided to leave school. By the time I realized that learning was good, it was too late. So at fourteen I quit school. My sisters were ready to get married. Both my sisters got married within the same year. As I was the only girl left, I quit school at fourteen to stay with my mother because she was sick – to help her.

I remember my mother as somebody continuously sick since my childhood. I remember that one day my mother arrived in a black car. I saw her getting out of the car. I was very happy to see her so I said, "And my mama?" She had just had an operation. She got operated on in 1947. She says that she was operated on due to a miscarriage. I was five years old and since that time I remember my mother as always

127

sick. When she started feeling better, after her operation, she began to sell things. This is when we started to work. My mother baked the *tamales* at night and the bread early in the morning. She worked and worked all the time. My father was working, but labour was cheap and there wasn't enough money.

My father had storehouses for corn. When I was a little girl, we used to shell the corn. We would work with my father. He had a lot of milpa. He used to harvest a lot of corn that they would sell. My parents also had pigs and hens. In those days, my mother raised 125/160 hens. She would send us to pick up the eggs and we would bring them back in cloths. We had quite a lot of them. We never got hungry because even late at night, if there was nothing to eat, my mother would send us to get a chicken. She would kill it, fry it and we would eat it. We even ate pigs. We sure ate well in those days. My father always had pigs for sale. He sold his last pig in 1963. He had four huge pigs which were thoroughbred and castrated. My father raised them on concentrate only. He liked pigs and he took care of them. He quit raising pigs because he was getting older and he said that pigs require a lot of work.

When I was a little girl, my father wasn't a cane farmer. He became a cane farmer in 1965. He bought his cane land from the Company. Only a year after they bought their cane land from the Company, they began to sell. They sold quite a lot of cane. He bought a field with my two brothers – I think it was in 1972 – and a truck. It increased rapidly. Both my brothers were working in those days – they were older then and married. The year that my father died had been a good year for sugar cane. They got a bonus: prices were high because sugar cane was selling at seventy dollars a ton. My brother told my mother that he wanted to build a house for us because he had heard my father saying that he was getting older and that he wanted a house for us. My mother remembered my father saying that the day he sold sugar cane at a good price, he would build a house for us. As they got a good bonus and my father was dead, my mother agreed to it. The house was built in 1974.

As he was a good father, we didn't forget him when he died. I don't have anything to complain about him. It was hard when he died because we didn't have a father who would bring things back to us any more. Since my father's death, my brothers take care of his work: they give the money to my mother and that's how we live. My father was sixty-four years old when he died. I was thirty years old when he died and I was married.

I got married when I was twenty-five years old. I had worked for eleven years with my father and my mother. I was not thinking about anything – only getting married. I thought only that when I got married I would work hard to have a good home. That's all I was thinking about: to take care of my husband, my children and my animals. When I got married, I asked my mother if she'd give me a turkey or a hen. I bred them and after seven months I already had animals. I thought that by working together we would be able to make our home, but it was not possible. He brought me to a house made of mud and thatch.

Two days after we got married, he closed the door against me and didn't want to let me in. I went behind the house and started crying. I thought, "Well, why did I get married?" I started crying because this shouldn't have happened after two days of marriage. He should have loved me but he didn't.

That's the way my life was with him. If I was taking a walk with my mother, he would walk by her side and me on the other. It is different today – when I see newlyweds together they hug each other and everything. We were always apart. When I was expecting my son, he told me that he was ashamed of me because I was big. He didn't want to be seen with me. I asked him, "But why are you ashamed? Aren't you my husband?"

But that's the way he was with me, never happy. He liked to quarrel with me when I was home. He was jealous. He said that I had another man, but I didn't have anybody. He even said that my son was not his. I said, "But how can he not be yours?" Well, the kid didn't get his father's eye colour. He got mine.

I had to ask for his permission to go to my mother's house because she had recently been operated on. I didn't want to get married because my mother had been operated and I had to take care of her. I told him, "I told you that I would take care of my mother and

I have to do it." He was upset because I was taking care of my mother. I had to do it. I didn't want my mother to be sick. First thing in the morning, I would prepare his bath, clean and sweep my house – I left it clean. I would then go to give my mother a bath and something to drink. I even cooked my father's meals. At four o'clock, I would give them something to eat and at five-thirty, I returned home to attend my husband. When he came back from work I never gave him cold tortillas; they were always warm. As soon as I saw him arrive from work, I warmed up the earthenware dish because he didn't like cold tortillas – they went right from the earthenware dish to his plate.

He was Mexican. He was working for the Watkiss Company. In 1978-1979 he was cutting sugar cane. He never left me any money, not a single day. He hid it from me. When I would ask for some – because I had to go shopping – he would tell me to go outside and that he was going to give it to me. While I waited outside, he would look for it. He didn't want me to know where it was kept. He never left any money for me. My mother even told me that I was stupid. She said, "Why don't you stay to find out where he keeps it?" But what could I do? He would close the door. When a man acts like that, you don't think about challenging him because he would hit you.

My husband used to get me up at four in the morning to prepare his lunch. I would get up to grind and to crush the chili and the onion for his lunch, but one day, he woke up and he didn't go to work. So I asked him, "Why are you getting me up early if you aren't going to work? You shouldn't do that because I could go on sleeping," I told him. "If you are not going anywhere, don't get me up."

Sometimes I was in bed and the things that he was doing to me – there was a shelf, beside my bed, where he put the radio: he would play it over and over again; he didn't let me sleep. I was pregnant with Carlos and he didn't let me sleep and believe me, I fainted when I delivered Carlos because I hadn't had enough sleep. One day I got up to go to church. I hadn't walked very far when I fell. I was very weak because I couldn't sleep.

He only started doing those things when we got married. I never had what one might call a happy life with him. He was always fighting, even though I was cooking for him, washing his clothes and ironing. That life was never good. He would go to the bush and come back. Well, the only thing that I would do was to smile at him. I was only smiling because I was happy to see him and because he was coming back from work. In return, he insulted me. I don't know why. I only smiled and he answered with insults. I didn't say a word because he would have hit me. I had bananas for sale and when the person would come to buy he would give them away. He would give them and wouldn't give me any money. And I said, "You are giving it away: you have to sell it so I can buy flour." After I told him that, he started insulting me – with him there were always insults.

I was washing his clothes once when I found two little seeds. I went to see my father and asked him, "Papi, what is that in his pocket?"

He answered, "It's a seed."

Something then came to my mind; when he would leave, his eyes looked fine, but when he returned they were red. So I told my father, "That's why his eyes are so red." That's how I found out that he was smoking (marijuana) and why he was doing those things to me.

One day I was with my mother here. He had already returned from Orange Walk. He started insulting me, saying that he didn't want to see me any more in his house. I don't want to repeat the words that he used. He told me that he didn't want to see me in his house – ever. So I told him, "Since you don't want to see me, I am leaving."

"Just go away because I don't want to see you any more," he told me.

I grabbed my things and left. My son, Carlos, was born eight days after he kicked me out of the house. I was staying here then. My father went to look for the midwife because I was ready to deliver my son. My husband had already left for the Mexican side when he learned that I had a boy. He came to see him, he glanced at him and then took him and put him aside saying that this was not his son. I told him, "Leave him here since he is not yours because I know that he is."

131

He came to see me again and wanted me back with him. He brought me to Obregon, on the Mexican side. He was worse with me: he didn't give me a thing to eat and he never bought me any food to cook. I would ask him to buy food so I could eat beans, but he told me that he was not going to buy anything. I used to eat with a neighbour over there. I would go and stand over there and she would give me something and I would eat. One day the lady told me, "Can't you bake me some johnny cakes because I don't know how to do it and I will give you some."

I forced myself to do it, to be able to eat a piece of cake. I baked it and brought it to her. She then gave me a little piece of cake. I even ground and made tortillas for a soldier's wife. I had to grind for three days to get a can of milk for Carlos. He was young and my husband didn't even buy it for him. I am the one who had to grind and make tortillas for three days.

I couldn't even breast-feed him when he was crying because I didn't have any milk. How would it have been possible since I was not eating anything? He would grab Carlos and beat him up to stop him from crying. I told him, "Why are you beating him up? You could kill him. He is hungry. It's killing him." He didn't bother. That's why I decided to separate from him.

One day he grabbed me and pulled my hair down. He was pulling it while he had a can of milk in his other hand. I managed to escape because he would have hit me with the can. When he did those things to me, I started crying. I was not hitting him back because if I had done so, he would have beaten me more. He was only giving me blows, nothing else. I was telling him, "This life that I'm living is hard." I was losing control and I thought: what I am doing here? Only suffering.

Then I went to the house of a soldier who lived close by. I told him, "Do you know what? I would like you to do me the favour of driving me to San Miguel because you know how much I am suffering. I even have a pain in my stomach. I can't pay you, but if you do me this favour, I will pay you once I get to my father's house." He told me that it was fine and that somebody was going to come and get me. The same soldier came. He went into the house and grabbed

132

my bag that was already ready. I grabbed Carlos and wrapped him up. That's how I got separated from him.

I will have been separated for nineteen years, on October 16th. Carlos was six months old when I brought him to my parents' house. I got pregnant with Carlos three months after I got married. He came once more to ask me to go back with him. I told him no and asked him to leave me alone. From now on, I told him, I will live as I wish and the same thing for you. I have not seen his face around since. He has never come back. He didn't give me a single cent to help me. I worked very hard.

When my father was alive he took care of my son. When my father died, it was even worse. I had to take care of him and educate him. The only thing that my father asked me was if I was pregnant again and I said no. "You are welcome then," he said. I went back and I never left. I still live with my mother. My father told me to take care of my mother because she was sick. That's why I am still living with her. I was sad because my marriage had been useless. I think that my son is sad because his father is hiding from him and doesn't want to see him any more. The man just ran away and never came to see him again. Carlos thinks that his father might not like him – otherwise why would he be running away?

The father of my daughters came along and said that he loved me and that he was not going to do the things that my ex-husband did to me. His name was Melchiades Chan. He was a Mexican worker. My father told me that I shouldn't go with him and that rather I should stay with my son. I told him, "But Daddy, if I am alone, who is going to take care of me?"

That's what I told my father, when he was alive. I had been with him (my father) for four years when he died and after his death, I stayed three years alone. Afterwards, I agreed to be with the man because he would support me and everything. Otherwise how was I going to survive?

At the beginning, he was good to me. He was working, he was taking care of my mother's coconut plantation and he was bringing back coconuts. My mother regarded him as her son. He didn't have to bring any food to cook. As my mother had money, she would give us food – we ate, drank and everything. One day he went to the other side – where he had been living before – and brought back a thirteen year-old boy. He told me that it was his son.

(One day), after the people (cane workers who were taking meals at her house) had eaten, he told me that the boy – his son – told him that I was flirting with the men. I told him that it wasn't true and that speaking with people is natural. "People talk to me and I have to answer because they are eating," I told him. So I got mad and told him, "If you don't want me to feed workers, I want money in my hands every week," I told him. "From henceforth, I will stop having people over to eat, but I want the money in my hands weekly to eat and live."

When Monday came, he had packed his bag already and he had left. He was supposed to come back in fifteen days, he said. My little girl, Angelica, was one year old when he left and to this date I have not seen his face. He has not written me – nothing. I was expecting Modesta when he left. I have not heard anything from him. I told him, "If you are thinking about leaving me just tell me because do not think that I am not able to work with my hands. I can work and take care of my daughter because I don't care."

He even wanted me to get an abortion – I was two months pregnant with Modesta – and he wanted me to take some pills to kill her because he was leaving. My mother then told me, "Don't do that," – because I told her what he had said. My mother told me, "If one can raise a puppy, one can raise a Christian; let it be born and we will take care of it." That's why I obeyed my mother and why Modesta is here today. When I told my mother, she said that I shouldn't do that because it was a sin. That's why I didn't do it because I know that it is bad.

I know that when you get married, you have to take care of your husband. You have to be united with him. When he talks, you have to listen to him. The same thing with the woman: just because he is a man, he can't do whatever he wants; both have to talk together. The duty of a woman when she gets married is to take care of the meals, to wash the clothes and to feed the animals. The duty of a man is to support a woman. He has to find a way to get money for the food supply: flour, butter, sugar, the things that sometimes are lacking in a house. He also has to give her spending money because what about if she finds some meat or a fish and he is not at home, or he is working? She has to have the money to buy it, she has to eat. Another duty for a man is to work on his milpa in order to have corn.

We have to obey him and avoid doing bad things because a lot of women don't have any respect for their husbands and sometimes they look for another one. But when a woman is committed to her husband, she is loyal to him. He also has to be faithful to his wife because when you are getting married the priest says that you have to love each other till death separates you. I knew what my obligations were when I got married and that's why I can't explain why he didn't love me – because if he had wanted to take care of me, I wouldn't have been as stupid as to leave him. I couldn't handle the way he treated me. Even though I loved him, I couldn't take it, I couldn't. That's why I tell my mother, "God knows whose fault it is, his or mine." I was not going to stay and die there. The last thing that he offered me was to slash me with a machete. I got scared. It was only a threat – I decided that it was better for me to leave and I came here.

When he (her second partner) left, I think that God wanted it that way. I went to confess again and to tell what I had done and to ask that God forgive me. I started feeling happy when I started serving God with my Sacraments. I am with God because I am not living a bad life any more. I don't know what happened to me. When you are a young girl, you are crazy. You don't know about life. It is only after that you sit down and start thinking about what you did. I wanted a man who would take care of me – that's why I got involved with the other man. It didn't do me any good. Well, I have decided not to look for anybody else.

My father already had the shop when I was born. He kept it till the day he died and then my mother didn't want to do anything with it and left it. I took it over when the father of Angelica and Modesta – my daughters – left me. When he left, we started working at the shop. I was pregnant with Modesta. I said to myself: it's better for me to stay alone. It's better to have my kids and to accept my life the way it is. I have been on my own for fourteen years, working to survive.

I opened my little shop to survive. I was selling refreshments and baking bread and coconut *empanadas*. I also raised pigs and chickens and sold them and that's how I made a few cents. I was the only one doing everything. I made a list of what was missing and then I would go to town – to Orange Walk – to buy what I needed, what the store needed. People told me what they needed, I wrote it down on a list and I bought it. I bought by the case because it didn't do me any good to buy by the dozen. I bought by the case – a case of milk, a case of cereal. I opened an account at Woolworth and every month I went there to pay the account. That's how I fell a little bit into debt. I still owe money there.

One day a man came. My son yelled to tell me that a man was coming. I went and the man told me that he was the control officer. He told me that my balance was not good. I told him, "And how come my balance is not good?"

He said that it wasn't. "If I put you in the hands of the law, it would cost you more money," he said. "All you have to do is to give me two hundred dollars." As I was scared and didn't have much money, I looked for everything I had and gave it to him. My financial problems started after giving him that money.

My brother came to see what was going on. He went to talk to the police, but the man was already gone. He came back again on another occasion. He told me that he had to check the shop. I then told (my sister's) son: "Elias, go and bring back the police. Let's find out if he is a control man or not."

He left. He was coming to rob me once again. I never saw any identification showing who he was. The police told me afterwards to ask for them when one of those control men came to check the shop. That's why I called the police when he came that day.

So that's how I started the little shop: I would look for a sack of flour, a bag of rice, a bag of flour, the essentials that people buy. So when I had a little extra, I used to go and buy a little bit more. One day my brother came to the store – people would come to buy what they wanted – and I would tell them I didn't have it. My brother asked me, "But why don't you buy it?"

Susanna

I answered, "And how am I going to buy it if I don't have any money?"

He then went and told my mother, "Mama, what if I give a thousand dollars to Susanna?"

"Well," she said, "If you want to give it to her, do so." That's when my brother helped me with a thousand dollars. I expanded the store a little bit more when my brother gave me a thousand. Eventually, I had nine thousand dollars invested in the store. I had a little bit of everything. Every year it was going well.

I made something out of the shop. Do you know how many years of my life I worked at the shop? Twelve years. I worked, drank and ate there. It helped me quite a lot because there was something I could do with it. I was the one in charge of doing business there. The owner of the truck would load it up and I would pay him the transportation charge. Sometimes they would charge me seventy-five cents for a pack of sugar and fifty cents for a case of milk. Sometimes I carried up to two thousand dollars worth of goods in a regular load – and sometimes up to three thousand, in the good days when people were not going to Chetumal (in Mexico). I sold quite a lot and on Saturdays, I would take in up to one thousand five hundred dollars. People would ask for credit and I would give it – and on Saturdays, they would come to pay me. Then I would put my money together and would go to pay my account and get more. That was the life I had at the store. I liked it.

I felt sad when my store went bankrupt because I had nowhere to support myself. When my son went to high school and everybody began going to Chetumal, it began eating up the money. It is cheaper to buy goods in Chetumal. People go to Chetumal: ham is cheaper. Here it is sold at up to a dollar and there it costs fifty cents. Everything is expensive, but over there it is cheaper – that's why people go there. Three or four years ago, it started to fall off. In 1973, business was good, but it started falling off in 1983-1984. Before, there were a lot of foreigners who came when it was the *zafra*. I think that people are up to drugs now – the weed. They don't come any more to cut sugar cane, they go somewhere else – but they used to come. We have sugar

137

cane, but people don't want to come. We had a few workers this year who came to cut it. They left and I wasn't doing any business. I was not selling any flour.

Since I left my shop, I have worked making *recado* and bread. I sell it in order to be able to survive because, if there were no bread, there would be no earnings to buy my supplies. When my son graduated, they didn't give him any work; he then started cutting sugar cane. He was making up to a $110 dollars and was giving me a hundred out of it. That's how I was able to buy things to eat, but now that the sugar cane harvest season is over, he went to apply for a job and he got a teaching job for a month. He went to get his pay cheque today. That's how we are living. He sometimes gets a job with his uncle, planting some sugar cane. He earns some cents and brings them back to me.

I am happy now because nobody insults me or tells me things. I get up in the morning and do my chores: I give my children something to drink and I don't have to worry about anything – that's what I tell my mother. When I had a husband, I was never happy because he treated me badly and he never gave me a bite to eat. Now that I am alone, I eat three times a day and even though I have to work, I feel fine. When my work is over, I go to bed. Sometimes I sleep and nobody tells me what to do. It is not bad to be single. Men talk to me, but I tell them not to bother me. They come and tell me that they love me – but I don't want anything, nothing else. I am very fed up about what happened to me. So they don't say anything else.

I tell Angelica, "When you have a job, it will replace any husband – because when you have money, you don't need a husband. If you succeed in graduating and look for a good job, you won't need any man because your money will be your husband." That was the way I was talking to her. Education is a gift, but most of the time girls get married. When she was young, she used to say that she wanted to be like her teacher, who was making money, and I would tell her that I would send her to get an education and carry on with her life.

That's why I sent her (to high school) but she tricked me and left almost two years before finishing. I felt very unhappy when she left because I had made a lot of sacrifices and I had worked very hard to get her educated and she didn't want it that way.

I even lashed her. I lashed her three times and the last time it was her brother who lashed her. She didn't obey me. She went to take her exam one day and I waited and waited for her, but she didn't come back. They told me that she was living with that man and I didn't know anything about it. I am not guilty. I didn't even know what she was doing. That's why I am so bothered – because she cheated me and she shouldn't have done that. I went to talk with his father and mother. I told them that I didn't want their son to give my daughter a hard time because, you know, she passed from primary school to high school and she doesn't know anything about working. This future wedding is not a game, it's till death separates them. I don't want her to have a hard time tomorrow or the day after tomorrow. They said yes. I hope it is going to be that way. The man may love her and take good care of her. She won't have to do what I did. She will only have to take care of the man, to wash his clothes, to feed him and to iron. That's all. This is the work she will have to do.

If I were a young girl, I wouldn't get married again because I already saw all the bad things that happened to me. I wouldn't get married again. I already had a few failures. Less work! Less headaches!

Six months later, Angelica was married and living with her in-laws. Susanna had re-opened her shop.

Bianca

Bianca was born in 1955 in Orange Walk, where she has lived most of her life. She lives with her partner, Charles and her son. Her son's father lives in Jamaica. Bianca owns and operates her own business.

I was born in Orange Walk. There were nine of us kids, five girls and four boys; I was the second oldest. My father was a farmer. He grew plantains, beans, bananas – many things – on his land. Later he grew cane. He still plants cane in the bush. He is a hard-working man: we always had enough food.

When we were growing up, my father didn't have a steady income. He got other jobs. My mother made things to sell – crochet, food – and us kids would sell it. We were happy kids. We had happy Christmas, even though we were poor.

We always worked when we were growing up. My mother always told us that if we wanted anything extra we had to work for it, so we worked for books, clothes, shoes. We worked in the Indian stores on the weekend. They used to pay us three dollars for the weekend. For three dollars you could buy the material for a dress.

My mother was a very good woman: she was hard-working, a very outgoing person, a very pretty lady. She used to love to have parties at the house. Lots of people had house parties then. Now people just go to the Lounge (a local bar), places like that. I don't like that as much. My mother tried to put us all through school. I'd say that half of us made it through school, through Sixth Form. We all had a chance. I liked school. I did good in the subjects I liked: math, science – I loved history. I even used to get honours, but I used to hate literature.

We couldn't have boyfriends when we went to school. My father was very strict. I had it hard because I was the second daughter. My older sister had a boyfriend and my father told her she could either go to school or get married. She got married. My father always watched. We thought we were fooling him, but he knew when we had a boyfriend – it is obvious. You have to be very tricky to fool a parent.

School was hard because I had a lot of work to do at home. My mother from when she was twenty-eight was very sick. They removed one of her kidneys, she lost a baby. It was years before she could do work, so the responsibility was mine for my little brothers and sisters. They would help, but I did most of the washing, the cleaning, the cooking. It was hard to do all the work at home and go to school. I felt like I was going to die. When my sister got older, she would help me. My father made the bread. In those days, they didn't have the tortilla factories, so we had to do it all ourselves. I had a lot, lot, lot of work to do.

I was eighteen when I graduated – 1973 is when it was. I missed some years because of money problems. I got a scholarship to Sixth Form. I didn't go because I wanted to work to buy the things I needed and I was near the oldest and had to help the others out.

The week after I graduated, the chairman of the Cane Farmers Association asked me if I wanted a summer job. I started working then. It was good. I got sixty-five dollars a week. That was good pay then. After I started working, I didn't want to stop because I liked having money. I used to give my mom thirty-five dollars a week and I used to love to buy clothes and shoes and gold jewellery. I saved five, ten dollars a week. Not much. I started putting it away so I could go on trips. After the first year, I had two weeks in Jamaica. I was in the Jaycees. I went with them to a conference there.

The following year we went to Merida and the next year a girlfriend and I were planning to go to Guatemala, but my parents said no, said it was too dangerous. Then we wanted to go to the Cayes.

I told my father I wanted to go. I had to ask permission for everything, even though I was a working girl. He said no, because he didn't want me to go there with the boys. My boyfriend was going. I said, "Well, I am going," and he said, "If you go, then you can't expect to come back to this house."

I said, "Fine, I'll stay in Belize City." I was very independent. He brought us up that way.

I went to the Cayes and then I got a typist job at Belize Estates in Belize City. I typed all day. It was so, so boring and only $55 a week. I lived with a friend. She charged me $100 a month. We had a lot, lot of fun, a lot of parties. Many people came to our house. Nothing came of the boy I had left home. My parents were right about that: they told me it wouldn't work out. I realized that I left because I didn't want to ask permission to do everything.

At that time, I met the father of my son. Timothy is from Jamaica and was doing construction work. His boss offered me a job at the office. It paid $95.00 a week. That was very good at that time. I worked there for two years: I was in charge of the office, all the payroll, typing, organisation. It was a lot of work. I was the only woman. They were very good to me.

It was a family business. Timothy wasn't in the family and he thought he was always getting the dirty end of the stick. He had a lot of trouble with the boss's son. He quit and somebody offered him a job in Orange Walk. So we came back here.

At that time, I was pregnant. I got very sick when I was pregnant, so I didn't work, but I was close to my family and they helped. And Timothy worked. I had a son, Keith. My parents were very mad that I didn't get married when I had a son, but they said I was always welcome in their home.

When the baby was six months, I got a job doing books at a store. After that, I started working for British Fidelity Insurance. By that time the economic situation in Orange Walk was going down, so no one was buying insurance, but I did it for two years. Then there was an opening at BSI. I applied for the job and got it. I was the secretary for the one of the managers, Charles Gordon. I liked working at BSI.

You had a good pension scheme, good insurance. Even the starting salaries were good. After six years, I was making $960 a month.

Charles was a very strict person to work for. I learned to do things the proper way. And BSI was a good place to work. The British don't take advantage of you: they give you all your rights: a pension scheme, good retirement, insurance. They treated us good. We had access to the pool, tennis courts, the BSI club – because we were on senior staff. And we got Christmas bonuses, depending on what the sugar price was.

From when I know Charles, we have a very open relationship. When I was working with Charles, he was getting a divorce from his wife and I was leaving my boyfriend. I needed to leave because during the time I was pregnant, Timothy started drinking and we started to have problems. I couldn't do anything about it. He needed help.

I used to stay with a friend who had just broken up with her boyfriend. Charles would visit us because they were friends. Charles would talk about why he was getting a divorce. I'd listen. He was a big man. He always thought I was a little girl and empty-headed, but then when he started listening to me, he saw that I was smart. He tells me now that he was amazed with me. He'd sit and listen to me tell about how bad things were with my boyfriend and how I was still cooking for him. And he saw that I was slowly making plans to reconstruct my life, instead of just cursing and railing up at my boyfriend. I used to tell Charles that I didn't know how to separate myself from Timothy. Timothy was so dependent on me, especially emotionally. He was very emotional.

I must say that Charles never said anything like, "Well, if you leave him, we can get together." He never ever pushed himself on me. He let me do what I wanted. I never realized that he had intentions for me – he never tried to lose his respect for me. We spent a lot of time together. Charles used to help me a lot. Timothy started to get jealous and I said that there was no reason. By that time, Timothy was already working in Belize. He just came home on weekends. Sometimes he'd come home during the week to just check up on me. That made me so mad! He had no reason to.

Then one day we went to some celebrations. Charles and I went together. Then we went to a dance. At ten or so, he dropped me home.

When he dropped me home, my boyfriend was there and he was drunk. He was mad and he asked me where I'd been. I told him that I'd waited for him and he hadn't come, so I'd gone with Mr. Gordon. He slapped me. He thought I was fooling around. I was shocked that he'd slapped me; he'd never done it before, but he was very desperate. He knew that I was going to leave him. I had already told him that I was and that I was just giving him some time to get himself together to leave. I told him after he slapped me that he had better not set foot in my house again and if he did I was taking my son to my mother's house. You see, at that time I was paying most of the rent. I told him to get out. And I told him that as of that day, I was going to live my life as I pleased because I don't want to have anything else to do with you. He couldn't believe it. The next morning he woke up and pleaded, pleaded, pleaded, but I didn't listen. He left. I never went back to him as a woman.

Timothy finally went back to Jamaica and got help for his drinking, but by that time I was very disillusioned with him. I was out of love. I wasn't going to fool myself and say that I love him and want to live with him when I don't. And that was a very hard decision because my son adores his father. I have taken him three times to Jamaica to visit his daddy. Now he goes on his own.

That year I started seeing Charles. After his divorce, he felt really bad and he started seeing a lot of women. He had all these women on a string – he would only be with them for a while.

Two of them had his child. He complicated his life, but slowly he and I ironed things out. My mother used to say, "Ooh, that man has had a lot of women!" But I would say that from when we are together he hasn't, but women follow him.

If I wasn't a mature person and we didn't have a good relationship, I don't think I could cope with it. Women used to phone, call here, look for him. I used to have to just let him be and not pressure him. And he made his choice and we live okay, we live happy. We have a good relationship. We tell each other everything. I would say that now our relationship is better than ever. If it were not going to work out, I think I would know by now. We have been together for eight years now. We like to do many of the same things. We do a lot of community work, like with Rotary and Rotarian. There is always some kind of fund-raising to do. And we like to travel, like to Cancun. We also like to swim and Charles is teaching me how to play pool. We like to stay home a lot. We read a lot. And most weekends we do things, either go to football games or take care of our horses. We like to visit with people and we spend a lot, lot, lot of time with my family. We have our problems, but we work them out. If there are certain things he likes that you don't like, you must not try to stop him because then he feels cornered. I can't do that with him and he must not do that with me. I must feel free.

After I had been at BSI for a few years as a secretary, they offered me the senior clerk's job. He had left. So I had that job and my job too. They gave me a raise. When I took over the senior clerk's job, I had to deal with a lot of the managers. They didn't think I could do the job because I was a woman. There weren't many women there and all were secretaries or timekeepers or clerks, but they saw that I could do it. They had to deal directly with me – I had to do inventory, pay cheques, many things. I liked that job. I was in charge a lot. After a while, they got to respect me.

When the cane prices went down, they made my post redundant. They offered me a job at Libertad. I'd drive back and forth, but Charles told me that they'd be closing that factory and that he was stopping in a year's time. So I decided to stop because we were going to start a business. I tried a lot of things to make money. I tried to buy clothes from the States to bring down and sell in shops. I used to go every six weeks, but the economy was getting worse and worse because the sugar cane prices were going down and down and so I really started business at the wrong time. I didn't make very much money: no one had any money to spend and they could just go to Mexico to buy clothes at a lower price.

When the prices went down, I don't know how people used to live. I was affected by it because I lost my job, but I got some money to continue to live on and Charles got money from his retirement, so we had enough to get by and invest, but I don't know how the farmers made it. People just abandoned their cane because they couldn't sell it. There was no money to plant or fertilize.

I invested my money in a little ice-cream parlour and an agricultural supply store. That didn't work. Everybody said that the agricultural supply store would do well because BABCO was coming. Ha.

BABCO is a USAID agricultural project that is supposed to teach people how to diversify from sugar, but it is a joke. They go around and they pick farmers that have a one-acre plot and they tell them to grow cucumbers and green peppers and other things. Of course, people are going to be successful with one-acre plots. You cannot live off of one acre – you can't make any money from that.

BABCO was a four-year project. They only have two more years. They said they would be able to tell Belizeans what they can grow here and how to grow it, but Belizeans already know that, or they can find out for themselves. What they need is a market. They need for the U.S. to secure them a market. Without that, what's the use of growing any crops except for food? We don't mind for the U.S. to subsidize us some, but they mustn't come out with bullshit like, "Oh, we spent fifty million dollars in Belize." What have they given us? Half of the things we know already. The concept is good, but the method and the results are terrible. I don't see how they will succeed.

Our agricultural supply store failed because they brought down all their own equipment and seeds from the States and they brought it all duty-free, so some farmers had to compete with farmers that were getting everything for free. And Americans grow with cheaper duty-free equipment, so of course they can sell it cheaper. And they ask, "Why don't those lazy Belizeans grow anything?" It's because they can't afford to, the competition was too high. And our store failed.

The Americans say that they are helping us out. The Americans won't come to help unless you are really in trouble and they are usually the cause of the trouble. If they hadn't reduced the sugar quota, then Belize wouldn't be in the trouble it's in now. Like we wouldn't have the drug problem: there were hardly any drugs in Belize before the cane prices went down. Most people went into drugs when the banks started taking away their houses, their tractors, their fields. What else could they do? The Americans came and offered to give them money to grow marijuana and they were between the devil and the deep blue sea. Most of them knew it was wrong, but their children came first. They had to feed their children.

I don't condone what they did, but I don't blame them. They did it to feed their kids – all because the U.S. cut the quota. What could that money mean to them? Maybe they would have lost two million dollars or so if they hadn't cut the quota, but that is nothing when you think about how much they are spending in aid now, doing feasibility studies and so. They come and they bring this expert and they pay him this big fat salary and he lives in a big expensive house and he has a car and air-conditioning – and he is studying something that Belizeans, who have lived here all their lives, already know. They do that all the time. It's a waste of money.

People say that when the cane farmers get money they only do foolishness. Who are they to say? Cane farming is not easy work. If a man has a store in Belize and makes money, it is his right to do anything he wants with it. But the Belize people, they say that the cane farmers throw their money away. A farmer works plenty harder than a shopkeeper. He has a right to buy what he wants. He works bloody hard. He feels like he improves himself by buying things like cars – it makes him feel better. Everyone thinks that the cane farmer has a lot of money, but that's not true.

Now, even if people start getting a good price for cane, it will take them a few years to get their fields back to good standards to get a profit because you have to take into account all of the money they've lost.

The cane farmers used to be uneducated, so people could take money from him: deduct money that shouldn't be deducted, etc., but now he is getting an education, or his kids are and he can watch out for himself. But people still take advantage of the cane farmers: the banks expect them to pay income tax for the last three years. How can they pay taxes? They have no money. USAID, they put a lot of funds available for people to borrow. They weren't putting the funds direct to the people – they gave it to the banks and the banks could charge people for it, so it costs money to borrow money. Then they give you money and they say you can only use it for certain things and those things aren't what the people need. I'm sure USAID has done a lot of good, but there is nothing of real significance.

The cane prices going down really affected Charles and me. Before, we were doing very well; now we are just surviving. I have tried to do many things to make an honest living. I have tried many business ventures. Now I am doing okay because I have a cement business. Charles has the tractor which he rents out and he works with the papaya people, but we are just surviving. I'm glad I only have one kid. That makes it easier. Everything is so expensive now. Most people have to do without a lot of things to get their kids through college or to buy a house. It is so hard to buy a house now and it is expensive to rent, like we are.

When things are hard, people tell me, "Well, you can always go to the States." But now, even that is expensive. I always say, "I am not going to go live in another man's country to live illegal or whatever to hustle a little job." It would be too hard. Belize is a paradise. Why should I leave my country when I can do what I want here? I can do most jobs, but I don't think I'd do much better in the U.S. It's so expensive.

Jobs are very hard to find here now. Labourers can usually get jobs, but a lot of jobs have been taken by immigrants. There are few industries. Belize needs more industries. That's the only thing that will generate money. We are basically dependent on two industries now and we need more. At least we have a minimum wage. The basic salary, by law, is $50 a week. That's what I pay my maid. In Belize, we don't take advantage of our workers. That's one thing that bothers Charles, when Americans come here and say, "My God, these people are expected to do so much!" But in Mexico and Guatemala, people are paid $4 a day and sometimes even less. We pay well, that's why we don't have the problems they do. And in America, people exploit the people from Mexico and Central America. They take advantage of them.

When it comes to people who have finished school, there are no jobs and there isn't much for women here, no opportunities. I can get a job because I have experience, but people can't get any experience. About eight hundred students graduated from high school this year and there is nothing for them to do. Only ten percent of the graduates get jobs, so the women, they get married, or take a man. Or they get pregnant because they have nothing to do. Or they go to the States. I tell my youngest sister to go to Sixth Form, so at least she'll have something to do and maybe she will get a job. It is very hard for women who don't have an education.

I would like to see women in Belize becoming more independent and not just doing what they have to do, but not everybody has had the opportunity I've had. I've had a very supportive person behind me. Charles always gives me support: he encourages me to do what I want and he takes care of me. He washes up and cooks when I'm sick and he is a good father to my son. My son likes him.

I always feel that if you are independent financially, then you are halfway because that is what always gives you the worries and the stress. I would say that women have more opportunities now than they used to. There are more things to want and when you want something you are more ambitious. You work harder to get the things you want, like to put your children through school. Even the poor, poor, poor people want to send their kids to school now. I am in the Rotarian Club and we give scholarships to kids. Last week, I was reading the letters from mothers who need money. They were so sad – we only had six scholarships and so many letters.

It was very depressing. As a matter of fact, I think I am going to pay for one girl, if she doesn't get the scholarship. She is an orphan and she did quite well in school. She left her foster family because she had trouble with one of the boys. Now she is living with another family. They are good to her, but they can't afford schooling. She works really hard and she wants to finish school. She paid her own tuition for a whole year, but she had nothing. She made only $10 a week. I want to help her out. She only has one more year. In Rotarian, we almost always give scholarships to girls – girls are at such a disadvantage, any way they turn.

We haven't reached that point in Belize where men and women are equal. Women have to always prove themselves, but they usually aren't even given a chance. It is easier for men to fend for themselves. Given a chance, I proved that a lot of men were inferior to me at work.

I made a lot of friends and a lot of enemies, but when it came to my job, they couldn't tell me nothing. So we always should give women a chance, but I think we still need good housewives to take care of the children. If my mother was a working woman, maybe we would have had more material things, but it wouldn't have been so good. We wouldn't have been so ambitious.

All the women in my family came out very outgoing and ambitious. My sister – she got married, but she married a bank manager, so she did well. My other sister – she got pregnant when she was in school, but now she has a good husband who works at the factory and she has a kindergarten. My other sister – her husband works at the factory and she works at a bank. The other sister is at Muffles College now. The boys in my family haven't done so well. My older brother is just a basic labourer – he doesn't have anything. He has five kids and his wife is a nobody. She doesn't have an education. She is not an asset to him. My other brother is okay: he went to Sixth Form and he has a job at the factory. He married a girl that is just a housewife. My other brother – the little one – he is just a social outcast. He is in drugs, he doesn't work, he is lazy. It is strange that you can all have the same mother and father and be so different.

I think women these days can find more of themselves because of the way the parents are now. I don't know how I would treat a daughter now. I don't think I would be as disciplined. I'd tell her how to take care of herself. I would never force a girl to get married to a man because she was pregnant. And in those days they used to do that. They still do. I wouldn't. I don't think I'd even allow my daughter to have a child. I think I would have the relationship with my daughter, so she could tell me early on, so we could take care of it. I'm very modern that way, even though I was brought up in a strict Catholic environment. Sometimes even now I have some guilt conscience, but I wouldn't bring up my children that way.

With my little sister, we all look after her good since my mother died. She works, just like we did. If she doesn't do well in school, she gets grounded. But we allow her to do things that our mother didn't, like go to the Benque festival – not with a boyfriend, but she goes to places with crowds of girls and boys and they all stay together. We have to give her the feeling that she has to watch out for herself. Most girls, if you restrict them, right when they graduate they will just find someone and get pregnant and they will have very frustrating lives because they will feel that they have missed something. I'm glad I was careful not to get pregnant. I could have spoiled my whole life. I knew how to take care of myself – I was twenty-four when I had my child. I was ready.

My son is thirteen now. We have a very good relationship. He tells me everything, we are very close. I tell him things too. He tells me even if he thinks I'll be mad. He is a nice child. People like him. He is thirteen now and lots of girls like him. It's funny. He is very independent and he is very good. He does what I say. I hardly ever have to lash him and I don't like to do that. We have a good time together. He helps me around the house. I think that this mentality that there are certain things that only men or women should do is bad. I think we should learn to do everything. When I was growing up, it wasn't that way – the boys would haul the water and the girls would wash, but in my house, men wash the dishes.

Marta

Marta was born in 1959. She is unmarried and lives with her mother in Orange Walk, where she supervises the family business.

In my family, there are four boys and myself. I enjoyed my childhood days. We lived in a small wooden house in this same area. We didn't have a business at that time. My father was a cane farmer and did small retail sales.

My mom used to protect us a lot. She would never have us go out in the neighbourhood and doing craziness, like stealing. We were good kids. I think we enjoyed ourselves more than kids now.

Sometimes it was hard for me, being the only girl. It was hard for me to play with them sometimes, but I did. We would play circus and Tarzan. When we played Tarzan, my brother, José, was Tarzan and the rest of us would yell, "Oooh," like the Zulus. We got the idea for this from the cinema. They played many jungle movies there.

When you are a kid, you want to do many things; you want to experiment. From when we were very small, this thing about business was already on our minds. I remember when a friend of our family sent us a big box of comics. We read them all and then we said, "Let's sell them."

We had something like a little store there. We would take lumber and build a little store. We hung some strings and with clothespins we would put the comics up. We sold them good. And then we would take that money and invest it and buy more comic books and read them and sell them. We did it because it was entertainment for us to read comic books. Up to this day, if you give me a comic book I will read it and enjoy it. And we did it so we would have a little money to go to the movie, or some ice-cream – so we would be independent. And I think that is like that with every kid: you read comics and you see Dennis the Menace with his little lemonade stand that says, "Lemonade, 5 cents" on it.

In my family, my mom did not show any preference because I am the girl. My mom loves all of us the same way, except I think she loves my younger brother more because he is mentally retarded and she loves him and cares for him so much. He gets more attention. When I grew up, I was a bit stubborn and I wanted things this way or that and my mom used to give me some beatings and I think I needed those beatings because she thought maybe I was growing up in the wrong way – wanting things my way. I am grateful to her for that. I think that in every child that happens, that they want things their way and if the parent doesn't get involved, they could turn out to be a bad egg.

My parents were very strict. My dad worked a lot. It was my mom with us mostly. My father made the decisions about the store; my mom made the decisions in the home.

She was more strict. I remember this: one time my father was in Belize City; I was running behind my brother. That house to the rear of us was just the upper floor then and there were some zincs and other things under it. I was chasing my brother and he fell on one of the zincs and cut his throat – if it had been a little bit more cut he would have died. My aunt rushed him to the hospital and he got stitched up. My mom gave me a nice little beating. When my father was coming home he stopped at the toll and one of the men there told him that something had happened. He came rushing and I got it bad. I guess it was just kids' play, but from that I learned that I should not be chasing him. When you are a kid you do some crazy things. After that I thought about things more. He still has a scar. I am glad that my parents were strict with me.

All us kids went to school. When I came out from Primary, I was eleven. I attended Muffles College. I really liked Muffles – I made some good friends. I was sixteen when I graduated from school and then I went to Belize (City) to study at St. John's for two years. I was studying to get an associate's degree in secretarial science. That was the first time I moved out of home. It was hard because I was so attached to my mom. I stayed with a real nice family there and I visited home a lot. It was tough, but it helped me to grow up. My parents started to treat me like an adult. They still took care of me, but they were beginning to trust me a lot.

When I finished at St. John's, they began to really think I was grown up. When I was twenty or twenty-one I started making decisions on my own. They started making me be more responsible. I wouldn't have to ask to go out. It was similar for my brothers, but maybe they could do things on their own a year or so earlier because they were boys.

In 1977, I came back to Orange Walk. By that time we had the business for six years – the hardware and auto parts store. My three brothers were working in the store with my father. When I came back, I thought I could join the business. It was not big then. They wanted me to help, but they could handle it, so then I joined them for a month or two. Then Barclays Bank asked me to join them and I told my dad that my dreams were to assist him in the business and to be a part of it. But he said if I wanted to go get the experience I could go. So I went there, to Barclays, and worked.

At that time, the business was picking up very fast. My father was a good businessman. At that time, the cane industry was excellent. People had cars, trucks and needed the auto parts from our store. There was a need for it – because of the cane and we did really well. We were the only ones in Orange Walk to have an auto parts store. My dad invested his money from cane farming in the business. That was a good thing.

Now business is not so good, but still people need what we sell. In 1981 or so, we started building this house. Our house is big and very beautiful, I was still working at the bank. When the house was finished, I decided to come back. My dad said he needed me to take care of the paperwork. I joined the business then and I am still here.

That next year, my dad turned very sick. He transferred the business to the rest of the family. He was very ill for a year and half and then he died. It was very, very sad. We loved him dearly.

We have all worked together as a family to build the business up. We have really worked hard for what we have. I am proud of that. I tell a lot of persons, "You can achieve something if you work hard." I have seen that in my family.

When I started working in the shop six years ago, my job was to do mostly accounting. At that time, the business was under the sole proprietorship of my father and then he changed it so we are all share holders. My father had the most shares and then my three brothers – each one of them have an equal share and I have a little less than them. When he died, all of his shares went to my mother. Now my mom has the most.

My job started to change. I started to learn more and do more. I was gradually coming into it. We had to do decisions, all of this. My field is accounting and I also do office work and type. I took over general administration of the office, like bills. And we run an agency for insurance and I am the one who is fully in charge of that. I have a lot of work. We are one of their best agencies. I am also the financial comptroller for our business: I do projections, etc., and I do supervisory work. We had to get a secretary and a cashier and I am the supervisor.

A lot of customers like to deal directly with me. Sometimes it seems like too much and my desk gets so messy! We just got a computer. I am just learning to operate it. It will surely help us out.

I love my job. It is a challenge. I have to make decisions on my own. I am a person who like to do things good, in everything. In my family, sometimes my brothers say, "You are a perfectionist."

A normal day, my mom is the first one to get up. She gets up early and goes to church. Then she gets back and starts knocking on everybody's door. "Wake up!" We have breakfast and then we dash downstairs and open the store at eight. We take care of the business. My mom takes care of my brother, Peter – the one who is retarded. My mom will start getting things ready. She cleans and starts preparing for lunch. Sometimes we will come up and talk with her. Sometimes I come up here five or six times a day looking for things. At mid-day if you are lucky you will close, but most days we don't because we are busy. On those days we will take shifts to eat lunch. Then we will go back to work. Then at five-thirty we close and we come up. My mom is watching her TV, her novella. She takes that rest. And I lie down for a few minutes and then go and have supper. Then sometimes we will discuss family affairs. We have a girl who works for us and sometimes you just can't talk around her, so that is the only time we feel we can discuss private matters.

If I am not going out, I help in the kitchen and we watch TV. Often, my nephews will come over and I play with them. Then I take a bath and go to bed. On Saturdays, we do all our heavy house cleaning. And at night we might get together and have a drink. Sunday, we go to church.

I keep very busy. Along with work, I am very active in Rotaract. I joined Rotaract in '76. I am the oldest person in it. I really like it. I am the treasurer of the club and the international service director. Rotaract in Orange Walk is the oldest in Belize – it is the oldest young people's group in Belize. It is a community service organization. We have a variety of activities for the community – national and international. We give scholarships, old people assistance, many things. They usually give scholarships to farmers' kids because they need it the most. They donated an incubator to the hospital – it cost $4000. It is really a good project. We sponsor a career day for the schools.

It is an international group. Rotaract wants to encourage peace and family values. I think that Rotaract has really changed me as a person. It is part of who I am. I think that when I was young, fifteen or sixteen, I was real shy, afraid that people might laugh at me, but Rotaract made me change. In Rotaract you have to do many things. It's like being in school: you learn many things from other people. It teaches us to be responsible for ourselves and our community. It changes your personality or character when you become responsible. In Rotaract, I have learned about other cultures. I have visited many countries. To me, that is important.

There is a lot to explore in Rotaract. That has changed my life. It really gave me a push. I think it made me a very good person. I can go anywhere in Central America and I have friends there. For example, I am going on this trip to El Salvador. I know people there. There it will be a conference – it is the changing of the representatives. It is the handing over of positions.

I have been going to conferences since 1980. Every time I go, I learn everything new. We had the conference here. I was in charge of the committee to organize it. We proved to the rest of Central America that we could do it. It was the first time an international conference like that had been held in Belize. People loved Belize. We had a cultural programme, took them to the Cayes – it was so successful. People said to me, "Who would have thought Belize is so wonderful?"

Most of my friends are from Rotaract. I do have some that are not from there. With my friends, I like to talk and to visit places. Sometimes we go to have a beer, but I usually do not like to go to dances – I like to go to parties and to talk to people. My friends, they come to me sometimes for advice. I give it to them. I like to give advice. Friends can do that for each other.

One thing we always do in my family is go to church. We follow the Catholic Church. We are very religious. I go to church every Sunday. I love going to church because I feel that we should be thankful to God our Creator for everything and we should praise Him and ask for His guidance and blessings. That's the only way I think we can survive in this world.

There are a lot of people who don't think that way, but there is a God. Without a God, then what would be of this world?

I think that the Catholic Church was started by Jesus Christ, but a lot of people have chosen to do their own religions for their own faiths, opportunities and wants. Most people change their religions because they want something better for themselves. For example, here in Orange Walk there are many churches – so many that you get confused and you wonder why they are all here. Most of them are evangelical. If they are one religion, then why are they so separate? If they are going to adore God, then why can't they do it all in one way?

Many people belong to those religions for their own personal benefit. Some people say, "I can take my Bible and preach and start my own religion and I can live good: I will be important and people will support me."

Even the Anglican Church started that way: King Henry started it for his own benefit. And they make themselves important and people follow them and if they are smart in brainwashing people, then they will do well.

I would never think about changing my religion. Most of those are Christian religions, but I think many of those are false religions, like it says in the Bible. I don't know much about other religions like Buddhism. I don't know what they get out of it, what they are adoring, because they aren't adoring Christ. They are adoring something else. It takes all kinds of people.

Of the people in the Bible, I admire Mary the most. She is the mother of Jesus and is very special, very good. When God chose her to be the mother of His Son, He made a right decision there. Mary appears to people in different ways, like the Lady of Fatima. She really cares for the world and she is someone we should pray to constantly. I always pray to God, Jesus and to Mary. She is very special and miraculous.

I pray every night. I ask God for His blessing and help for my family. I could say that I get a response from Him and I feel satisfied They love me and my family.

It has been a tradition in the Catholic Church that only men can be priests. Woman can assist the priests and show their love for God by helping the poor, or being Sisters or doing other work in the church. In my church, I see women doing many things. I believe that they play a big role. For example, my mom is in the sodality: they participate in the masses, help the poor and pray together a lot; they do a lot of work.

I think that in everything (in the Church) women are the ones who lead things. Men don't get involved in those things so much. I am not much involved in any church group, simply because I have been very involved in Rotaract.

I would say that women aren't that equal in the Bible. I don't know the Bible so well. I read it sometimes – I have one in my room, but I don't know it so well. But I see there was not much equality in those days when the Bible was written.

I think that women are these days fighting for equality – women's lib and so. I think it is good; I believe in it. Of course, some women like to take advantage of the situation. I think that they feel like they can boss up the man. I feel like both have a role in this world, especially in a marriage. I dislike when a man puts aside his wife and I wouldn't like to see a woman doing that either. If a man is strong enough, he won't let a wife boss him up – neither should be above.

I love kids, but I don't know – it is a really hard question for me at the moment. I am already twenty-nine years old. I have only had one or two boyfriends, but I have never thought about getting married. Personally, I wouldn't want it. I don't know why. It would change my life so much. I don't say no. Maybe if I found the right person.

I think that marriage is something you have to really think about hard. And for me, I like to do certain things and it would not be good for a husband to rail up at me. I am in control of my life now. I do other things in my life. I don't want to be in the kitchen all the time. I like to do other things. My mom tries to teach me how to cook, but I hardly ever have time. I am so attached to my mother, it would be hard to leave.

I love my mother very much. She is my favourite person. I think what I like most about my mom is her sweetness. She is a very sweet person, somebody who I can talk to; she understands me. She is so loving with my entire family. She is a very caring person. Not only with us, but with other people. The relationship I have with my mom is not only a mother-daughter relationship, but we are sisters and friends. I can confide in her. She knows a lot about me and my life. It is very special. She is the person I love most in my life.

Perhaps I had an easier time than my mother did growing up. There is definitely a difference between my life and hers because I didn't have to pass through what she did: a lot of poverty. We weren't doing that well, but we were not poor. My mom's father died when he was forty. My grandmother's parents had been very rich and had left my grandma with a lot of land in Orange Walk. She and my grandfather set up a business, but he died young and my grandmother was alone with all her kids. At that time, it was very difficult for a woman to take care of papers and properties and so and she had to sell it all to take care of her kids. My mom was nine at that time. So my grandma got taken advantage of and sold things for very low prices. They were poor then. My mother grew up that way. My grandma had to take boarders and make bread to sell. They all worked hard. We did not have to work so hard.

I think all of us should love our moms, because they suffered so much for us. They cared for us. The person I miss the most when I go away is my mother. She attends to us in a very special way. And I am always proud of her.

My best advice for my mom is to take it easy, not to overwork. She works so hard. You can come here any time of the day and find her working, cleaning the house, cooking for us. And whenever she does something and it doesn't come out good, she gets mad. Like last week, she experimented with a new cake. She didn't like it. We told her, "Mom, it is okay. You made it for us and we like it." But no, she threw it out. We tell her to take it cool. She is already beginning her sixties and once you are that age, you can suffer anything. The love that we all have for her, we don't want her to get sick. We want her to stay with us as long as she can.

Sometimes I take her on vacations, but she gets a little tired. I put her to walk those shopping malls – she gets pretty tired, but she does it.

I have been lucky to be able to teach my mother general knowledge, things that I've learned in school. I am of a higher education. She was unable to get much schooling. I should say that my mother is a very smart person. Sometimes when I was young we used to go out and we would sit on the swing and talk about the skies and the stars and the sun and the moon and the planets. I would tell her things that she didn't know, but she knows a lot. I tell her that you are never too old to learn. I tell her about present events and why things are happening that way. I increase her general knowledge that way.

My mother has taught me many things about how to take care of myself. One thing I surely like about her is her cleanliness. From when we were young, she taught us how to be as clean and neat as we can. She taught me hygiene: night cream and perfume, using the right cream is important. Oil of Olay is good for wrinkles. She has taught me things like that. Sometimes she tells me, she says, "Why don't you paint your nails?" And I say, "Mom, if I spent the day painting my nails, the next day they are all chipped – I would have to keep doing it." But I always make sure my nails are clean.

In my family, we have always been UDP. It was a long struggle to get into government. The PUP was in power for many years. Myself, I'm not involved in politics – I like it in a way. I like to get involved in the community and in doing the right things, but in politics, you and your family are put into all kinds of discussions, lies and slandering.

We are a very united and honest family. We would never get involved in things like drugs, but that is what they say about us. They say that we are involved in selling and buying drugs. People talk about us because my brother is a politician. He was the mayor of Orange Walk for three years. He can take things, when people say slanderous things about him. I sometimes can't take it. If politics weren't so dirty, I would be more involved.

I think that our political system is good. We have to be careful about communism. Communism has already started in Central America, in Nicaragua. It could start in other countries here – it could even start in Belize. We understand there are some people with communist ideologies here in Belize. There is infiltration here. They have relations with communist countries. We have not really seen them working here, in the sense that they are converting Belize, but we have to be careful because, of course, we don't believe in communism. If you are Christian, you don't believe in communism because they don't believe in God.

I think that communism brainwashes people – especially the poor people – telling them that if they become communists they'll have it made because everything will belong to the state and you don't have to worry about anything. But of course the ones who have

161

worked hard and know what hard work is and have achieved something in their life, then they don't want that to happen. That's what I dislike about it: if you have worked hard and you know what sacrifice is and you achieve things and then somebody who is a lazy bum or something comes over and wants to take what is yours. I don't like that. The thing that I disagree with is that I'd hate to see it here. I don't think that Belize should ever think about becoming communist. We are not that poor here. If you have been to other countries you can see more poverty and those countries aren't communist.

I don't know if I'm right, but it seems like, with communism, you live a closed life. You have to get permission to do everything and you are not free. I don't know that much about it. I don't think I would like it.

Belize needs development. We are a beautiful country. We have good resources: land, sea, natural beauty and warm and friendly people. We are very peaceful. It is very unique. We need to develop investments and tourism. We need roads. We have the land to feed everybody.

The sugar cane has helped Belize. It was bad when the prices went down. Many people were made poor. Some people say that some of the farmers began to grow marijuana then because they did not have any choice. I do not think this is true. I think it is wrong to grow marijuana and that those people had a choice. They could have done something else to make money.

I think my life is very good. When I grow older, I would like to start painting, painting pictures. When I was young I liked that. I don't know if I will be good, but I should try. If I can paint and it is well received, then I will try to send my paintings to exhibitions.

PROFESSIONAL WOMEN

Ana

Ana spent her early years in the bush as the daughter of a chiclero *and later went to school in the United States. Now living in Orange Walk with her husband and three children, Ana is the manager of a local financial institution.*

I was born in the western part of the country, in San Ignacio. My dad, his family came from Mexico – they immigrated here when the war broke out. My mother is from Guatemalan descendants – they immigrated into the western part of Belize.

My father used to be a *chiclero*. He went to the western part to work chicle. That is where he met my mom and that is where they got married.

He went to do chicle work all the time. When we were born, he took us along with him. My mom, my older sister and myself, we would go with him every time he would go up. We would go up on mules and horses into the bush and we'd have to travel and travel. I can always remember sitting on the mules, behind whichever men were taking us up, and we would spend six to eight months in the bush and then we would come back down. We did that for several years off and on.

When we went up to the chicle bush, my mom went as a cook for the crew that was going up and so she would cook sometimes for about fifteen or twenty men – and of course, that would only be cooking. The men would take care of their washing and everything.

Us kids – that is our life. We would wake up in the morning and help around – we'd help our mother as much as we could. My sister,

164

she helped my mom to wash dishes and, myself, I took care of the younger ones. We would go down the creek to do the washing and we spent much of each day collecting wood from the surrounding areas. We were told not to go too far, unfortunately, because there were tigers[1] around and we would always keep the fire on to keep them away and there were baboons, many of them. They would holler a lot.

Us kids, we got used to living out there and it was not so bad. It was only us and every now and then another *chiclero* with kids. My mom would take the time – the little time that she had left because cooking for twenty men wouldn't leave much time for her – but the little time she had left she would spend with us, teaching us our 123s, our ABCs – how to add one and one. So we had more to do than to just run around and play and that's why when we went to the school it wasn't hard for us because she took it upon herself to teach us.

Apart from that, working and learning, there is nothing really, nothing much that you can do up there except live the life. You know, it's different: when you come down here you appreciate what you have. When you are back there, when you are forced to live with the mosquitoes, sickness and everything, life is tough. We would take as many medicines as we knew, for cough and diarrhea, etc., and in the bush they would find leaves that could do certain remedies, but there was only so much you could do. My mom – that was one of her big fears, that one of her kids would get sick and she wouldn't be able to bring them out to the doctor. But we were used to the life. She knew before it got worse what she would do. Fortunately, we never got very ill.

It was just that type of life. My dad would go because that was where he could make the money to maintain us. He worked there until he had enough money to come down and get a small lot to build a small house where we could live and when my mom decided that it was time that the kids start school, she brought us down. We rented for one year and then my dad decided, "I can't live up there without you guys," so he came down to be with us and that is when he left the chicle bush.

After my dad quit working as a *chiclero* he became a cane cutter. In those days it did not pay much, so my mom would bake bread or anything we could sell. My sister and I knew what it was to go out and sell the things Mama made from when we were six, seven years old.

When we came out here and started going to school and my dad started working, it made us a closer family. Since then we have always worked for each other. My mom and dad had three girls first, then three boys and therefore the girls had to be the boys. My older sister, she was the most feminine and she would stay at home and help my mom and then I would go out and help my dad chop the wood, build the house and all this. That was what I used to do. We didn't have electricity at that time – it was many years before we had electricity. I remember there was once some tourists that came when I was carrying wood and they said, "Oh, can you stand there for a moment?" I have my arms full of coal and wood, I am all covered with sweat and black coal and they took my picture. I said to my sister, "Just look at that. I imagine that they will put that picture in *National Geographic*. Can you believe that?"

Anyway, that is the way we grew up. Of course, our kids don't have to go through all of that because at least now life has changed quite a bit. We are more advanced. The introduction of the sugar cane factory in Orange Walk really changed things completely. My dad worked there for many, many years, up until eight years ago.

Growing up like that was a real good experience because I think that since I lived that life, I learned to appreciate the little my parents could give to us and I learned what it means to have to work together. To live that life was good. Because of living that life I am a striver: I am a determined person to go and get ahead in life and I can relate to those people that live in such circumstances. I wouldn't say that it was a misery. It was a way of living – it was a way of making money. That's the way our parents worked for their living. It's just that now things are more modernized.

When I was twelve years old, I came out of primary school. That's when I had my first job. I worked as a clerk in a store. I always knew that my mom and dad could not send me on to school after that because we did not have the finances and in those days, after you finished school, you had to go out and work. That's the way it is here. You are expected to work because the family needs it, but my parents

166

were always positive about education, which was an asset to us. We have many people here, especially the older people, who couldn't afford education and so told their children it wasn't important. I was fortunate that my parents encouraged me to try to get an education although they couldn't afford it.

Fortunately, I had a friend who went to the U.S. and finished high school and he suggested that I go to the U.S. He said he would get a family for me to live with. He found a family for me and they took me in for four years. I was able to finish my schooling there. If it wasn't for them, I wouldn't have been able to finish.

I stayed in the U.S. for almost four years. I had a scholarship to go to a university to study nursing, but I was called upon to come back down here and help my family. My youngest sister had to leave because she got married to an American and there was only the older sister working and my father was ill. We couldn't expect him to work much. We always have worked as a family and felt the responsibility of helping each other, so I had to make a decision. I made a choice to come back.

I always thought that if I wanted to be somebody, I could be somebody in my own country. I think that as a Belizean that you can take the opportunity to learn in the U.S. You can get advantage of what the U.S. has to offer financial-wise and knowledge-wise, but you should bring it back home and make yourself someone at home – teach your fellow Belizeans that what they do is important. If you are going to invest, why not invest here, in your own country? That is why I always knew I would come back.

As for my family life, I met my husband, Jorge, just after I returned to Belize. At that time, he was already working at BSI. I didn't have a job and I really wanted to be a nurse – I had wanted to come back to this country and serve as a nurse. I couldn't do that, so I thought that maybe I would like to be a stewardess. I applied for a job as a stewardess and was sent to Honduras for interviews. I got the job. Jorge said to me then, "Well, if you go, forget it because I'm not just going to stay here and just wait for you." I told him, "Okay then, that's the way it's going to be because I want to be a stewardess." I knew that he wasn't serious about not waiting for me. It turned out that it was my mom who did not let me go. She started to cry on the very day that I was leaving for Honduras to start work. She started crying, saying, "Oh, I wish you wouldn't leave."

My sister had everything planned. She called up the boss in Belize City and told him that my mother was sick and that I couldn't go, so I didn't go. I don't think that I really wanted to do that anyway. At that time in my life, I didn't know exactly what I wanted to do.

Jorge and I courted for about three years and married in 1978. I had my first child in 1979 and then I had my second child in 1981. I had my third in 1982. We have two girls and one boy.

Fortunately, Jorge has accepted me for who I am. I grew up in a Christian home. My mom and dad accepted the Lord from when I was very, very young and they committed themselves to serving the Lord in the Nazarene Church when they came here. At that time, the church building itself was not there—then it was the Gospel Missionary Union. I grew up in the church and that is the reason I felt that I couldn't just leave because there is so much need in the church, so much need in the community and the only way to reach the community is through the church. And when I met Jorge, I wasn't the girl to go out to dance and party, but he accepted me like that and he learned to go to church with me and to make it his life also.

Around the time we were getting married, I started as a machine operator at a financial institution in Belize City. Jorge was at BSI. Fortunately, about six months later, I was transferred to Orange Walk. At the same time I got a promotion. Over the years I've worked hard and have climbed the ladder. I heard a lot of people saying, "She wants to take away my job," or "she's looking for a position." It was always men ahead of me. Sometimes they seemed angry at me, but I knew I could do it. I have gone from the bottom to the top, striving very hard.

Now, praise the Lord, He's given me an opportunity to manage a branch of our institution in Orange Walk. I feel fortunate because I feel that I have the support of my fellow Orange Walkeans; they say that they are glad that I took the post because they know me and trust me. They don't have the fear of me. I have worked with them and I know the people in the community. They have respect and confidence in me.

As the manager, I'm in charge of the whole operation. Of course, it's not only me. I have a very good team of people to work with. I think a manager should always give credit to his or her staff because we do the planning, but they are the front line. We have to be behind them, making sure it all happens. I am proud of my staff. I have two people who are my assistants and eleven other workers: nine women and two men. I am proud of them.

When you are a working woman, you find that you make a lot of decisions on your own. At first, it was a little problem between Jorge and myself because men always want to make the decisions in the house, which I agree with. However, having my own pay cheque makes it easier for me to decide what I should get and what I shouldn't get. We eventually got to the agreement that we will discuss what we need and between the both of us decide what is the best thing to do. In the beginning, when we first got married, it was hard because we were always striving. We didn't have much and we always found ourselves short, but we always knew that we had to go on and it would get better from there. And we've done it. I think it worked because both of us worked towards it. I'd get discouraged, but he'd say, "It will get better." And if he would get discouraged, I would do the same for him. We'd both encourage each other along the way, but it was hard for a while.

Now we know what the expenses are and we know what we need to set aside for emergencies. We try to save as much as we can. Beyond that, we need to discuss what else we need. He is not as petty any more about what he gets.

It would tend to be that when I think I need something and he agrees, I will actually go get it and get it home faster. He tends more to wait until I go with him for something he wants. That's his way. Like if we need a new mattress, as soon as I can budget for it, it gets home. And when he comes home, there it is. When he wants something, we decide together also. He will always come to me. Like the last time he wanted to buy a lawn mower – it was his idea. He came to me and said, "Why don't we buy a lawn mower?" I said, "Do you know how much money you need for a lawn mower, for repairs and so," and he said, "Yes, but it would help so much." And I knew it would help. You know, he works all day and when he comes home he doesn't want to take a machete and do the lawn. He feels better using the lawn mower and we ended up going to see it together. He hardly ever buys a piece of equipment or anything without me being there.

He makes his contribution to the house and I make mine. It's not that I wouldn't be able to make decisions on my own – I know I could – but I think that as head of the family he should always be involved in decisions, so we always make decisions together.

By saying that he is the "head of the family," I mean that I expect him to run the house. He is the one I want my kids to look up to because he is the head of the house. He is the father of the house and I want him to be the moral support of the family. It's like many times I'll talk to him and show him that our kids walk in our own steps. Whatever path we take, they tend to take it also, so it is his responsibility to be the strong arm of the house, the example of the house. Even for me. For as much as we women do, we still need to know that there is somebody there who we can lean on. I am a career woman and I tend to have a very strong character, but I still need somebody. I need to know that I don't have the whole responsibility on my own. I need to know that I can say, "So and so is happening, what do you think?"

At work, it's ME – I have to make the decisions. At home, I am glad that I don't always have to make the decisions. I can lean on somebody and that's what I mean by saying that he is the head of the household. He is the one we expect to be the problem solver, somebody we can hold on to and that's what he is. I need his support. Even at work, I want to know that I have his support of my being the boss there.

Although I am the boss at work, it was up to me to make Jorge realize that I don't want to be the boss at home. I would never say, "Well, Jorge has to wait on what I decide." I don't want him to ever feel like that. I want him to feel that it is his decision that counts. It's important for him to feel that way because, really, I'm not supposed to be out there working, much less being the manager, but it was my choice to do so, with his okay.

I believe what the Bible says: first comes God, then comes man, then comes woman. I want to keep it that way because there is a certain reason why God wanted it that way. He made man first and why should I try to take away man's position? I shouldn't and that's the reason that in my home I want that Jorge always be respected as the head of the household. That's what God wants and what I have, what I am, I can only attribute it to God's goodness.

All I have is because of Him. I really owe my life to Him. I dedicate all of my work and my life to Him. Before I had so many responsibilities I used to teach Sunday School. It's important for kids to learn when they are small that God loves them and that there's more to life than just walking around and just living every day. Jorge and I try to teach our kids that there's a reason for life. Actually, God brought us here to give Him back what He has given us and if we don't do it, then we are not serving the real purpose of life. We need the kids to learn that when they are very small, so when they grown up, they will not forget. That's the reason we go to church. In our church, we don't baptize people when they are babies: we dedicate them. They are taught what baptism is. They are taught what salvation is and then you are free to make your decision of being saved. Then we ask them, "do you want to accept Christ as your personal saviour?" If you can understand that Christ really loves you and that love is the reason He left His home in Glory to come down here to suffer, to die on the cross, to pay for your sins, to pay for my sins and to earn us a way back to Heaven – if you understand that, then you know you are ready to be baptized. He said, "I go to prepare a place, that where I am, you may be also." And if I want to spend the rest of my life with Him, then I must accept Him.

And how do you accept Him? It's only by faith. Christ said, "For God so loved the world, He gave His only begotten Son, that whoever believes in Him should not perish, but have everlasting life." After I believe that I have accepted Him, there is one more thing that God asks us to do: He asks that we be baptized. And we are not forced into that. We are taught what baptism is. Myself, I accepted the Lord when I was nine years old. I was at the age of twenty-six when I made my decision that I wanted to dedicate my life to Christ. And so I made the outward demonstration of being baptized.

At that point, when you are baptized, you are at a point where you are called into fellowship as a member of the church. You are taken into fellowship with the other members and you can also be disciplined by them. The reason for this is that the Bible says that we should be exhorting each other. And how can you exhort me when I am not your brother or your sister? If I am not a member, a part of you, how can you do it? So whenever you become a member, then you are in a position to do it. To me, its good because it keeps me on the alert. I know that God has others looking after me. Even at work, sometimes I feel so unsure, sometimes I say, "Lord, if you put me in this position, it's because You know what I should do. Please help me." I depend on God a lot and, praise the Lord, up till now I can't see that He has let me down.

A lot of my life is based around this church and when I tell you I want Jorge to be the head of the household, I want it to be what God wants. I don't want to take his place. That's where God wants him, so in the home, I am second and Jorge is first and God is the most. It's important. You know, you have children and they must learn this also; at the same time, they must learn that they are an important part of the home, the church and the community. And I think each child, must be taught that he or she is important. We must not always say, "No you cannot do that." They should be given the opportunity to prove themselves.

And apart from the role that Jorge is setting, I am setting an example for my kids, especially for my girls. I have two girls. I am setting for them the example that they have an important part to play in life also. I don't think that anyone should ever feel that a woman is not capable. I grew up in a very poor family and now I am a manager. I think this is a good example to set.

It is unfortunate that in our country religion is mostly left for the women. Most of the organizations in the church are run by women. Very few men are dedicated to the work of the church. The men are not as involved as the women are. When you are going to go evangelize, more women are out there than the men. When it's time to visit the sick, there's more women than men. When it's time for prayer, there's more women than men. Why? I always ask that question. Why is it that men are so hard to turn to God? Maybe that's the reason that women are so blessed. But I'm glad to know that so many women are going to go to Heaven. That will be fun to be with so many women!

There is much room here for development in Belize and I feel that we should take advantage of it. As a woman, I believe that Belizean women are just starting to become part of the development of the country. There is a lot of room for them to get involved and I want to see younger women growing up to form part of this development because they are an asset. I think women are the backbone of the development. There is so much that they do. If you notice, there are a lot of women right now becoming teachers. As a teacher, you have a responsibility, the great responsibility of training kids.

To me, many women are conservative, mostly the older ones. They are conservative in keeping the tradition of "Women are to be seen, not heard." In the U.S. nowadays, women are trying to be heard. That is what is going on. I don't say no to that – fine, we need to be heard, but we need to know when to be heard. We shouldn't always try to be the boss.

Women are being educated now in Belize. Before, parents would think that if you have to send anybody to school, you should send the boy. That was the way of thinking. We still have some parents that think that way. I don't believe in that. I believe that girls are supposed to be given the same privileges as the boys. There is so much that needs to be done to improve our country – literacy work, teaching people hygiene and many, many other things. We all need to help out with that. And women can play many important roles: teaching, social work, politics, business, etc.

But people didn't used to think this about women. Before, the parents taught that the girls are to go to the washtub and the boys are to go and work. That's the reason why men, especially the men in the Latin American cultures, have this machismo in them. Before, women were beaten like anything. You don't find it as often any more because women are starting to speak up for themselves. Women are starting to show what they can do.

Men have to recognize that women are valid. They are not just another child. I mean, who takes care of them? Even if it's a domestic woman, what's her job? Doesn't a man depend on her? Sure he does. So why should a woman be treated like a child? Being beaten and being treated like an animal. Even a child shouldn't be treated so. So I'm glad to see that women are more involved. I'm glad to see that men can realize that now.

As I said, it is important to have both the men and the women involved in community work and business. Like for example, at my institution I wouldn't like to only hire ladies to work there. I like to hire both because the world is made up of both of them and there's always a more balanced environment when you have both male and female there. If you're going to have all female, it's more likely that they are going to overlook something that a man would not overlook. And if you have only men, then they will overlook things that women wouldn't. So in anything that you do, I think it is necessary to have both men and women. In the past, it was mostly men involved in everything. I am glad there are women now involved. I also like to have men involved for one more reason – for them to realize that women can do it. I hire men and women also because men need to see that women can do the work as well as they can.

In my work, I have noticed that women are becoming much more involved in our country's economy. For example, I think that sixty percent of the people who work in all of the branches of the institution I work for are women and many of those women are in leadership roles. And you notice, you go into our businesses and a big part of them are managed by ladies. Many times husbands and wives own stores together. The husband goes out to do the public relations and the wives manage the store. So I'm seeing women getting more and more involved in the everyday growing of the community, which is very good.

174

I've also been really surprised at how many women have applied for loans from local banks and financial institutions: but of course, we have more women working now. We have lots of married couples with both working now. And that is the reason that you can see more development because they have to take into consideration the fact that both of them can contribute. The women may not have to work all her life, but in the beginning it is necessary that they both work together to get their things done.

Also, a lot of women have been going in with their husbands for loans together. They get loans for businesses and for cane. In many cases, the husbands are getting loans for parcels of land in their wives' names and cane licenses in their wives' names. This gives the women some worth, even if they are staying home. This is what I like about it – the village women now feel that they are part of the development. They have a role to play. Because the licence or the land is in their name, there is reason to help the husband to do something. I am glad for this. The women in the villages know that there is more to living than just being maintained. Of course, what we expect – we expect men to be the bread winners, but there is a role for women in life. They can improve their lives, their homes. There is a role for them in the home and I think that apart from being wives and being mothers, they can contribute a little bit more and I see more women taking part in that everyday.

There are quite a few women I have noticed that have become cane farmers, either because their husband died, or they have been able to acquire it on their own. I know a lady right now whose husband has been very ill and for the past three years she has worked hard. She has even gone out to plant a field of rice with her kids. She has made sure that the fields are going okay, that the men cut the cane, deliver the cane. She has really been going good. There are quite a few women like that right now in Orange Walk. I am proud of that. To me, it's because they have the opportunity to work with their husband, to know what they have to do in the event that something would occur. They were made a part of it, so they were not left helpless and this is important. It's important in a developing country to have women involved, not to just leave them to the mercy

175

of whoever happens to be there. A woman cane farmer right now knows exactly what she has to pay for cutting her cane, what she has to do to clean up the field, to fertilize that cane, and when it's going to be ready and when to plant. She has that knowledge.

Even young women are taking the advantage of loans being given to acquire assets for themselves, to buy land, or start businesses or go to school and I am glad to see it. In a developing country it's necessary.

My life has been a commitment to my family, my church, my country and my work. My country is important to me because this is where I grew up. I know I have gone from what little I had to exposure to everything, and I've thought about what I would really want my kids to do. I think I would want them to have the same kind of exposure that I did because I'd like them to know what it is to live with a little and what it is to have a lot – for them to know, to learn to appreciate how it is that we live. I appreciate it.

To tell you the truth, I think that there is no place better than Belize. People say that you have to go to the U.S. to do things. It's true, we are not as advanced as them. Someday probably we will be, but I hope when we do, it's going to be for the good of Belize.

Right now, we have quite a bit of unemployment, but I think it's because people don't want to go to work because during the cane season there's a lot to do and you find a lot of people not doing it because they don't want to do any hard work. They have actually left the hard work for the aliens to do. It is very hard to get Belizeans to go and cut cane. Very hard. That's why the aliens from Guatemala, Mexico and so do that work and now it's costing us because they have realized this and they have taken a better price. My daddy used to cut cane for two dollars a ton. Right now, they are cutting cane for ten dollars a ton.

What I am trying to say is that the Belizeans have been influenced by the U.S. and are starting to get the idea that only the lesser ones do the physical work. This is what I think. Another thing is that there are more educated young people. Before, you didn't have that. Back then, people would go into the fields to work, but now, young men are getting educated. They spend their time in school, or

176

looking for jobs that are not out in the fields and a lot of the older men can no longer do it. They are tired of doing it. They are finished and so we use the aliens.

I feel like agriculture, as a whole, is really good. Our people should get into it more. There is so much we can do to diversify and they are not taking advantage of it. As it is, who cultivates the corn? Who cultivates the beans? Who cultivates the rice? It is the Mennonites. Our own local farmers don't do it. Some say, "No, it's good for the Mennonites to do that because they're Belizeans too. They need to live off something." But I think that we have depended too much on the cane and when the cane goes, then there is nothing else. The farmers are learning that now and they are trying to diversify.

I love my country. Most of the people in my family have gone to the States. It was hard for them to leave, but they all had important reasons. I want to stay here. I love it here and my country is my home.

---

[1]*In Belize, "tiger" refers to what is more commonly known as a "jaguar."*

Gabriela

Gabriela, born in 1951, is a widow and the mother of three children. She lives with her parents and children and works as a community health organizer.

I remember that when I was a little girl I had to go to school. Before I went to school, I first had to get up early and help my mother to clean the house – I always had to help her with something. When I grew up in San Miguel, we lived far from the well. We only had one well, called a public well, and the water had to be carried from there. We were only ten or fourteen years old and we had to help my mother to carry the water because all the water that we were using at home had to be brought from that place. We didn't have any water tanks then. It was far from our home. Everybody in my village had to go to that same well.

I had to help her so much that sometimes I think that she bothered me by having so many children. My mother said that I was doing things for them. I moaned and talked back to her. I said that they were not even my sons but hers and that she wanted me to take care of her sons. I was like their mother because I had to help so much. In any case, I had to do it because there were a lot of us at home and I was the first girl in the family.

I remember that even when I was a teacher my mother lashed me if I didn't wash the clothes or sweep the floor – she threatened that she wouldn't let me go to school. I think that I was lazy or maybe I waited till the last minute to do it. I would get up around six o'clock. My mother would tell me that we had to wash clothes and clean house till around eight o'clock. My mother would lash me and afterwards she would say, "Go away!" In spite of the fact that I was a teacher, I would go to school with red eyes from crying so much. Even today I remind my mother about it. That's why I tell my children that they have to do something with their lives. I cried at school if I didn't do my chores at home! That's how my mother treated us. We just had to do it.

We had a small thatch house – even the beds were made of palm leaves. The house only had two rooms and in each of them there were palm leaf beds and a few hammocks. As there were a lot of us at home, the ones who didn't have beds used hammocks. Life was hard because my father was not a cane farmer then. My father shelled corn – the work that was available. And when he went to shell corn we even had to help him to earn money for food because he wasn't a cane farmer. He was a *milpero*.

He said that he was not interested in cane. He could see people planting cane, but he only went to work with them. He got interested later and then started to plant his own cane. A lot of them were already cane farmers. When he saw that others were planting cane, he started to do the same thing. He got a block. Since the boys were already growing, he planted it with their help. When they grew up, my father tried to get more land. There was no bush available in those days, so he looked for blocks (already planted in cane). Now that the boys are older they all own their block except for the youngest. But my father said that he would get the one that he owns, so each of them has his piece of land. Only the men in my family have it. I have one, but it comes from my husband who passed it into my name. My father only cared about the males, not about the females. I have one because my husband left it to me.

So my father started to plant and to harvest his cane. My brothers cut the cane and worked on my father's piece of land, which extended from here to San Vicente – it was all cane. I was a teacher at that time. My father had already started to sell his cane. After the sale of the cane, the money that was left over went into the bank. My father, my brothers and I put our money together and even though it was almost nothing, it was deposited in the bank and kept there –

it was money then! My mother also helped. As we were all older, she provided meals for the cane workers; there were a lot of Mexicans and part of her earnings were going to the bank too. On Saturday, we all pooled our money and my father deposited it. We did this for many years until we saved some money.

My father then decided to buy a truck and he bought a second-hand truck. He planted more cane because he saw that it sold well and that he was going to get a good bonus. He then sold the truck and got a new one. He went to Belize to buy a new Austin, the same year I got married. But before that, he built a house, the one located behind his other house. He built a concrete block house and made a big tank. We could see that he was getting ahead with the money. I decided to get married. My father installed a cassette in the new Austin. He provided transport for people in his car to Orange Walk when it was not the harvest season. He kept his Austin for a long time and then he decided to sell it because the boys told him that the truck was not working very well.

The thing is that my brothers got tired of it and as they had seen other kinds of trucks on the market – like Ford or I don't know what – and saw that people were buying them, they also wanted one. They didn't want the Austin any more. My father sold the Austin and bought the Ford. Like everything else, they got tired of it after a short period of time and they didn't want the Ford anymore. My father then bought a pick-up because he realized that he needed it to be able to transport the workers because at times the truck was slowing down and it couldn't carry them.

They sold the Ford after five years, I think. They didn't want it anymore because they wanted a better machine. We thought, "How can we do it?" So we all got together to buy it, my three brothers who are cane cutters, less one brother who didn't want to – he is not a cane cutter – my father and I. And we went to ask for a loan to buy the machine, a John Deere tractor. My father bought his tractor and sold the house in San Miguel at the same time. He paid for the tractor with part of the money he got from the house and with another part he bought a trailer. With another part that they loaned him, he bought another trailer. He then had his machine and his trailers. My father

180

found out that the pick-up couldn't go into the bush when it rained and that consequently it was not useful. When he learned that Jeeps were good buys he said, "Let's sell the pick-up and let's buy a Jeep." After a rain, even though the land was muddy, it was possible to go in with the Jeep. They always found out what was new on the market, sold what they had and then got what was new.

They used to have horses before. When the bicycle appeared they said, "Maybe next year, it won't be a bike but a truck." From one year to another, one could see changes occurring due to cane. A lot of people now have their house, their vehicle and transportation to carry their cane.

But when prices went down (1981), it was terrible for us because as is well known here during the cane season each worker has a little bit of money every week to buy food. But when those five or six months of the cane season end, there is no way to earn money and when there was no bonus it was that much more terrible because there was no money circulating to pay people for weeding, etc., so there was nothing else to do but go to the other side (Mexico) to find work. They went to the other side to clean the cane lands. They said that they had to clear a lot for almost nothing, but they had to do it because it was their only way of surviving. A lot of cane farmers, even the big ones, had to abandon their cane and go to the other side. They had to work for two weeks on the other side before they were able to buy their provisions. I went with one of my cousins to the other side the year that no bonus was given. She was surprised to see that even rich cane cutters also had to work on the other side for nothing. It was terrible.

He (my father) always had a little corn, even now. It is near San Esteban because his block here is full of cane. When there wasn't any money everybody thought, "If we have beans and corn, there won't be any problem because we can eat with that." During the rainy season we had to walk for two or two and a half hours before we could even reach it because the road was bad. In summertime, we used the vehicle to go. At other times, we had to walk and even I would go. When we used to go to the *milpa*, about twenty-two people would get together. More! Sometimes there were around forty of us. Quite a few families had their land and a house to live in during the week that they were working in the bush. There was meat! I liked to go because they would shoot so many pheasants, deer, that there was never a lack of meat -only fish was lacking.

People came to the conclusion that by having some corn, beans and rice, things were going to be easier. And now, even though my father has his own cane land, he stops cutting the cane for a week and goes to clear the bush. Then he comes back later and plants for two or three days. He clears the milpa land for two or three days and then he comes back. After that everything is in God's hands. They thought that the price of the cane would never go down because when the price is good we can buy food, but everybody makes sure now that they have a little bit of corn and beans.

I was fourteen years old when my dad took me out of school. The exam was given in June at that time and my father took me out before the exam. Maybe education was not very important to him. My teacher didn't let it pass: he went to talk to my father and told him that I was very advanced at school and that I had to take the exam because I was ready to do it. My father understood and he put me back in school and I took the exam. When the results came out, my teacher told my father that I had passed it. A short time after the exam, my teacher came to the house and told me that there was a vacancy for a teaching job. He then added that he thought I should take the job because he had made all the arrangements. I didn't have to go and tell the priest that I wanted the job or anything. I just went to sign the papers – my teacher had everything arranged. My father then said that it was okay. I told him, "Do you remember that you took me out of school before I took the exam? I only went on because my teacher was interested in me because, without him, it would have remained that way." He said that he thought that education was not very important for women.

My teacher told me that I wrote good compositions. He did everything in his power for me to become a teacher and when classes started I began to teach. Eduardo Martinez was my teacher. He told me that if it was my wish to carry on, I would have to study and take a test called the teacher's exam. He started to instruct me. He was quite interested in having me progress with my studies. I was also interested. I studied, and when the teacher's exam day came, I passed the whole exam. My teacher was very pleased about me having taken everything at once because some people only do half of it and the other half later, but I did everything the first time around. "Keep going," my teacher would say.

Mr. Martinez always advised me to finish my studies: "Go as far as you can; don't think about getting married now." He saw that boys were always escorting me home and he didn't like it. If he noticed that a boy came along with me, he would come and talk to me about it. He told me that I should finish my studies, to forget about boys and about getting married. He talked to me straightforward. That's why I always remember him. I think that my teacher was doing more for me than my father. My father never sat down to talk to me or to advise me. My teacher sat down and advised me as if I were his daughter.

(My mother) told me not to get married before I finished my studies and she kept saying it to me. When the second teacher's exam came, I went and passed it. I only had to take three more subjects to finish my second teacher's exam. I even passed the practical teaching. My teacher told me, "Don't be discouraged." He noticed there was a boy hanging around and every day he came to talk to me before his class. His everyday counselling began to bore me. The boy was telling me that he loved me. My teacher was married and I thought, "Well, he is married and he doesn't want anybody else to get married." I remember that I was always thinking about it. But my teacher had good intentions.

But I didn't wait for long and I got married. I told my husband that I wanted to carry on with my teaching. I taught even after I got married. Six months after the birth of my son, my husband told me that he didn't want me to continue with my teaching any more. He said that the baby was crying a lot and as my mother-in-law was not patient enough to take care of him, I had to give up my teaching. I then realized what my teacher had been advising me about and that he only wished the best for me, that he wanted a better life for me.

But at that time, my mind was not working all together and I didn't understand it that way.

I could have carried on with my teaching, but we lived far from my mother's place. I say that if my mother had taken care of my son, I would have been able to carry on and get all the education needed. I even might have obtained my training and everything. I was breast-feeding my baby. After six months of maternity leave, I was back at school and I had to return home to breast-feed him and everything. After a while, the baby wanted more milk and I had no idea what to do. Nobody explained to me what I could have done. Now I know that you can extract the milk and keep it, but before I didn't know anything about that. If I had known it, it would have helped me, but nobody knew about those things. I know that I can advise a person about it now, but before we were backward. We didn't have enough information. It was an obstacle.

His parents noticed that the baby needed to be breast-fed more often, so they were upset when the baby cried and I was not there to take care of him. In the end, I left (teaching). I felt awful because I knew that I could have helped with the finances at home. I had to leave.

We worked as a team after we got married. Aurelio didn't have land nor cane. Absolutely nothing. He was not a cane farmer – he only helped his father to take care of the cane. After our second son's birth, we went to see the representative (of the Cane Farmers' Association) about becoming a cane farmer and he got a license. Aurelio knew that he was going to die because the doctor had already told him what kind of illness he had and that there was no cure for it. He also felt very weak. So he told me, "Let's go to the Sugar Board and put everything under your name and my children's. When I die you won't have any problems." My in-laws didn't know that he had done it. When he died, they went to the Sugar Board because they wanted to put his licence under their name even though they knew that he and I had three children. But my husband had gone ahead and transferred everything into my name and my children's names. They told them, "We are sorry, but Aurelio left everything to his children and his wife." And they were mad. Really mad!

After two years, I had another boy. Then two years after, I had a girl. We got our house the same year, maybe because I talked to my parents so much about it and I was tired of the situation. Even though my husband was the only son and I had a father-in-law around, I didn't feel comfortable when I had to get a coconut or an orange. I didn't feel at ease - I felt like I was doing something bad, so I said: "Let's build a house" and my husband listened to me.

I had another son who didn't survive. I was pregnant when we moved to our new home. I never felt bad during my pregnancies, I never threw up, but that pregnancy was different. I stayed alone at home and when I had to grind cornmeal I felt pain. I suffered terrible pains for two or three months. I told my husband that I didn't know what was going on and that I felt bad. He brought me to a woman doctor. After that the pain didn't last, it faded away. Time passed.

They brought me to the hospital because I had labour pains. I didn't want to go to the hospital because the pains were far apart and they were not strong. We went upstairs and the nurse told me that she would examine me. I felt that the pain was worse now and she told me to lie down on the bed. She lifted me; the baby didn't wait and he was born. He was born dead. The nurse told me that he was dead for sure. He was tall and his head was very soft. When he was laid down, his eyes bulged out. All my kids were okay except for this one. The bones in his head were not hard, but everything else was fine. When they grabbed his foot, it seemed like his skin peeled off. It seems that the baby had died days ago. I felt that there was some movement, but they told me that the baby was dead. He had been dead for days.

I didn't feel very bad. After he was born they brought him home to bury him in San Miguel. The doctor talked to my husband and told him why the baby was born dead. I went back home the next day, but my husband didn't try to explain to me the cause of the baby's death; he thought that I was sick. He came and hugged me, saying that he had never lost a child before and I cried because when I had come back from the hospital in the past I had my baby with me. I cried and he couldn't find a way to comfort me. A few days passed and he said, "Do you know that the doctor told me that one of us is sick – that's why the baby was born like that." In his mind, he probably thought that I was the one who was sick. The truth is that I didn't think more of it and as soon as he said it, it was over.

A year passed and, thank God, I didn't get pregnant again before he fell sick. He had fever, a fever that didn't go away. When we realized that he was very sick we decided to go to Belize. We waited for a long time. The doctor said that we had to wait for the five o'clock consultation, so we stayed. At five, he had the results. He said, "I feel sad about this, but it is better to tell you the truth. You have cancer and there is no cure." As soon as he said it my husband started to cry; he cried all the way back home and we didn't know what to do. Then my brother said, "I am sure there is something that can be done." So we went back to see McClery and he said, "There is an agreement between the Government of Belize and Mexico which says that they can take care of some cancer cases. It is free in Mexico."

He got his first treatments and the doctor said that he had to come back for more. I went with him on the second trip. We went and came back without the children. November came. December. We went around the second of December—we thought that we were only going for a consultation and that we would be back soon. As we had a few dollars and Christmas was coming my husband said, "My poor kids. I'll get a Santa Claus for them. I'll keep it and I'll give it to them for Christmas. I'll buy for the boys and you will buy the gift for the girl." As I thought that we would need the money later on, I bought a little doll for my daughter and my husband bought big noisy guns for his sons.

We went to see the doctor. "Now," said the doctor, "you can't leave. You have to be treated every day with cobalt for a month, so you have to be here." We thought that we would go back the next day, so the idea of staying was terrible for us. We travelled every day to get the cobalt treatment and as a result of this, other illnesses arose. I don't know what they were doing, but I think that they injected something because every time it was effective. I don't know if the nerves were touched or what, but he jumped on the bed without any control like a hen who is going to die. I don't know if it was due to the treatment. I had to be with him and I cried because

186

I could see that he was dying. That's how the treatments were every day.

My husband knew that he could die after one of those treatments. We always prayed besides his bed. I said, "God, if you want him to die what can I do? If it is Your wish, let it be, even though it is hard for me because I see that the man is suffering too much. But, there is one thing that I am asking You: don't let him die here in Merida alone with me. If you love him, God, wait for him to be in his country. Everybody is there to share our pain. Here I am alone. What can I do?"

The doctor said that he was going to get him ready the same night. As the doctor told me that it was his last treatment, Aurelio said, "Doctor, you know that I have not seen my children for quite a while and it is Christmas time."

So the doctor said, "Aurelio, that was the last treatment that you needed. If you feel that you can stand the long trip, you can go now." He gave him the last treatment from seven to eight at night. We left the hospital and went to collect the things that we brought with us. We then went to the terminal. We arrived here on the 24th of December. It was my mother's birthday – they had killed a pig and I don't know why, but when I arrived I felt like crying, so I started to cry bitterly. I thought, "Here they are, they killed their pig and nobody knows how much my husband is suffering and that I was suffering, over there alone." I cried and told them, "Aurelio was close to death every time he had a treatment over there," and I explained to them how terrible it had been. They had planned a party for the night of the 24th until the 25th in the morning. I felt so awful that I didn't stay with them at their party. They didn't share my pain and I thought that they didn't know how much I was suffering. I suffered just by looking at my husband suffering. I was not in pain but I suffered inside, remembering how cheerful my husband had been before. That's the way things are. People thought he was being taken care of properly because he was in the hands of a doctor.

We went back to Merida once again and we continued travelling back and forth for a year and four months. In that period, the agreement between Belize and Mexico on the insurance was cancelled. When we were on the insurance plan, we didn't have to pay anything. They were not going to take care of Belizeans any more in Mexico. One day we went to consult with the same doctor on a private basis. We continued consulting him for about four months, until one day the doctor made signs that I should enter his office and he said, "You know what? We can't do anything for Aurelio. You must find ways to take care of him. Tell him you're going to treat him with herbal medicines, but we can't do anything for him."

I didn't want to tell him the truth. I couldn't tell him that the doctor couldn't do anything else for him, but I couldn't hide it. After we left, we went to look for the luggage and I cried all the way home on the bus. "What did the doctor say?" asked my husband. "He told you something." "No! A lot of things hurt me," I answered. When we arrived, I went to see his family and I told them the truth. I said there was no hope for him and that the only thing that we could try was to give him some herbs until he dies. A short time after, he died – after sixteen months of pain. He suffered a lot. It was a terrible year, without a single happy day.

In the course of time, we loved each other more and more until he died. Up to now, I am afraid to look at another man. My husband was so good; he never mistreated me or yelled at me and I find it difficult to look at another man here. I might have problems now that I never had with my husband. He was a good husband. He always worried about my family. We always got along. You don't find this kind of husband a lot. I say that good people don't last in this world.

On the 24th of August, he will have been dead for ten years. We got used to it. At the beginning, I felt strange to be with the family, but after that it went back to normal. We were all together, as a daughter and with the children. There was no difference. They always made sure that the children were entertained. It is hard enough when somebody dies, especially a husband. It hurts – even after one or two years I could still feel it, even though my family said that I looked happy. They couldn't understand how I felt inside because I felt his death inside me. I felt lonely and sick and I thought that if I remained like that it would be terrible. I had the opportunity to leave for a week to a marvellous villa so I went. The trip helped me quite a lot. I came back with a new spirit – before I always secluded myself by thinking all the time. I can feel how I changed after that trip. That's why I tell my father that people have to go out to change their mind and forget about their problems and to get over their sadness and their loneliness.

After my husband's death, Father Gomez, the local school manager, came to my house and asked me what I was planning to do. I didn't care about a thing in the world. I think that it was good of Fr. Gomez to come to my house and talk to me because he was worried about me. "Don't you think about going back to teach?" I couldn't have cared less about anything. I felt lost. I regret it. I think that Fr. Gomez came to see me at the right time. It was ten years ago. I would have been able to do a lot with my studies then. I regret it now, but it was difficult because I couldn't get over my pain. My children had also lost their father and I wanted to be close to them.

After eight years, the project MAC (Mothers and Children) came along and they wanted volunteers, so I offered to do it. I think that they realized that I could share what I knew with the people. They explained the working conditions and I said, "Well, let's try." As I had to ride a motorcycle, I saw it as an obstacle to doing the work, but I did it. My boss came to me one day and said there was a vacancy as a community health organizer and she thought that I could do it. She explained to me the working conditions. She also said that they were going to put me on probation for three months and if I could do it, that would be fine, but if I couldn't that would also be fine. And after three months they said that they were satisfied with my work, so I started working on the 15th of September, 1987.

I talked with one of my brothers first. What do you advise me to do? I was a little scared to tell my father because he didn't really want me to go outside the house to work. He (my brother) told me, "Don't be stupid. It is a great opportunity." So when he said that I thought that I had at least the support of one person, and I told my father.

I had been a health volunteer for eight months. They taught us about nursing babies, diarrhea, how to prepare the intravenous, about family planning and the preparation of meals for four-month-old babies. They also taught us subjects like acute respiratory diseases.

We had two sessions for each subject. Let's say, for example, if we were learning about immunization, we had to attend two classes. We held a general meeting after these two classes – the meeting first was with the volunteers only and then we called a general assembly with the village. The volunteers then shared with them what they had learned about the importance of immunization and the illnesses that result from (not having) it. That was what the work of a volunteer consisted of. We were going from house to house telling people when there would be a clinic and a general assembly. We always had a movie related to the subject that we would talk about to present to the assembly meeting.

(As a community health organizer) I have to know both languages, English and Spanish, because I may have to talk in Spanish in the villages and in English in the office. CARE pays for the programme. They get money from the USAID. I think that it is a good programme. When we talked about immunization, for example, we noticed that a lot of people made sure to bring their children to the clinic because they saw the effects of polio, diphtheria or tetanus on the children. They were asking when the clinic would be available. You can see a change.

I sometimes leave at seven or at five-thirty or at five (in the morning). I come back around five-thirty, six. If I am in a village far away, I arrive later. I prepare my work schedule for the entire month. If we have a week on immunization, we have to see six villages. I have to do two sessions, two days for each village. I'll do one session in San Miguel and one in Trinidad in a day, for example. Besides that, I have to set a general assembly for each village. I have to see six villages in a month. I have to plan them, six general meetings and twelve sessions, no matter what the subject is about. I sometimes have to plan a day of support visit and go with the volunteers to visit the families from house to house. We first have to see families with kids under five years old and if we have any time left, we see the other ones. We also provide service to pregnant women. The volunteer goes and visits the expecting mother: she explains to her how to breast-feed the baby, if it is her first time and she also gives her advice.

I am happy now. I have my friends, I am meeting more people. It is a real pleasure to go out and meet them now. You learn fast. Last month, or the month before, I was at a workshop with the Breast Is Best in Belize. People came from all over Belize and we shared everything – who does what. We met people from all over Belize; we met representatives from all the districts at this workshop. I did things that I have never done since I was born, like staying overnight. They sent me for the Breast Is Best and to another community development workshop last month. I stayed one week. It was really interesting. You learn how to improve your work.

When I want to go out – like the other day when we had a little party, I told (my father) that I was going to the party and he didn't say anything. I let him know where I am. I just want him to know, so if something happens, he would know where I am. I told my brothers yesterday that I felt more satisfied with my life. I am sharing my experience. When there is a celebration, like the Independence celebration in Orange Walk, I say, "Let's go with the girls. Later on, they'll get married and they won't even be able to go out with their husbands." As I have a daughter who is a teenager and a niece who stays with my mother, I want to bring them.

I have a lot of pleasant moments – before I got married and now. I feel happy because I am meeting a lot of new people. I enjoy being with them. I am so happy that I don't want to stay at home. I don't know if my happiness is due to the fact that a lot of us know and trust each other now. It may also be because of my work or my family. My girlfriends find me more cheerful. Sometimes we plan a party and my friends come to my home and at times I go to theirs and it is always fun. My mind is on something else. Maybe that's one of the causes of my happiness.

Sylvia

Sylvia was born in the Cayo District of Belize. She is twenty years old, unmarried and lives in Orange Walk with her parents. At the time of the interview she was serving a two-year probationary period preparatory to becoming a full-fledged police officer.

I was born in the Cayo District. There are eight children in my family; I am the oldest. I had to help a lot. There was a lot, lot, lot of work. I had to wash, cook, take care of the kids. My mom had a baby every two and a half years.

I went to the chapel school and then to Muffles. When I was young, I always wanted to be a journalist, but when I was at Muffles, I messed things up so I couldn't. I failed my third year. I failed the first two terms and passed the third, but I would have had to do the whole year over again. I had a chance to go back, but I didn't. I was tired of studying. Then I wanted to go back later, but my parents, they couldn't finance me because they didn't trust me.

I was sixteen when I came out from school. I stayed home for one year, then I decided to do something for myself: I joined the police force. I wanted to help my family. My father, he was a captain at BSI, a supervisor. He was dismissed in 1986. That's partly why I got a job – he didn't have a stable job and I had to help.

I was scared of joining the police force, but my mom convinced me to. I used to be afraid of them. I didn't like them. You always hear about police brutality, but then when I got on the force I found out what it was all about: you have to keep serious so the public will respect you.

I was eighteen when I entered training school. The training was four months. It was very difficult: it was physically hard and we had to do a lot, lot of studying of law books. We had a test every Monday. They wanted us to be neat and clean all the time and we had to run and march for miles and miles. They said that they wanted to stop us from thinking and acting like civilians and start acting like police men and women; they said we should stop acting like boys and girls and act like men and women.

In my class there were fifty recruits: forty-seven men, three women. That was very difficult. I have mostly sisters and wasn't used to being around boys and most of the boys were Creole—they were TOUGH. They like to curse. I just wasn't used to them. Sometimes it was so hard I wondered why I was there. I nearly resigned about two times, but I stayed.

The squad before us, they had to take out all of the girls because they were caught in compromising situations, so they were very strict on us. There were six instructors, only one of them was a woman. There were two men sergeants that I liked. There was another one that none of us liked. He used to tell us that he hates women. He was one of my squad teachers. We didn't get along. He was very strict – he used to follow us wherever we went. He didn't do that to the men. We knew if we slipped one inch he'd get us. He would punish us for small reasons. To punish us, sometimes he'd have us women running around the parade square at noon carrying these heavy, heavy guns over our heads. It was hot, hot and he wouldn't let us rest. He was awful.

But on the whole, training was okay. The men in the training always kept their respect for us. They keep their distance. In words they lose their respect but not in actions because they had people watching them too. All the other male leaders were okay. They were more fair, but they were all strict on us: we couldn't get many phone calls, we couldn't go out much, we couldn't have relationships with anyone in the school. The men couldn't be alone with us. We had to be in our barracks by six. The men didn't have to do that: they could go to the recreation hall, or the mess hall. It was unfair. They had more freedom.

But the three of us got to be real close. We talked about our problems and studied with each other. The woman instructor, I liked her. She took care of us. She would advise us and help us. Sergeant Leona would push us a lot. She said that since there were only three women in the squad we had to do very well. Once I did really bad on a test. I didn't study for it and she got so mad. She told me that I had to prove that women were as good as men. And the boys and men in the training would harass us – like when you hang out your under- wear and they see it and steal it or laugh and say obscene things – she'd help us then and talk with them. In that case, we ended up hanging our underwear inside because it was too hard to deal with them. There were so many of them.

When I was in training school, the one thing I was most afraid of were the men. They want to make you fall into temptation. They wanted to test us to see if we were strong enough to resist them. We proved that we were because three of us went into the training and three of us passed out of it. And I did really well: I pushed myself hard and I came out fourth in the squad, out of fifty, and I was the only one who didn't have high school. No one ever believed that I didn't graduate from high school because I did so well and it was tough. The law books we have to learn are tough and you have to really know it 'cause they test you good on it. A lot of people who had graduated from high school didn't do as well as me. I am proud.

After training school, they only gave us the weekend off. So two days after we finished, I had to start work in Orange Walk. I was fortunate to be shipped back here. The commissioner decides where to place people. You don't know where you are going and they can transfer you any time. They usually transfer you every two years. The nice thing about the job is that you never know where they are going to send you. You get to know all the different districts.

At first they weren't going to let me work here because I grew up here and people wouldn't respect me. But I told them I didn't go out very much, so not very many people know me, so they let me come here. A lot more people know me now.

On the first day I reported for duty, the other policewoman was sick. One of the things policewomen do is send and receive radio messages. I didn't know anything about sending radio messages or anything. I accidentally hung up on them and didn't know what to do. The men expected me to take care of everything: they'd say, "Do this, do that," and I wouldn't know what the hell they were talking about. I felt like crying. It was so hard, I wanted to quit.

I used to feel bad all the time, but I like the job now. I like interfering in other peoples lives, asking questions, and I want to try to stop crime, to help my country.

They tell us that we are policemen twenty-four hours a day, that we have to be an example. Our working hours are eight to five, but the policewomen, we come in at six in the morning to do the dispatching, to report our situation to Belmopan. The other woman and me, we take turns doing that. When I do that, I go home at three. We also send and receive radio messages during the day and give out permits and take down statements and we take care of the women prisoners. We do mostly what the men do, but we usually don't go out on operations. And we don't always do all the things the men do, like escorting prisoners, so the policemen tease us and tell us we're not doing much. But we do a lot.

Sometimes the men try to protect us. If they see someone on the street being tough to us – some guy trying to beat us up – they help us. They are defensive and protective. If they are going somewhere on an operation and we ask them if we can go, they say, "No, because you are a woman." But sometimes they take us.

The men expect us to be tough. We went through the training to learn to be tough. That's the one thing I like about myself, that I have a wall built in me. Sometimes people say things that really hurt you, that are mean. The thing I like about myself is that I think I am strong enough not to listen to them, to listen to insults. I don't give them no mind.

What I like best about the job is dealing with people. Like if a young girl ran away, I like to know why she did it. When I am taking down the statement, she tells me things like she ran because her parents used to beat her. Sometimes I think the parents are at fault when the kids run away. I like to find out what really happened.

I take down statements on all kinds of things. For example, we have a good amount of domestic violence here. There have been about ten cases of that since I got here. But what happens is the husband beats the wife, she comes and tells us about it and then when the case comes to court she says she doesn't want the case because she gets scared. Like there was a woman who reported to us about her husband – he beat her all the time. The time she came to us, she had asked for some money for her child and he had beat her up bad. We arrested him, but then she dropped the charges. We often refer them to the Social Office. We often don't arrest because they always drop charges. Same thing with husbands that beat children: wives don't go through with the charges.

What I get mostly is girls who run away. Most of them run away with their boyfriends and their parents report it. A lot of times they drop the charges. The girls say that they ran away because they loved the boy. Then the parents say that the girl should marry the boy and so they don't want to take him to court. I get mad then because I feel like they wasted our time. We went through all the trouble of finding them and then they don't want to press charges. Most of those girls are so young, they don't know what love is.

I like being a policewoman, but there have been many times when I wanted to quit. One of my squad sisters, she is going to resign in October because it is so hard. Where she is, they have to work nights and she doesn't like that. She wants to teach. But my mother encourages me to stay. When it's hard, she encourages me to ask for help. That's hard for me. And now my father has an okay job and I told my mom that I wanted to quit because I am tired of it, but she says, "No, you're getting older and have to take on responsibilities." But someday I'd like to finish my schooling and maybe become a journalist and I would like to travel.

I'd like to know how people on the outside live, but when you're on the police force, they don't like you to just quit like that. I'm on trial now for the first two years. They want to see how I behave, if I am fit. After two years they'll decide if I am fit to stay, so it wouldn't be wise to quit right now.

It is a good job. It pays okay. The salary goes up in increments, like there is an increment for married men. Men and women are equal in this job. We get paid the same. What I make is enough for me because I am living with my family. I spend a lot of money travelling. I like to travel in Belize. I should save more because I could be transferred and I might not get as much money in the new place as I get here.

There are not many policewomen – it's mostly Creole men. There are some women in high positions, but not many. I think there should be a woman commander because women have a lot to offer. We can make decisions as well as men. We should be given a chance. I think if a woman wants to become a police officer, I would tell her not to do it. Ha, ha – I don't mean that. No, I'd say if they think they have something to offer they should do it and not pay any attention to them men who insult them. A woman can do anything men can do. Even if men do a lot to abuse them, a woman can do it and be proud of herself.

Gloria

Gloria was born in 1962. She is the eldest of a family of ten children. At the time of the interview she lived with her parents and was a teacher at the village primary school. She told her story in English.

I was born on the 5th of December 1962. As far as I can recall, my parents used to live with my grandfather and my grandmother in my grandfather's home. They had a house built – but like the cooking, they used to do it together with my grandmother and when it was time for sleeping – when the night comes – they would go to their own house. It was in the same yard, but when I was at the age of four, they moved the house and transferred it to the lot where we are living presently and that is where they are still living today. I can remember it was a board house – lumber.

Then I can recall being in classes, and my grandfather, he used to like me. He had a shop – a big shop because we had to pass by his house to go to my house. Whenever I passed, I went inside there. He gave me biscuits and sweets. He and my father worked together. Whenever he planted corn, he used to make a lot – more than a hundred mecates of corn – and that was what sustained them for the whole year. At that time, the village wasn't that big – they could take land wherever they felt like. He cleaned the lot – he paid people to clean the lot – and then planted and so forth. He used to sell them (corn). They would take all the corn and sell it in Belize. My father always tells us that they used to wake up early in the morning and clean the corn, pack it in bags, put it in the truck and they would go and sell it in Belize. They would eat from it also.

He (grandfather) paid workers to work with him because he only had my father and my uncle – only two of them – and (at) that time – when my father was a little bit bigger – he went to high school. When he stopped, he started to work with my grandfather. He planted cane and so forth. Since the land was free, he took a piece of land and he cleaned it and planted cane and from there he started growing and growing. It was behind here – behind the cemetery – where he made his first planting. I would say that my father, when it was cane season, he would barely stay at home, always spending the day in the cane fields. He got home late at night. You see, they had a lot of cane – it was a very large work. Most naturally he had to stay out and whenever it was Saturday, he would go out and come back in the afternoon – half day. He would stay at home. Whenever he comes, he gets his pay and everything and sometimes when he comes in he would bring everything that he can find and bring it to us so we can eat.

I can recall I was the first one to go to school. And since I was the only one, I was a little bit spoiled of leaving mummy by herself at home because I would usually stick to her when I was small – because I was the only girl. I was the first-born child. I kept on thinking of what was at home. I can recall that when I was at school I used to cry – my mother usually made my bottle – to cry for my bottle and they used to send me home to drink my milk. But after a month or two, I forgot about it and could do without it. That was when I was very, very small.

I came out from primary school at the age of thirteen and I started to help my mummy a lot in the housework. And then I went to school in Belize. My mother didn't oblige me to do anything because I can recall that my father always used to tell her that I was too small to be working, so she did all the work. If she was sick, I would bathe my little brothers and sisters, or do a little bit – only the small clothing, not the big ones. That is what I used to do and do the sweeping in the house.

In order for us to qualify for high school – at the age of thirteen, I took the entrance exam for high school. I made a seventy and at that time the high schools were restricted and accepted in the eighties and nineties. My cousin was at Belize, working with the Palatine Sisters, and he came to my father and told him there is a high school for only girls in Belize, if he would like to send me over there. And my father talked to me and I told him – because my cousin was the one that told him about it. So after the results came in, my father went to the convent and talked to the principal and she said it was okay and I was accepted.

So when I went to Belize – I can recall, at the age of thirteen, first of all I used to be scared not knowing anybody. Before school was opened, I went one week ahead to get used to the house – I used to stay in a boarding house with a lady. My cousin recommended her to my father. Before I went to school, I can recall that I put on my uniform. I was lonely by myself. She had a daughter and the daughter was in Sixth Form and she used to come and talk to me and give me like a little bit of consolation. I didn't know how to go to the school in Belize City, so when she got ready she took me along and left me by the school and she went on and I stayed at the school.

There I felt very, very strange because what I saw was only Creole girls and that was very, very strange to me. And I knew I had the Sisters and I talked to them. I made more friends with them the first year, and then afterwards I got to know the girls. Later I got to know that they were in the same situation as I was. Not all of them were from Belize City. Some of them were from the districts and so forth and they didn't know each other, so I made friends with them and that's how we went along. It was a four-year course.

(I studied) commercial subjects. I used to enjoy it. When we first entered high school, the seniors used to organize Freshman Day and the second formers, they were the ones who were supposed to perform. There were games, like tug-of-war, blind man's bluff, etc. In the third year and fourth year, we were the ones who used to organize the things for the little ones and that was quite interesting.

It was a Catholic high school. Because it was a strict high school, we were not allowed to go to the discos. We were not allowed to be in our uniform, let us say, at six o'clock in the evening, because it was one of the rules of the school and we had to see that all the rules abide. So we were the ones who used to look after those in Third Form. When we wore our uniform we had to wear a whole slip, like the Sisters wear, and that was – especially in hot weather – quite hot. And the student body used to go and check to see who has only got on a half slip and those who only had a half slip, to send them home to put on her entire slip. It happened to me once when I was in Second Form.

The merit system was for the girls who didn't abide by the rules and so forth. I can recall that when I was in Fourth Form, there was a freshman in First Form and she used to be rude to the teacher. As my cousin used to be rude to the teachers – I can recall that she was standing in the sun holding a book over the head of one of her teachers – so that was the job she was given. Depending on how you behaved in the class, depends on the teacher the kind of job that you have been given to do. That was in the merit system. We used to get five demerits – after five demerits, you got a jog, working in the compound at something that needed to be done.

That was the punishment that you used to get. Those girls that filled their cards, they were suspended for two weeks. Or let us say that if one of them didn't abide with the rules, they were not allowed to go to the discos, and if one of the teachers saw one of the girls entering a discotheque, that girl would get expulsion. But for minor things, like wearing your uniform at late times of the day, you were given a suspension – that is two weeks out of classes. That means that you're going to stay home. When the time of the exam comes, you still have to sit the exam.

And, for example, let us say that – it happened in my class when I was in Third Form – girls got pregnant. Immediately the Sisters noticed. They suspended her from coming to school anymore. That is one of the rules of the school. So she didn't abide by the rules of the school. But there is another high school where they allow the young girls who are pregnant. After she delivers, she comes back to school and finishes her schooling. But Palote was not that way: once you fall, you fall and you are out. The government schools, they weren't that strict, you know. The girls could go anywhere they want to go. At the government high school – let us say that one of the girls gets pregnant – they are allowed to go back to school. It doesn't happen very frequently. When I was at school I can remember only one time when a girl fall and that was when I was in Third Form. She was the only one that fall and had to leave.

I don't know if it's so common right now, but when I left the high school – when Melva (her sister) was going to Palote – she told me about several of the girls who had fallen and were out of school. So I should think that it is happening more regularly now.

For us as girls, I think that the rules were quite protective. If one girl in the community goes to high school and the people in the community always see her going along with a boy – every day he or she passes and goes to school – they have to come in walking sometimes, to go by bus and so forth – and people in the community look at it and they start talking about it. And it so happens that the girl falls, gets pregnant and the people in the community are noticing it. Let us say that one of the girls wants to go to high school. They (the parents) will say, "No, if you go to high school the same thing will happen as the other one did. You had better stay home and learn to cook and learn to wash."

That is what they say. The boys, they don't have any problem. Boys can go to high school. Let them go. That is what some families think. The girls stay home and do the work at home. That is what some of them think.

It happened here in the community once. I think the girl was at Muffles and every time she used to come from school late, accompanied with the boy. And it so happened that she falls. Her parents were quite annoyed. And he was right from here also. It went on like that. She had her baby. They lived together, but afterwards – after living together for a little while – she decided that she wanted to finish her high school. So she went to a government high school here at Corozal. She got to finish her high school and right now she went to the United States and is there now with the boy. The baby is here with her sister.

202

Well, I graduated and applied for teaching. I taught one year here at San Miguel and then I got transferred to San Vicente. In going to San Vicente it was a great experience for me. I did one year – that first year was a little bit hard for me. I didn't know anything about teaching because I took the commercial subjects, so I didn't bother about the others.

My plan was being a secretary, but when I came down here to San Miguel for a secretary job they told me there wasn't any. I told my father there isn't anything to do, so I will have to go into teaching. I just intended to teach one year because the first six weeks I still didn't get into the spirit of being a teacher.

So the months went by of the first year. Father (the priest) came to me and he said I had to get transferred because the school is overstaffed. So I went there to San Vicente and in San Vicente there were more teachers and more qualified. They were able to help you. And that was the first time that I saw that parents used to come to school about their children. It was what brought my attention how parents' interest comes in. That's how I stayed in the teaching profession – because of the help that I used to get both from the parents, the children at school and the teachers. Because it's a big school – there are ten teachers – and whosoever passes by, you just hail them and say, "Help me with this, help me with that," and they were willing. And I did in San Vicente two years and afterwards I got transferred back again to San Miguel and I am still working – three years.

When I was at San Vicente, my first month it was a bit hard because I had to go out – not coming back home till classes were over, let us say at four o'clock, or five o'clock, when I couldn't get any buses to come in. I had Standard Five – both years I had Standard Five. And the children were quite loving.

For example, if they had any problems at home they would come in and say, "Teacher can you help me? This and this is happening." For example, they used to come with a problem that they didn't have blanks (notebooks), they didn't have breakfast in the morning, or sometimes the mother is fighting with the husband. And probably that his father is drunk and when he came in beat him.

That was quite a great experience for me, the children coming to me – like they had confidence in me telling me their problems, so I didn't neglect them either – just gave them some consolations with the help of another teacher. I didn't let them know that I went and discussed it with the other teacher. Let us say, whenever they came to school without any blank and so forth, I would get money and give them their own blank.

(If) they didn't have their breakfast I would know. He would always come and tell me he didn't have his breakfast, so one day I went to one of the child's house and asked what was the problem that the child didn't get his breakfast. So most of the time the mother will tell me that she got up late and wasn't able to prepare the breakfast. So we discussed it with the lady and she said she would try to make it comfortable to get breakfast ready before they go to school. I asked her if they didn't have the money to buy anything. She said no, that wasn't the problem. So from then, the child was punctual to school, had his breakfast.

But let us say, in the case that the father beat the little child, I didn't dare to go to the house. I just wrote a note in telling (asking) him why, because the little child went to school all bruised – his back, his foot and everything. So I signed it and made the principal sign it also. It wasn't quite so healthy in meeting the child's interests in such a cruel manner. He answered back and said that he was sorry about it, but it was because of the liquor that he had drunk.

Let us say that the mother is having some type of problem. The mother, in taking all her anger out – only a minor little thing the child does and she takes it out on the little child. The mother beats the child and, in some cases, when the father comes drunk he beats the child for probably nothing that he did. Mostly it's the mother. Sometimes it does happen that the husband does beat the lady and the wife doesn't have the courage, or the strength to beat the man – she goes and she takes it out of the child.

For example, some days the child doesn't want to go and get a bucket of water and immediately she takes the child and starts beating the child only because of that – because the child doesn't listen immediately.

204

In the class, we have to know the parents of the children because in working with the child you cannot only centre yourself on them, but you have to learn something about their experience on the outside. And once you get to know the parents, the parents and the students and the teachers can correlate together, so the children's progress can go up day by day. And that's the way we should work, both the community, the parents and the students and teachers.

That was at the time when I was in San Vicente – the visiting that I did with the parents, I think it helped me, helped me a lot to think seriously about a teaching career. And after that I decided to come back to my village and give the utmost to the children here and that is how I came here and I started working. I followed my same pattern as how I was working in San Vicente.

Last year, I had a boy and his father – he rarely goes to the farm, but he wanted the child because he had a piggery, you see – and he wanted the child to stay at home and watch the pigs, feed the pigs. And he came one day and he said, "You know what, my father takes me out of school because he alone. He cannot manage the pigs himself." So I said, "Well, tell your father to come and speak to the principal." The father didn't come, so the boy took his bag and he went home. Up to today he is still working with his pigs. That was a boy.

In some cases it happens with the girls also. Girls – at the age of twelve – the mother says, "You are too big already." Even though she is twelve years old she has her big body. "You are big enough, so you'll be out of school, so you can work." So she puts the child out of school. What I tend to see – not here in San Miguel, but in San Vicente – once the girl is menstruating, the mother thinks that she is not supposed to be in school and they take them out of school. They say, "It is time for you to start working, knowing your responsibilities at home," and that's what they do.

In September, if I am accepted – we do not know yet who will be accepted – I will enter the Belize Teachers' College for training. It is a three-year programme, two years in Belize City and one year of practical work.

While (in) the course of two years in Belize City, the student will be instructed on better methods of teaching and how to abide by school board rules and also in the academic field. Since I have chosen teaching as a career, to me it is compulsory that I do get more training because with what I have I don't think I have a good training background yet. So I think that it is quite reasonable to go to training, in order for me to bring to the children.

I asked her if she hopes to get married.

It depends. For example, in the situation we are in presently, there are a lot of financial crises – not exactly in my family but in the entire country. A lot of problems and, for example, men coming out from other countries and diseases and whatnot, so you have to be careful to see what it will be like. That's what I think.

Take, for example, the case of Maria (a married teacher)—she is doing her work here at school and doing her work there at home. I feel that it is a little bit tiresome (tiring). Very tiresome and I think that you should have sufficient resistance. It is better for you to attend to your family and school problems. And I don't think that I am strong enough to have two things at once.

Let us say, if I am teaching, I will continue with it. If I had my family, I don't think I will be able to give everything to my family and just a part to the school. I don't think we should go half-half. When you are in school, you should give your everything and I think this is quite too hard. And let us say that once you have children, you have to attend to your children – sick – and your husband. And I think it is too tiresome. And I don't think that will go along with me. I have to choose one of both (one or the other).

From my point of view, a girl goes to high school, she finishes high school, she goes to teacher training and whatnot. If she gets married one time, she has a child, stops teaching, stops doing everything. Let us say that her husband wasn't quite responsible, paying attention to her. One day, she might leave the husband. That could be for her lifetime because she didn't get proper treatment

206

from her husband. Since she got that treatment, if she wishes, she can come back and defend herself. She doesn't have to depend on him.

You get married and you love your husband. I think it should be quite reasonable that you should have children. And with a child, if you have only one or two, I don't think it will be quite a big work to do. That is what I think.

The Church is offering some classes whereby – not exactly birth control – but the rhythm (method). I think that every month a pair of couples come in and teach them how to go about working it. If you ask for it and you don't know anything about it, they will surely help you because the chemicals are quite dangerous.

Today, it is a great problem for girls to find work because of the big number of girls graduating from high school and most of them don't continue their studies any further. So especially those ones that live in the town get the first benefit to get into the offices, get into the government departments – they are the ones who get the work. But here in the village, even though you are a bright student, leaving at Fourth Form, you have a hard chance getting into a type of work being a secretary or a government job because they consider the travelling, going and coming, they consider things that may happen on the way. A caution about things that might happen to the girl – that is what they think of first.

They (parents) do not have confidence in their own daughters. That's what I think – they don't trust their own daughters. Probably I would say because there are some parents that always would be thinking that their daughters would be going out and doing all kinds of mischief. That is what I would say.

Likewise, my parents, they would sit down and they would advise us what is good and what is wrong. Once they have told us what is right and what is wrong, I don't think they have any say if we go out.

Like the Church group. I just started with them about three years (ago) and I entered because we were a group of youths and the older people didn't want to take care of the church. So we went outside, inviting young people to enter, and we managed to get a group of fifteen. Fifteen young boys and girls – most of them at high school – and we started working.

The group would assist in cleaning – for example, in cleaning the cemetery. The group would go and do the cleaning of the cemetery—the cleaning up is being done by the girls. Or, like on a feast day or something like that – like Easter – the boys would go out in the bush and they would cut whatever needs to be cut and used for the Church and so forth. That's what is the work. The tablecloths and so on. I think it was the way I was brought up at home. They attend Mass and take part in the Church. And since I went to a Catholic high school, that opened me more or less to religion.

We used to have our meetings whereby villages from all the parishes would participate, plan for the district. Later on, as we were working together, youth conventions were held and every two months we would have a youth convention and every village was responsible to prepare food. And where the convention was hosted, the group had to prepare food for the visitors coming in. That was quite interesting. And that was the first group that attended the Jamboree when it first started. That's the Youth Jamboree, whereby youths will go out and share with others.

A little community does have to develop and it can develop with the help of the people living here – that is the only way it can improve and if people do cooperate, there will be development. I don't mean giving money and so forth, but they can do a lot.

When I returned after two years, Gloria had left the village to join the Sisters.

Sister Grace

Sister Grace is a member of the Order of the Sisters of Mercy. She did her novitiate in Rhode Island, beginning in 1962. The second oldest of a Creole family of eight children, she teaches at a high school in Orange Walk Town and is active in community affairs.

I grew up in Belize City with my mom and dad. There were eight of us kids. I was the second oldest – there's more or less one and a half years between us all.

My mother was a teacher before she met my father. Once she got settled in with her family, the neighbours, knowing she was a teacher, brought all their little kids for tutoring. And then before we knew it, she had started a little school in our house. All of us kids went there.

My father worked at the sawmill. He drove a crane.

Both my mother and father were active in the community. When I was young, both the credit movement and the union movement were getting going. I remember going to meetings with my family. People from all walks of life would be there to talk about unions and credit unions and how they affected people in other parts of the world and how it could affect us. Us kids were always there with my parents and we'd listen and soak it up.

During this time, the Second World War was happening. I remember that during the war we collected everything that was aluminum – wrappers and so – to send off to the front. Our school got a little plaque thanking us. It was from Winston Churchill and it said

something like, "God Bless You – Britain's Future is in Your Hands."
I also remember some of my brothers joining up and going to
Scotland. I think they did timber work there – it was somehow
connected to the war.

After World War Two, the dollar was devalued. That helped to
bring around the political awakening, that and all the men coming
back from the war and not having any jobs. That is when people
really started to talk more about credit unions and such and also
when the political groups started forming. That was when I was in
Standard Six.

The kids in my family, we got on well. We played football,
climbed trees, played cowboys and indians and all sorts of things. We
also would put on little shows where we'd sing and recite and so on.
Our parents would reward us with little prizes.

My father was on the disciplined side. He had been on the front
during the war and was strict. In the house, we all had our chores:
sweeping, doing the floor, the dishes, the washing. We all pulled our
own weight; we worked hard. We had a little roster to keep track.

We did a lot together as a family. My father would come home
in the evenings and we'd eat together, then he'd go off for a while
with his cronies to listen to war news or whatever. On his way home,
he'd buy little things for us to eat, then we'd have what we called
"talking parties" when he got home: we'd eat the snack and talk.

My mother got sick giving birth when I was in Standard Four.
She was in the hospital for almost a year. For a long time when she
was in the hospital, we stayed home. My father had received permission from the school to give us our lessons. We'd get them done
lickety split and then go off to play.

When mom was in the hospital, she met a Sister of Mercy and
became good friends with her, so we ended up going to the Holy
Redeemer Catholic School. We did well in our classes. My older
brother and I were competitive sometimes. I hated being worse than
him in anything and hated being compared to him. I used to admire
him because he was so outgoing: he lit up the room when he came
in. No inhibitions. I was shy – I always felt like I was in his shadow.
But I learned a lot from him. Now I am less shy.

We did well in our classes. When we finished, my brother and I got scholarships, then I got a government scholarship to St. Catherine. Us older kids also worked to help pay the way for the others. In this time, we still did a lot together, even when we started dating. We would go out on group dates, all of us together.

My parents were both very encouraging about education. They put a lot of stock on being educated and pushed us a lot. They used to boast about us. Right after I graduated, I started teaching. I had decided to become a Sister but waited so I could help the others through school. I was also a little bit worried because there were very few black Sisters of Mercy.

I wanted to be a Sister because they were doing good things for the community, like my parents had taught us to do. My mother was a very big influence on me wanting to teach. I idolized her. And my favourite teacher was a Sister of Mercy. I really admired her. She did good work and I liked her way with people. I very much wanted to be like her. I had a very good feeling about being a Sister – I knew it was what I wanted to do. A lot of these things I didn't realize at the time. I didn't know exactly why I wanted to do things, didn't realize I was being influenced. But this is what my hindsight tells me.

I taught for seven years before I went off. During this time, I still lived at home, not like in the States where kids move out so early. My parents would have been scandalized if I'd moved out right after I graduated. That idea was foreign to our culture.

My novitiate period started in 1962. I did my novitiate at the Mother House in Rhode Island. There were twenty-six of us in my novitiate. That first year was dedicated to the study of the vows and the Bible. At the end of that year, we went to senior novitiate. At the end of three years, we took our first vows. We take five vows. The first three vows are common to all Sisters: the vows of celibacy, obedience and poverty. The last two vows are unique to the Sisters of Mercy. We take one vow to serve the poor, the sick and the needy and another vow to persevere forever.

That first year was the hardest. I liked it, but it was really strange at first. I KNEW that I wanted to be there, but I felt dislocated for a while in a strange culture and a strange house. There were three of us there from Belize. People were always curious about Belize – most of them had to be told where it was. Sometimes, especially on holidays, I missed being in Belize with my people. I also didn't always like the discipline: I was older than most of the girls and didn't need the strictness that the younger girls did. But I liked the life. It felt right to me. I felt pulled towards it.

In the first years, we would get up at five-thirty and have prayers. We meditated, said office and heard Mass. Then we had breakfast and did our chores. Then we did our charities and went to classes from eight-thirty until eleven-thirty. In the afternoon, we'd have spiritual readings and say our stations and do the rosary. The prayers took a good four hours a day. We did them at different times, spread out during the day. In the afternoon we had what we called "common recreation" – it was fun – we'd go for field trips as a group. Then we would have free time to pray, or write, or whatever. After supper, we would have another recreation period and then say prayers and go to bed. We were usually in bed by nine-thirty.

We were isolated from the surrounding community. The whole idea of the novitiate is to be away from the rest of the people so you have time to think seriously about things. But our days were so full that you hardly noticed. I found that in that sort of life you tend to appreciate the simple things, like a conversation with a friend or singing songs together.

We lost about one-third of the girls by the time we took our first vows. Some of the girls left after the first month. It was very hard: a lot of self-examining, searching. It was hard when people left. We'd all get sad.

After we took our first vows, we started to go to college. The college was about an hour away from the Mother House. We'd spend almost all day at school. It was a good atmosphere of thinking and learning. Also, it wasn't as strict. We had more seniority and in my third year, we were feeling the effects of Vatican II and so there was more talking things over and asking us what we wanted. The Church was a bit more gentle.

I had to practice teach to get my degree, even though I'd already taught for six years. I taught the final term of my fourth year. I taught sixth grade at a Catholic school. The year after graduation, I taught for a whole year. I was planning on going on for my master's, so I did evening classes and finally got it. After that, I did church work and worked at the Interracial Centre at the Parish. There wasn't any prejudice, except people bent over backwards to make me feel comfortable. When I went out teaching, the kids would call me "the Sister from Africa." After a while, I gave up trying to tell them the right way.

I like being a Sister because I can be a vital part of a community and I can do the work that I love. I am doing what I know is right for me. My work is teaching. I have been at Muffles for twenty-one years. I teach English. I try to bring out the best in these kids – I want to help them be their best selves and do good work in the community.

In being your best self, you realize there are values that you should follow, eternal values. I try to teach kids that they should capitalize on their gifts and use them to help out their community. And I try to teach them that they are tops: they are good and talented people and should respect themselves. I think that these attitudes are "caught, not taught," so I try to live them. The chief way you can show that is in your relationship with people. I make time for my students. I don't act impatient with them, or like I really don't want to speak with them. I show them respect. I also try not to put people down. And growing up, my parents both had strong personalities so much so I go out of my way not to be overly disciplinarian.

I help the kids realize that they don't need to be tops in everything: each person has his or her strong point. If there's something that a kid does well, I ask her to do that. Like if you discover that someone can draw, you have him or her draw the decorations for Christmas.

With teaching, I know that there's a lot to learn from other people and I try to listen. For example, it wouldn't be beneath me to ask the kids for advice because they are experts in a lot of things. It's also not hard for me to tell the kids that I've made a mistake. I'm not worried about impressing them.

I teach full-time. I try to update my classes often, so I don't get bored. I think if the teacher is bored, then the students will be. I also

213

teach summer school sometimes. Other times I go to Belize and do some volunteer work there or stay around here and work. Apart from school, I do many other things during the school year. I very much like to go around and visit with the older people. I learn a lot from them. I like to hear them reminisce. I also work with young girls in Girl Guides and am very active in the Church. It seems like sometimes every day I have a meeting for one thing or the other, but I also like to take time off, to read or to write letters or to enjoy nature. Sometimes I just go and lie down in my hammock to rest. And every day, Sister Mary and I try to play a game together, like Scrabble or cards. It helps us both to relax.

I am also the manager of Muffles, so I am active in all of the decisions that are made about the school and the students. Most of the time I trust the principal to take care of the day-to-day running of the school, but he always consults me and we make the big decisions together. He is a very good person and a good principal. Sometimes he is more strict than I would be, but I think that usually the strictness helps the students.

I usually have thirty or so kids in my class. When I first started here, the ratio of boys to girls was two to one. People weren't as well off, so they had to choose who would go to school and they chose the boys. Now there are more girls. Everybody is getting a chance at education. And the girls are much more confident – they used to be mostly very quiet. Now they are right in there with the boys in discussions and are sometimes even more vocal. Last quarter, I had a class of all girls and they were so strong and confident in comparison to classes I had five or ten years ago. But we still have a long way to go in women's rights: too many women still believe that men have more rights than them and are better off than them. But luckily, the modern girl is becoming more and more demanding of her place in society.

I believe in women's lib to a certain extent. I don't feel that I have to prove to men that I am as big and strong as they are, but I do believe that each human being has dignity and many gifts to offer and we should all be able to offer them. I believe in respecting each being: you don't have to prove yourself to anyone, but you have to be your best self. We should all have equal rights. We all have important contributions. The other day I was wearing one of those WAV (Women Against Violence) shirts that say, "You Can't Beat a Woman." The boys were saying, "What do you mean by that, Sister?" And I said I meant that women are tops and they said, "You think that women are better than men?" And I said, "No, men are tops too. Everybody's tops." I am number one, so are you.

I think that if men and women operated in the same way this would be a very boring world. We all have different things to give. I still believe that women are more tender than men, more sensitive. Men don't usually have that, but some do. It sounds like I am contradicting myself, I know. But women are mothers – they usually develop those skills and qualities of tenderness, etc., more than the men do. Men are certainly capable of it but don't develop it as much. We complement one another. Women can certainly do what men can do.

It is a trend in the community of the Sisters of Mercy to work against sexism. Our organization was founded about a hundred and forty years ago by an Irish woman who had a concern for women and their welfare. Within our community, we work on making religion not so male-oriented. We also work to stop men from making decisions that harm women or interfere with their rights. Even in the liturgy, we try to make it less sexist and we are working for women to be able to become priests. For too long that has been a sacrosanct area for men and we need to challenge it. There's nothing in the Bible that says that women should not become priests and they are certainly able to do it.

We are considered an avant-garde group in the States because of our thoughts on this, as well as the other work we do. For example, we do a lot of work with AIDS, the sanctuary movement and with the gay and lesbian community. We don't refuse women who want to enter our community just because they have been lesbian, just as we don't refuse women who have led a married or sexually active life. We agree with the Church that this (being a homosexual) is not the "normal" way of doing things, but our community does not ostracize or judge them in any way. I notice in our literature every month there's usually mentioned a workshop or lecture dealing with the issue of homosexuality, like looking at how homosexuals' civil rights are abused.

The main thing I like about the Sisterhood is that you can be what you are. There's a freedom to be whatever your talents call you to be and there is room for uniqueness. There's not any profession that's not open to the Sisters, except we try not to get too political. Some of our Sisters have had to make the decision whether to choose to continue their political work or to stay in the Sisterhood. A couple of them were lawyers. One of them was running for attorney general. Rome thought that was too political and so they gave her an ultimatum. She chose to keep running. She thought that the thrust of the Sisterhood was to work for the poor and needy and underprivileged and that running for attorney general was in keeping with that. She thought that was her calling, so she chose to leave the Sisterhood community. We had another Sister who was working on an urban programme which gave funding for abortion. But as you know, the Catholic Church is pro-life and Rome felt that she was not giving the true witness that a Catholic religious should give. The Sister said that she herself wasn't advocating abortion but was only supporting free choice. She saw no conflict with the Catholic ideals but Rome did. That Sister also chose to follow her heart and leave the Sisterhood. I can see why Rome would ask them to leave and I don't know what I would have done in their case. It was really heart-rending. There are some things that I don't agree with that Rome does.

When I speak of Rome, I mean that all religious communities are, in the final analysis, answerable to the Pope. Briefly, there is a group called the Sacred Congregation that regulates religious communities. The individual communities make their own policies within the guidelines of the Sacred Canon and then the policies are submitted to Rome for approval. The Congregation is made up of all men – European men. It is my hope that soon women and people from other places will be represented on the Congregation.

Here in Belize, we are not as active as the Sisters are in the U.S. We don't get up on our soap boxes so much, but we still do a lot of work. One of my sisters, who is also a Sister of Mercy, is the director of women's affairs in Belize City right now. She's much more vocal and involved in those things than I am – I don't have a burning desire like she does to keep my finger on the pulse of things.

I very much enjoy being a part of an international community of Sisters. There are hundreds of us, some in almost every country. We try to maintain contact with each other through letters and newsletters. We also visit each other. Like this summer, I will go visit some of the Sisters in Miami. And last summer I went to my 25th reunion. Many of the women who were in my novitiate were there. We also invited the women who had left the Sisterhood. We still keep in contact with them and are involved with them. Many of them came with husbands and children. It was a lot of fun.

Because I work here, my friends are mostly lay people. There are only two Sisters at Muffles. You develop bonds with the people you're working with and living with. I like that. I also like to get together with the other Sisters and priests in Belize and Orange Walk. We keep in touch and help each other out – like recently we have been having meetings to discuss how we can draw more young people to services, how to make it more interesting and involving for them. Sometimes we just get together to go on a picnic or to go boating. Last week I went boating with some of the people from around here. There were lots of mosquitoes, but it was fun – it was good to talk with them, to share experiences.

My family, we still are very close. My father died a few years back, but my mother is still very much alive. We have a few reunions each year. It is interesting: three out of the eight of us chose to go into the religious life. We all see each other two or three times a year, at least.

There have been many changes in Orange Walk since I moved here. Because of the influx of the tourists and TV, radio, etc., we know a lot about the rest of the world, especially the U.S. The teenagers really pick up on the trends there, like they'll all start wearing certain clothes or talking in a certain way. Sometimes it is quite funny. It seems strange when they do it, out of place.

There has been progress, but with the progress comes the ills. Since Independence, there's been more communication with the outside and we are becoming more involved in the world. People are taking responsibility for issues within the country: people are more alert and are taking stands. Politics is still immature here, but I guess that's true of most countries—look at the Republicans and the Democrats back-stabbing all the time in the States. But I would like to see us become more mature politically, like being able to belong to a political party and not being the sworn enemy of everyone in the other party. We've come quite a ways, but we have a ways to go. We need to allow for mistakes without damning each other.

I was glad to see Independence. It was a beginning. I am concerned about our lack of resources – we don't have any minerals or anything, just people and land and agriculture. We need investment. But I am apprehensive about all the aid coming down here – there are so many strings tied – I think about Nicaragua and Vietnam. It might not be as drastic as that, but no nation gives so much without expecting something in return.

I have had mostly good experiences with Americans – there's Americans and there's the ugly Americans, you know. There's the volunteer system, which can be good. We are fortunate at Muffles that the volunteers, like the Peace Corps, haven't been the ugly Americans. They have come to ask how they can be of service here instead of saying, "We know what is good for you."

I believe in the universal brotherhood, that there is no need for anyone to be poor because we certainly have enough resources to go around. So in that way, the volunteer programme (Peace Corps) is good. But I have heard some bad stories, like a volunteer in Hopkins who said some very racist things and treated the people with a lot of disrespect. One body can do a lot of harm.

I am very satisfied with the way I am and with my life. One of the things about religious life is that people ask me how could I give up the right to be a mother and do other things – but it is a choice you make and you have to live with it. I am doing what is right for me. Like those two other Sisters I talked about: they made choices about their lives and their choices forced them to leave the Sisterhood so they could follow their hearts. That is what you have to do: follow your heart.

218

Part II

CONTINUITY
AND
CHANGE

THREE GENERATIONS OF A
RURAL MAYA FAMILY

Estella

Estella did not know her exact birth date, but she was about seventy-nine years old when she narrated her story. A widow, she lives with one of her three daughters. Estella is the mother of Clara and the grandmother of Juanita.

I did not know my father nor my mother, only my grandmother. We had to live in poverty.

People say that my father fell into the well. That's what my grandmother who raised me said – he fell into the well and broke his neck. When my father died, my mother met another man. He was a drunk and he was a bad man. He hit my mother over there – on her ribs – and she died.

She died and we stayed with our grandmother. I grew up under her authority. She used to lash us. She also complained, "Let's cut some wood, let's do that, let's grind." She gave us food. That's how I grew up – I grew up poor. My grandmother raised us on her own. She worked quite a lot – she baked tamales and other things; she also sold them to get money and to feed us. She sold the eggs, the chickens and the pigs. That's how I grew up – when I was young, I baked, ground and washed. We also fished then.

I don't know what school was like. My grandmother didn't send me. There was a school, but we didn't attend it – we just played around. If you wanted to go, that was fine; if you didn't want to, it was also okay. If my mother had been alive, she'd have said, "Go to school, daughter." My grandmother would say, "What school are you talking about? Here there is a kitchen. It gives you food to eat."

She said that we had to work in order to eat and to buy clothes and shoes.

My grandmother never let us go out. We only used to go out during the carnival – it is a festival that we have here. They would come to get us to go to the carnival. Boys and girls would get together.

He came to my house to talk – that's how we met. He wanted me to marry him. He asked me if I would marry him and I said yes. We knew each other because both of us lived at the same place, in Santa Cruz. I said that I would marry him, so he went to talk to my grandmother. My grandmother said that if he wanted to marry me, he would have to wait for two or three years. He didn't want to.

He got a piece of land and built his house. We had a great life, really! I had one happy year. One year after, he started to drink and to hit me. He said that we had to move to San Joaquin with one of my aunts, so we went there. We came to San Joaquin, but the same thing happened there: he was getting drunk all the time. After that, he started chasing women. Then the bad luck started, the fights began.

They said that I was stupid. "You are so stupid to stay. I would leave him if I were you." I didn't. I stayed. When I looked at him, the anger faded away. We were trying to make up. Time flew once again.

I had quite a lot of hens in San Joaquin. I had quite a few of them before everything went bad. Then he started chasing women. I raised my hens. I sold them and sold their eggs. My life was good. I was selling some corn too. But after that, things started to get bad. He was chasing women. We had to find food for them (the hens) all the time. My husband had a cornfield in the hills and he would bring it (corn) back. After a while, he didn't bring any. I asked him, "How are the hens going to eat?" Instead of bringing it to me, he was giving the corn to the woman's children – she had two young sons. He told me that he didn't have time to cut the corn. I said: "No?" He cut it for the other woman. That man was bad. That's why, I think, he died the way he did.

Someone came one day and told me, "Do you know what? Your husband has another woman." "It is not true," I said. "Yes, he is going out with a woman." I said no. She said: "Yes, I saw him one day with her; I saw what she looked like." I felt hot and cold. I saw with my own eyes that it was true: he would sleep there and come back at four in the morning. He was saying that he had been out with his friends. I said: "No, you are sleeping with such and such." He said no. I said yes.

Once he went to a place where they cut *caoba*. He brought the woman along with him. She kept the money that they made – when he came back, he didn't have anything. "I only made a little money." It wasn't true. Some friends – other people – said that he had brought along a woman with him. She kept the money. He didn't send me any money. As I had my aunt and my grandmother, they told me to forget about him. "You won't starve to death. You will have food and drink." My aunt gave me food. He didn't send me any money because he had another woman with him in the mountains.

When he came back from the mountains, I said, "Why didn't you send me any money?" "It is because my work was not very good." "No," I answered, "It is because of the woman from Chetumal." "Who told you?" "Well, my friends."

That's how my husband was. He had like six mistresses.

I then learned that the woman was going to have a child, my husband's child. My daughter was born fifteen days after the birth of that woman's daughter. He told me a few times that it was his daughter. "Is it your daughter?" I asked him. "Yes."

My aunt told me, "Leave him, girl. Let him chase other women. Leave him, don't follow him, let him go to other women." That's when I came here – here to San Miguel. I left because of the mistress that he had. She laughed at me. They were holding each others' hands in front of me, making fun of me. They looked like husband and wife. I saw them so I told Luci, my grandmother, to look at them. She said, "Don't bother. Let them, girl. I am going to bring you with me. You don't have a father nor a mother; they are making fun of you."

So my grandmother said, "Let's go, girl. Don't bring anything but your clothes. There you will find things to do. You will find little things to do to support yourself."

224

Well, it was true. I came here with the three children. That's when I came here (with two daughters) and with the adopted baby – because I had an adopted one. He was small when they gave him to me. I raised him.

One month after I moved, he came and asked me to forgive him. I said, "Okay, don't do it any more. It's okay."

(But) he had brought that woman along with him, so she would take care of him. That woman had a daughter with him. She looks like my daughter. He nagged me. I answered back. He insulted me. I insulted him. We had a bad time. He didn't come home to sleep. He slept with the other woman. He slept with her at her house. He was just coming home the next morning. Sometimes he would tell me, "Get up and get my food ready." "But god," I said, "Since you stayed with another woman the whole night, eat there. I won't get up to feed you. You are giving her everything she wants, so stay with her." He was hitting me. I would run away. He didn't lash me when he was not staying at home.

He left me when I was expecting my twins. It was a few days before they were born. He left with another woman. He stayed there. I was going to die when they were born. I couldn't stand the labour. I was thin. They didn't tell me that I had two. One of them was born. I started crying. "The pain," I said. "I am in pain." The other one came then. I was going to die, when a lady came they told the midwife that I was going to die. I felt that I was going to die. I told the midwife, "I give you those two children to raise." She said yes. "I don't want them to be alone like that, I want you to raise them."

I was going to die. "I am dying," I said to various people who came to see me. They asked him to come and see me because I was very sick. (I said) "I swear that when you die, or if God gets you first, I'll never have another man. I'll stay alone with my family. I don't have a mother. I don't have a father. I don't have brothers. I don't have anybody except for my three kids."

But I came back once again to normal. God blessed me and I got back on my feet again.

I had to work hard to support (my family). Clara was very little when she started carrying and selling the water, about ten years old,

I think. I gave her a little bucket. "Go and get water," I was telling her. She would go to get it. She would cry and would say that she was tired. "How do you think that I pull the water out of the well? We have work to do." They didn't want to. They said that it was far, that they would fall with everything, including the bucket. I told them, "What do you mean that you would fall? You are strong. Pull the water out."

I washed clothes and made tortillas for Sra. Alejandra. I baked bread for sale. I washed and kneaded. They brought me the *nixtamal;* I ground it with a mill and I sat down to knead it. I also would go to their house to wash the clothes. She told me, "The water is nearby. Come here to do the laundry, woman." So I was going there to do the laundry: I washed the clothes and the next morning I rinsed them and hung them outside.

We had chickens, but not enough. There was no money for corn, so I had to find money to make tortillas for them (the children) to eat. I used to go to cut wood with the child. With her. We fished for little fish to eat.

Her first five children died young. Of thirteen births, only four lived to adulthood.

My son was born very healthy. He died at four years old – he had an attack during the night. He was dead in the morning. There was no doctor or any bush doctor, nobody. There was nothing available. I asked my aunt who is my godmother and my grandmother to come to see him. They gathered together some bottles of medicine. They looked for things to cure him, but he didn't get better. When my first son died at four years old, the other one was already born. He was three months old when he died. My four-year-old died and then the second one died at three months old. Fourteen days after Mario's death, José died.

An old man (came to see me). He was only an old man, a bush doctor. He said that he was bringing me some kind of medicine, some kind of water that I had to take to see if one of my children would survive. Then Clara was born and she survived. The fifth (actually the sixth) one. She survived. Afterwards, another was born and died, so

226

my husband told me, "But what kind of luck do we have? They grow up and then they die." I told him that I didn't know.

When we came to stay here, I got pregnant once again. The same thing happened: those two (the twins) died. My boy was born later – he died when he was young. Another one was born. I didn't want any more children. I said: "I don't want any more kids if they are going to die." I felt sad. One was three months old, the other one was four years old. They were older when they died. I felt sad when they died – I was sorrowful, I cried. I stayed that way. I didn't have any kids, so my husband went with another woman.

I then started to be alone. My (youngest) daughter, Natalia, grew up and got married when she was about twenty-six years old, so both of us (Estella and her husband) stayed. We had a good life. Well, we did fight but not as much as we used to. We were kind of young before. We quarrelled quite a lot. Later on, not that much.

We had a good life because I raised my animals: I had chickens, it was good. We had some corn. He was a cane cutter then. The only thing was that he liked to drink, but I stole the money from him – I stole it when he was drunk and I hid it. When he recuperated from his binge, I told him, "There is no money, you lost it." I had stolen it. We had a great life.

A lot of them (cane farmers) got good houses. They earned their living, but not him. He drank his money as soon as he earned it. The next day he was looking for his friends and was spending the money – he was losing it. When I told him, "Why don't you stop drinking?" he got angry at me. He said that he was the one who was making money, not me. "If I earn it, it's mine. If I spend it, it's mine, not yours."

I said, "And your work? Who is going to do it? You have to work. We have to eat." I threatened him. He threw the money beside the hammock and I grabbed it. He didn't remember it. I stole it and I hid it. I bought things with it – that's how we ate.

He asked me, "Where did you get the money from?" "But I have money," I answered. I had the money that he dropped when he was drunk. I told him that he had lost it.

I lied. "You lost it," I told him. "When you came here, you didn't have any money. You didn't have anything." He believed it. He didn't get angry at me. But I had the money and I hid it to buy food – the things that I needed.

I was happy because he died. He is resting in peace. I said, "Blessed be God." I am alone now. I can eat and drink. Nobody tells me that I am such and such." He was such a complainer. When he got sick, he got worse – he insulted me.

He never used my name: he never called me "Estella." When he wanted to yell, he said "Chicampel!" – it is Maya – "Didn't you hear me, I am talking to you? It looks like you don't have any ears. You look like a devil." He insulted me. I would go outside the house to cry.

When my daughter would come, I would tell her, "Your father did such and such thing to me. It seems that he hates me." I don't know – he hated me. He was sick for a month or two before he died and he was rough during that time. He complained and was angry at me all the time. I weeded and planted the land. I kept more animals.

I say that God didn't help me because my children died. A lot of women here live with their children and all of them are alive. It is nice to look at them when they go out with their children. Why is God bad with me? Why did all my children die? It is an evil thing. I have always believed in God. I never said, "I am going to take another religion." Never. Only Catholic.

Now, in my older days, I have a better life. I stopped working. Life is easier because now I watch my hens and they give me some food to eat.

Clara

Clara was born in 1936. Married and the mother of eleven children, she lives with her husband, her younger children, and one grandchild whom she adopted at birth. A married son, his wife and two young children also live in the household. Clara is the daughter of Estella and the mother of Juanita.

We lived in San Joaquin. My parents were very poor – we lived from selling oranges. There were a lot of orange trees. And then we began to live here in San Miguel, my mother and we three – myself, Irma and Adriano. There were three of us. I saw three die, three boys. Two of them were twins and a little one died in San Joaquin. I half remember. It was a great sadness for my mother.

My father used to like to go off to work far away and he earned very little. He would send money. He went to the chicle: he was a *chiclero*. My father had gone away to work and my mother was living from making bread for sale. We sold bread and then paid for the flour and kept the balance for ourselves. My mother used to wash clothes for the señora, for Don Pedro Arcurio's wife. And that was how she earned a little money for us, me and the little boy, Adriano. That's why I said that life was hard – because my mother used to go to grind corn in a house, the house where my godparents lived. She earned a little from the *masa*. And with that – she used to grind by hand, with her hand-mill, like that. After she ground it, they used to give her a little for us.

And so we grew up, little by little. And when we were about eight years old we would carry water for sale. It cost one cent the cube – the

229

bucket of water – one cent because in those days, when you earned twenty-five cents it was a lot because one pound of salt was two cents, a pound of sugar was three cents, a pound of lard was ten cents. So the twenty-five cents we earned yielded a lot. I used to arrive very late at school because I had to carry a lot of water. I used to begin at six in the morning. Sometimes I began at five in the morning. But the well is a long way from where the señoras lived. We used a little cart or carried by hand. It's hard. It used to hurt here, but sometimes we had to do up to twenty-five trips carrying one bucket each time – twenty-five buckets is a tank of water. And we had to carry them, me and my brother, Adriano. Sometimes we didn't finish until nine o'clock. But since sometimes we didn't know what time it was, we would leave it until we had finished and then we would go to school. Some days it would have been better not to arrive. We would go there, go in, and afterward the teacher would send us away – he would beat us with a stick. But I had to work out of necessity.

Then I would play with the children and learn a little because I learned how to read a little. Not a lot, but, yes, I can get along. I can read a little English. When I was a little girl, when I came from San Joaquin to here, I didn't understand Spanish or English, only Maya – only Maya, when I was a little girl of about six. I was about eight when I began to speak Spanish. Up to today I speak Maya with my mother. When we are alone we speak pure Maya. There are days when my children want to speak Maya, but when I speak Maya with them they laugh at me and I don't like it and I don't teach them. They don't understand it, either – none of them, nor my husband. Only me.

When he (my father) came down from the chicle and arrived in San Joaquin, he saw that we were not there – we were here in San Miguel, so he came to look for us, but my mother didn't go back to San Joaquin. She told him she wouldn't go: if he wanted to, he should come here to San Miguel because she was living very well here. And we liked to fish. We used to get ourselves beautiful fish. So we lived happily because we were eating a lot of fish and my mother was working. She made bread, she washed, she made tortillas, even *relleno*. So he had to stay. He said it was all right because we, the children, told him that we were better here. We ate well, you see.

230

With the fish. And we sold our water and we were well off. We had clothes, we had shoes. It was good. Yes, I liked how we lived. I liked very much to go fishing with my father. He taught me to paddle the canoe, so I went fishing with him quite a lot.

And we also used to go to the *milpa* to look for beans or something like that because we, the Indian people, the poor people, like to harvest beans, *jamote, macal.* He had all of that. My mother would dig and we would fill the bags to sell. A lot of women used to go. Now women don't go out, but in the old days, yes. Before, the women used to help their husbands a lot because they would go to fell bush with a machete to help the man. They went to the *milpa*. My mother used to chop thus, thus, thus. She used to clear the houselot. She used to like to plant. Chili, tomato, okra, papaya – she liked to plant since she was young. We would help with the harvest. My father used to like to plant a lot of watermelon. Plantain. Yes, there was always food.

And then the cane industry began. It was in the forties. He planted cane early. Then when he was going to harvest the cane – the first year he was going to harvest the cane – and it was raining. The truck came to get the cane and it was raining hard. All those who were cutting cane got under the truck until the rain stopped. And when the truck started up, he didn't warn them – it was Juliano Canul. Since he didn't warn them, my father tried to get out hurriedly, but he slipped and the truck rolled over his two feet. One foot was broken, but the other wasn't and he spent a year in the hospital in Belize. One year.

The cane never was a big thing for him because if he hadn't had the accident perhaps he would have been a big cane farmer because he began early. Then it was worse because when he got better he left the hospital and came here and he couldn't work hard any more due to his foot, so the Company gave him work – like a work captain. He didn't earn a lot, but he did earn for food because they were sorry for him because just as he was beginning he damaged his foot.

And thus we grew up until I was big. Then I used to go to work for Don Juliano and his wife. I worked with his wife, sweeping, washing dishes, taking care of the baby. I used to go very early – at six in the morning. I didn't even breakfast with my mother. I left and went to sweep, to wash dishes. Afterwards, I would eat with them. They paid me my little bit. Sometimes they only paid me three dollars or two dollars a week, but they did give me a bit of food. They gave me a bowl of rice and beans – a little beans – and I would bring it to my mother, so she and my sisters and brothers could eat. I would give it to my mother, so she could buy something for my sisters. Thus we all helped each other. I continued growing and working until I was fifteen: I would wash dishes and I could iron. I always worked in the same house until I was sixteen or seventeen, when I got married.

I had hopes of getting something better. I wanted to dress better, to not work hard and to have my own things – my clothes, my shoes. And my dream was to not stay here. It was to go away because I said, "If I suffer, they won't see me." My mother didn't want it. Since I was very little my mother counselled me, "Don't get married, daughter" – that I not marry so I could be with her. I said that I would marry and perhaps I would stop working hard – dress better, go shopping. I thought I would see someone who would work for me: he would work for me and buy my shoes and for that reason I told myself not to marry anyone from San Miguel. I would go far away so that if things went badly nobody would see me. And so I married.

It's perhaps that I didn't think well because my little sister, she went to work, but it was different. She and my mother began to cook meals for workers. At that time, a lot of people began to come to cut cane. In those days, a lot of Mexicans came, labourers. Up to forty or fifty people might come to work. There was no problem. Nobody bothered them. Nothing. Each owner had ten, five men – Don Ramon, Don Juliano, Don Felix, Mr. Chan, Don Roberto. They all had people. That was like twenty-five years ago now, something like that. In that period, there was a lot of freedom and people came. So my mother and Irma fed a lot of people and made money. They lived differently because during the cane season my little sister made a lot of money. They fed workers and when the people went away, she could buy shoes and clothes.

When I went to the dances, I liked to dance with foreigners – people who weren't from San Miguel, to seek a friendship with a boy who was not from here. Yes, I looked for him – I met him at a dance. At a dance I met him and eight days after I met him, he came to see me again and then he used to come back every eight days. When he came he talked with me and the three times he came, he came to speak with my father. He came with his mother and his father. He spoke with my mother and my father and they agreed. They only told him to wait three months – only three months – and we married. I was only sixteen. I got married the 3rd of October and I turned seventeen the 10th of December. I was in his power. I had married.

It was very hard. It was very hard and very sad because I believed that it was going to change, but it wasn't like that because after I married I suffered a lot, because after I got married I was far away from my mother, from my father – far away where there was no family. Only his. And he had a lot of sisters. I think there were four big sisters – older than I. And after I got married I felt sad because I wasn't accustomed to so many girls. I was lonely. I cried a lot. They weren't married.

It was hard because when we began to wash dishes, I was the only one washing. Since there were a lot of them, one would grab the broom, another would take the washtub, the other something else. I was only washing dishes. I couldn't do anything else until they had finished washing – there was only one washtub. Only when they had finished at one or two o'clock could I go and do my washing. It was then that I began to think that I shouldn't have done what I had done. I was sorry.

I regretted it because I was alone without my family. My husband would go off to dances. He didn't take me. No. I stayed. He would go alone. With his friends. When he came home, he was good and drunk and I couldn't do anything. Nor could I get him to change because my mother-in-law would scold me. She would say, "You knew he drank. You knew where he lived, Ramonal. Far from San Miguel. He's from here. He's used to going out. Now, you are not going to go where he goes. You stay." And I couldn't do anything.

What could I do? I didn't know what kind of a man he was. Nevertheless, later I learned, but it was too late. And I got pregnant very soon. In one month I was pregnant. One month. So I had to suffer because I was pregnant. Here I was, big – and he, well, he would go off. I couldn't do anything to make things better and very soon (I had) my children. I would say, "If I leave him, if I go, when my child is born who will I say is his father?"

And I had to bear it in Ramonal. And I used to come here to San Miguel. But I never told my mother. She never asked me, "How are you? Well, how are you doing? Well?" I never said to her, "Mama, he does this, Mama." Never. Never.

I think we spent one and a half years with my mother-in-law – one and a half years in one house. Then I began to ask him to make me a little house – even if it was poor, small. That he make one for me, so I could leave. Because when my baby she was little, I couldn't work fast. The baby was crying and I didn't give her the bottle. Pure breast-feeding. For that reason, I began to ask, "Please make me a little house so I can work at my own pace because if I am in my own house, I can make tortillas when I've finished breast-feeding. If I haven't finished when I stop feeding the baby, I can make my tortillas." And he – well, he paid no attention to me.

I fled from him. I took the boat, picked up my baby, took my boots, my cloths, my clothes and I came here. Here, with my mother. In eight days he came to see me. He didn't come at once. He came in eight days. He came to get the baby. It was Juanita. He said, "I want my daughter."

I said, "No. I won't let you. I told you: make a little house and I will live in the house. You don't want to do it. You don't hear me. You don't listen to me. You paid no attention to me, so I came here to my mother. If you make a house, I will go with you, but my daughter is mine. And you don't love me, nor my daughter."

Then he didn't reply because he came – he and his father. Then his father answered, "All right, daughter. I am going to make the house." And the old man went away and very quickly they made the house. In two weeks it was finished – not big, of thatch. But the house was finished and he came to get me and I went with him. So thus he made my house for me.

When I had my first daughter, I was very sick. I got measles when she was one month old – I nearly died. My little girl was tiny and they told me I should give her away. When I was delirious with the fever, I said to my sister-in-law, "Take my baby because I'm dying." And truly I was dying, but thanks to someone, my mother arrived – because she sent for my mama. She arrived there and went to look for an herbalist. He came and blessed me and gave me medicines – herbs. Then the fever left me and the measles went away. But then after a month – I was hardly better when my baby caught it. Measles. My baby nearly died. And you can imagine how I was – a young girl – when I was getting better and my baby got sick. I cried, cried, cried in my mother-in-law's house. But thanks to God, she didn't die and she got better – my baby, Juanita.

Two years after Juanita, Arsemio arrived. Well, he didn't get sick much. Then came Maximo. It was hard raising my children because every two years I had a child – every two years.

With the last children – I didn't want them. Like Marcos, Secundino. After ten children, I felt sad because I had enough. I had to work a lot. But still, when I saw that I was pregnant I would only say, "My God, I'm pregnant. Help me to have it and to not get sick." But I never wanted to get rid of them. No, nothing like that because I like the Catholic religion and I heard that it was a sin. So I said no. "If You in your power, tell me that I'm pregnant, then with Your power, let me have them fast and don't let me get sick a lot." Then I think He heard me.

God helped me – or else I was lucky when my baby came. That first son, Arsemio – the midwife didn't come and I felt bad. I said to my husband, "Go find me a midwife because I feel bad." And he went. When he arrived at the midwife's house, she wasn't there. She had gone to another place and he came and told me, "She isn't there. I'm going to look for a horse."

And he went to look for a horse in the bush so he could go and look for the midwife. When he returned from the bush, the baby had already arrived. Alone, alone, alone. When I felt that she was coming, I got into bed – alone, alone, alone. I took Juanita outside. I closed the door and Juanita cried and cried, "Mama, Mama." I was dying. And I went to my bed and – boom – my baby was born.

When he returned, he was shocked to see the baby crying among the blood. He spoke to my mother-in-law. He yelled, "Mama, Mama! Come and see Clara. She has already had the baby." "What?" said my mother-in-law. "She already had the baby."" And she was surprised. I was lucky. And my mother-in-law came and cut – she cut her umbilical cord. He didn't go to look for the midwife, since I already had the child – and everything came out, everything. What luck.

We were thirteen years there in Ramonal. And then he got sick. He was very sick, so we came here to San Miguel. He agreed because one had to make a living. He had five little ones. It had begun well. He had *milpa*; I had my hens, my pigs, turkeys. We were working well. I sold meat, chicken, eggs and we could live well. But that was when he got sick. Aha. If he had not got sick perhaps we would be there up to today.

Then I got cane. They were going to give a little cane to the people. So they advised me – well, friends told me – "Apply. Perhaps you will have a little luck and get some." Then we applied. My husband couldn't because he was Mexican. He wasn't accepted. So I applied and God helped me and got me a bit. That cane that I got is God's gift to me because I knew how to take advantage of it. The first year the cane that I sold – I sold six hundred tons of cane. When I got money, I bought my house, the next year I bought my truck, the next the pick-up, the next the boat. I never had money in hand because if I don't spend it, I will never buy anything – it will just disappear.

He began to be a driver. When he got the pick-up he left everything – he didn't take care of the *milpa*, he didn't take care of the cane, he left everything. He began to drive, carrying passengers. There were days when we bought the *masa*. There were days when we bought corn. We made *nixtamal*. We could no longer eat only tortillas. We had to buy rice, flour.

Then he (the eldest son) got married and he asked me if I wasn't going to give him something. So I thought that he is a man, so I gave him a little of my license. I gave him a hundred tons of my license – to the oldest. Then the next year – I don't remember what happened – I think it was the flood – the cane didn't grow. I only sold

236

two hundred tons of cane. It (the price) was going down. Then that same year I gave another hundred tons to my other sons – Maximo, Juan. I gave them my quota. Today I have only two hundred. I gave to Arsemio, to Juan and the Company took two hundred away from me when I didn't fill – when you don't fill your quota they take it away. The year that I didn't fill it, they took a little away – because each time a son marries, he leaves, he doesn't help me any more.

My life changed when my sons grew up. When they earned money, they gave me money. One of them would come, "Mami." Another would come, "Mami." I began to have my own money through my sons and thus we bought the things we have now.

But right now, over the past years, they have got married and now they have their own wife. Now they take their money. It's sad to say so, but it's the truth: I have five married boys and of those five boys, no one helps me. Not one dime. And nonetheless my daughter, when she gets a few cents – even if only twenty, thirty (dollars) is all she gets – (she gives me) five dollars. "Mamita, buy your sugar, buy." You see the difference? A girl is different to a boy.

My first son, my Arsemio, when he began to work at Public Works, each month when he came he would give me five dollars. "Take it, Mama." Five dollars was a lot then. You could buy your sugar, your lard, or something. I thanked him. I felt happy, happy to get five dollars. But now, for the past year, not even half a cent. Nothing. Nothing, not even a piece of candy. This other one also. Only once did he give me five dollars. Again nothing. One time, the señor (her husband) had a puncture and I went to borrow the money. Do you know what he said to me. "Ask my wife for it. If she gives it to you, fine," he said. You can imagine how I felt. They don't give me a dime. Not a dime, even though I need it – if I want to borrow it, I have to ask their wife for it.

There was one day when I cried because one child offended me. I borrowed twenty dollars and didn't return it, so when he was drunk he said, "You borrowed money from me and didn't return it." And I said, "Yes, son, it's true, but I didn't eat it. It was your little brother's illness and you can tell anyone that your mother borrowed your money. Due to your little brother's illness, I can't return it and you are going to feel proud because you helped the child and he didn't die. You can tell people." And that day I cried and I said, "Blessed is the mother who has a lot of daughters. It's no lie. It's true because these boys married, or not married, they have stopped giving to me.

But that's because they don't have any steady work. Where are they going to get money if they can barely get for their wives? But still, I believe that if they had work, like a teacher or someone who is employed by the government, then they would be able to give me a gift of so much – five dollars weekly. I don't ask for a lot because life is poor. But then, if they don't have anywhere to earn it, where are they going to get it?

I was thinking something very sad, but still I see that it's a reality. I really saw. Because it's past, it's like the story of my children: how I suffered at the beginning of my life – a lot of poverty, a lot of work. It's like planting a tree. You plant something. It has to grow and it will bear fruit. You will go to harvest it. The only difference is that the tree will give fruit until it dies. But the child, no – until he decides to get his companion. Once he's married, it's finished. There's no harvest.

At present I have others, but they are small. I'm beginning again to raise them so they will grow up again. At present, I have one who will be fourteen this year, the other thirteen, the other eleven. I still have work to do because we women – sure we have a lot of work. But you don't see what we do because we – what we do today, we do tomorrow, we do it the day after tomorrow. Every week the same thing: in the morning wash dishes, sweep, wash clothes, make tortillas. Today, tomorrow and the day after – every day the same thing. And you don't see because we eat the food and boom – the dish gets dirty and there it is.

On the other hand, they, no. They cut down a bit and it stays cut. They cut another and another bigger piece. You see? They only work a little and you can see the result. We do a lot of work and you don't see it, so there is a difference because on Sunday they can rest. We, no – there's never rest for the woman. Never, never. There's no rest from food. Food is every day – and washing. And they, yes, they can rest. A holiday, there's no work – they swing in the hammock or play ball. But we women, no. If we don't wash every day, the washing piles up.

My mother, despite being so old, has not stopped working. When I knew her, she worked hard to support us and up to this day she hasn't stopped working. Although I say to her, "Mami, don't sweep," she wants to sweep. She wants to work. She likes it because she is so used to it. When she's sitting down, she feels sad. She wants to work because I believe that it gives her energy or strength or she is accustomed to it. And when she doesn't do it, she feels sick. Aha. I notice that.

The only thing I want is to see my young daughter well off, my daughter who is studying (in high school). I don't know – I love her, maybe because I don't have many daughters. It hurt me because I saw how she wanted to study since she was very young. Since she was very little I saw that she wanted to help me in some way and she – I see her effort, the sacrifice she is making to get ahead. I hope not that she will support me, but perhaps even though married, she will have the means to give me something because I have struggled so she can study. Perhaps – because one doesn't know if one will die suddenly or will die of old age or perhaps I will be very sick – she can give me a gift of her company in that case. And (if) she has work, perhaps in time she can help me: give me food, even if ever so little, or even bury me. If she wants. But if not, then so be it. But then I am happy that I helped her to achieve what she so much desired. And I pray to God that she gets that work or that study that she wants so much – what she wanted since she was little.

The happiest time of my life is right now because I can go out with my young daughter. When my children were small, I never went out. Never, never, never. I didn't go to dances, I didn't go out to parties, I never went out. And now that my youngest son is already eleven and she is young and wants to go to dances, she doesn't say, "Mama, send me," or "I want to go." No, she comes and hugs me and says, "Mami, take me." She likes to go out with me. I go with her. I feel happy because I see that she's happy and going out. For that reason I am telling you that I feel happiest now because I have my daughter to go out with. I go to church. When there's a Mass, I don't fail to go. A rosary. We go together, so I feel very happy because I go with her.

Up to now – I don't know if we are perfect – but up to now, I think my life is good. My marriage – because we have been married for thirty-five years and we haven't separated once. I'm fifty-two and he's fifty-four and we are happy. Because I listen when the priest comes, he says that we have to look after them and they after us. True? Thus life should be.

And if a woman sees that her husband is sad, or put out, never remain silent because if you don't pay attention to him, he notices. But if he sees that you take good care of him, it's going to be hard for him to make you suffer. It's going to be hard to leave you because he has a good memory of you. He's going to say, "That woman takes care of me. I'm important to her. When I'm sick she loves me. So she looks after me." You see?

Never mistreat your husband. On the contrary, love him, take care of him. Love him with the love of a wife: when he arrives serve him his food at once good and hot. Don't give him cold food. Give him his hot food and serve him well, give him his bath, give him everything he needs. Thus, if you suspect that he is going with another woman, he'll see that she's not your equal.

He's going to say, "I left this woman who took good care of me. Why did I come to this one who doesn't?" You see? But if one looks after him badly he will say, "Thank God that I left that woman." Thus he will know what the love of a woman is. But if you take care of him well, it will be hard for him to leave you – if he has a memory of you that you were a good wife.

When I returned to San Miguel after two years her youngest daughter had graduated from Sixth Form, had married and was expecting her first child.

Juanita

Juanita, the daughter of Clara and the grand-daughter of Estella, was born in 1954. She is the mother of six children and lives with her partner and her five younger children.

My mother tells us that our grandfather liked us a lot. And they always lived together: my mother, my father and my grandparents – they were the grandparents on my father's side. They were Mexican. Only my mother's mother is Belizean.

My father was a *milpero*; he had corn. My mother raised animals; she had a little of everything. And as we were growing up little by little, my mother would tell us that starting life is hard because sometimes we had nothing to eat. And so my mother would get *masa* and she would cook it – it would become like *atole* and then we would make tortillas from the strained dough and that took the place of beans for us. She would give us a little piece of tortilla with something to drink and that was all. Those were the hardest days of my life. Thus we grew up little by little.

She would cook us *chaia* leaves: she would cook it with eggs. She would fry it and we would eat it. Sometimes she would cook us the flower of the squash – she would make it into a soup. Then she would throw the *masa* and fat and salt into the soup. That was our food.

He took good care of us because when my mother was ready to have another child, he looked after us. When my mother got sick he would cook for us: he made the tortillas and fed us. He looked after us: he would bathe us, would put us to sleep – everything that my

241

mother used to do for us. He always loved us and still loves us as if we were still children.

When we arrived here (Belize) I was twelve. We didn't come just for the sake of it – we came here because my father was sick. He got sick when I was eight years old and so he couldn't work the way he did when we were younger. It was his liver – it got inflamed because he drank. It got inflamed and he couldn't work well. So my mother was obliged to come here. My grandparents would help us. I was already big. We would carry water and they would pay us. My mother would take the money we earned in order to get things to eat.

And then my father began to work a little. He stopped drinking: his doctor forbade it. And so he could work a little. Then the cane began. My grandparents used to cut cane. He would go with my grandfather, my mother's father.

When we came here they put me in school. I went to school at the age of twelve. When I went to school they put me in Infant I – with the babies. They used to laugh at me. Here I was, big and they were little. That made me ashamed because I was big and they were small. But no matter. My younger brothers and sisters were little.

After we would get out of school, we would always go to get water to sell and the others found things to do, but since I was the oldest, I had to work more. (I was in school) until I was fourteen. Yes, two years. No more. And because of that I didn't learn much English. Sometimes I would stay home to help because she had a lot to do. Sometimes she had to wash clothes for other people and I couldn't do it. I could sweep, wash dishes, all that. I made tortillas and all. I would do that so that she could do other things. Since they were all brothers and I was the oldest, I had to work more.

When we came here, my father saw that there was more work. One could earn more money here in Belize because over there for one *mecate* of *milpa* they would pay five pesos – one cent per *mecate* to fell bush and plant there– whereas here, no. You cut cane and earned more than there. We came to live here and my grandparents always helped us and my mother worked for another lady. She always gave us clothes and she (my mother) mended them. And thus we grew up little by little.

242

When I married I was eighteen years old. I got married at eighteen. I went to a dance. My parents didn't like the boy because he was older than I – much older. I was eighteen and he was thirty-three and because of that my parents didn't like him. And because of that my mother always advised me not to get married and she would give me a "cleaning" – she would lash me so that I would forget the man. Sometimes when she would see us talking, she wouldn't say anything, but when the man left she would grab me and hit me with whatever she had. Sometimes she would hit me in the head – my mother, she would strike me because she saw me talking to the man.

I was in love with the idea of getting married, so I married at eighteen. And he was thirty-three. And later when we got married – the day that we got married – there was a fight and he fought. He wanted to hit my uncle because there was a tape-recorder that was playing and so my uncle said, "Let's dance for the last time because you just got married." He came to get me and I went out. And my husband, Julio, didn't like it. And then he grabbed me, he pulled me and took me to his house – with my clothes and everything. He took me there. Afterwards, on another day I went to see my mother. I didn't go to any more parties. He would get angry.

That was when I realized that he didn't love me. His mother would tell him that I was deceiving him, that I didn't tell him the truth, that I used to go to visit my mother without telling him. He said that I had to ask for permission to go see my mother. And whenever I would do something for him, he would hit me. And we lived like that on and on. We lived together in his mother's house and his mother used to tell him things about me. I stayed with him nine months.

The first time he hit me, I was pregnant. I was two months pregnant. But I still stayed. We never separated, but I went and I told my mother. She said, "Daughter, it's because of that, that we were advising you, but you didn't know how to listen."

There was a policeman who got along well with us and his wife would tell me, "Bear it for a while and see if he changes," and so I always returned to him. Then we borrowed another house and so we went to live in another house. For a little while, everything was going well. When he went out he would take me and all. I was already seven months pregnant – and that was when he hit me. That was when he pushed me and I fell next to a bed. I was already big with child and I couldn't get up. And he left me like that and went out.

He wasn't drunk at all, nothing like that. But his mother had told him that the child that I was going to have was not his and because of that he didn't want me, nor did he want the baby because (he thought) it wasn't his. And thus I went on growing and he would hit me all the time – all the time he hit me and the last time, when we separated, I was only one month from delivery.

When we separated he took all his things: he took his bed, table, the dishes that he had bought, even diapers for the baby, my wedding shoes, my wedding rings – he took all that from me. He took them. Animals – he took everything. He went away from where I was staying and went to his mother's. And afterwards, I stayed alone. I was left alone. But my aunt, my mother's sister, lived near me and she heard all the noise. So she went to tell my mother. It was ten o'clock at night when she told my mother that I was alone.

She and my mother came. I am on the floor. I have some rags and I am lying down. And so when my mother comes, she says, "Let's go home."

"No," I say, "because if I go, he is going to say that I left him."

Says my mother, "But how are you going to stay here in this state, without a bed, without anything?"

He took everything. And so that was when I left and went with my mother. The next day he returned but only to look for a pig that had stayed in the yard. He hadn't been able to take it and he returned to look for it and he took it.

He never spoke to me. On the contrary, the same month that we separated, my child arrived – the big boy. That same month I had him there at my parents'. My father sent word to him that the baby had been born. And he said that that son must be my father's child, because it wasn't his but rather my father's. He said that that little boy was my father's. He insulted my father and even threatened that he was going to hit my father, so my father told him to leave. The thing is that he said that it was not his because we had left each other.

244

He (her son) knows that I am his mother, but he never asks who his father is. But my parents told him who he is and he says that it is not true because he never loved him. "He is not my father, Papi," he tells my father. "If he had loved me, he would not have left my mother," he says. "Father" and "mother", he says to them. He calls me "Juanita" though he knows that I am his mother. They treated me well because when I had the child, my parents had seen everything and so my father bought the diapers and he replaced everything that he had taken. That was when they loved me – they treated me well. I was well off with them.

I stayed three years. And during that time we would go to dances. My brothers were young. None of them were married. They would take me to the dances so that I could forget the father of the baby. I was happy. My mother was working then. We would give meals to cane workers. I had to work with her to earn money and so to raise my kid.

He was three when I met this one (her present husband). He is Julio's cousin because his father is Julio's uncle. I was twenty-three when I met his cousin. I think that I was in love because we are still together. Many people tell me that if I waited a little to get married, I would find my partner. My mother and my father never liked him either. They didn't like him because he was Adventist. They would tell me that his mother was going to say that I am older than he – by one year. It isn't much, but since I was married and he not, for that reason my mother told me that I should tell him no because he is younger than I and I am married and have a child.

And so one day there was a dance here in San Miguel and he went to my house. And so we were chatting when his mother came around and she pulled him out – she pulled him and talked to him and said, "Antonio, come here. What have you got to do with that old woman? That woman is married. She should be ashamed to have a friendship with you because she even has a child."

He didn't respond. He didn't say anything. Well, I wasn't going to go to the dance. I wasn't going to go but because I heard his mother tell me a whole bunch of stuff, I said to my mother, "Mami, let's go to the dance." My mother got changed, I got changed and we left. So,

I danced all night and I told my mom, "I don't ever want to see Antonio again. Since his mother told me all those things, I don't want to join with him." And so he would always pass like that in front of my house and I wouldn't pay any attention to him.

And one day he returned to talk to me and so I said, "Why do you come to talk to me, if your mother doesn't want me? Your mother doesn't want me. Well, stay with your mother and leave me in peace."

And so he said. "No, but I love you. It is not my mother who is going to be with you. It is me." And I said, "No I don't want to be with you." And so another year passed. But his mother never wanted me. Even now she talks with me out of pure necessity.

This time we got married on the other side (Mexico). At that time my grandmother was alive – my father's mother at Ramonal, so we went there with her. We lived there a while. He worked and so there we were – we were there about a year. And so one day he met his mother on the road in Ramonal. She was looking for him and so when he returned from the fields he said, "You know who I saw? My mother." "And what did she want?" "She says that we should return to San Miguel, that from now on she is not going to get involved in my life and everything is going to change." Well, that is when we returned here. We returned here to San Miguel.

Since he was a child he was an Adventist; he was raised in that way because his mama is an Adventist. Antonio's father isn't. And afterwards when we got together, I had to join his religion. I left mine and got his, though it was harder for me because everything is prohibited. You don't go to dances, you don't drink beer, you don't eat pig meat and other things – fish without scales and the wech, as they call it, and the pechuinte in the bush. They only eat chicken and deer and beef and fish with scales. Well, because I was used to going to Mass, I found it a bit difficult because at Mass you put a table like that in front and there you put the statue, the crucifix and the other statues. But they don't – there is nothing of that kind. There is only the pulpit and the preacher preaches the word of God. That's all. But I found it different, as I was accustomed to the other thing.

I didn't choose. He told me, "You have to go to my church. I am an Adventist and you must follow my church and you're not going to the Catholic church because I don't want you to."

I didn't want arguments or fights because I was in love with him, so that is why I joined his church. Up to this day, I go. Now I am happy because I'm used to it because I see that he doesn't do a lot of things: he doesn't drink, he doesn't smoke, he doesn't go to the dances – nothing of that sort. For my part, it's better that way, because he doesn't run around the streets getting into trouble.

When they heard that I was going to get baptized into their (the Adventist) religion – because one has to get baptized in his religion; in the Catholic religion, they only baptize by throwing water on the head, but in the Adventist, no, they throw you in the water, in the river – so when I told them that I was going to get baptized in the Adventist Church, all my brothers were upset – more than my father.

My mother said, "If you think it is fine, it is up to you because you're grown already and you can do as you want." Well, my brothers said "I hope that when you're getting baptized you will swallow a sardine so that you will see that what you're doing is not good."

Well, I didn't pay any attention. I went ahead and got baptized and everything went well and now they have accepted it. At first, they made fun of me. Even my mother and father said things when I brought them bread or something. They said they weren't going to eat it because it contained vegetable oil. But later they accepted it because at my uncle's funeral – before he died – he said, "Don't make fun of Juanita because it isn't bad to love God." So he said that it isn't a sin to love God. It is only that we love Him in different ways. Now when I take them some food, they do eat it.

When we returned to San Miguel, first we went to my mother's. I spent about a week there. Afterwards, we went to his mother's house and we spent one year there with her. That was a very problematic year for me because his mother still didn't like me. From the start she didn't like me – she didn't want me. And when we were there in her house his mother would ignore me and when I would take up some task, they would have already finished. Since there were a lot of them, they would finish the work quickly. And they wouldn't let me make tortillas. And so it went day by day until we bought this lot.

At first, he didn't want to move to the house. I was getting tired of what they were doing to me. Also I was pregnant with the first (her second) child, Liborio. So I moved my things: my clothes, my dishes, everything. Only I couldn't move the bed. I said to him, "Antonio, are you going to move to the house? Tell me because I want to move. I am tired of this place!" He had to think because he didn't want to leave his mother because he always did what his mother told him. Finally, we moved to the house. But it has always been bad with them: they have never liked me. Sometimes she gets something and, instead of giving it to my kids, she gives it to the other grandchildren. She says that mine aren't her grandchildren, even after Liborio had been born.

Liborio had just been born. He was little, like two months old, when he (Antonio) took up with this woman. She was a Salvadoran. She was living in Orange Walk. They met in the bar. So he got her and began going with the woman. He says that he is Adventist, but he did things that he shouldn't because his religion prohibits it. But he did it. He took up with her. There were times when he would come with her rings, her necklaces. When I would talk to him he would turn away. He didn't want me to talk to him − like he didn't pay any attention to me. His mother liked the woman.

So in the end I left him. I separated from him. I went to my mother's. And so when he came to see me, to ask that I return with him again, I said, "Yes, I will return with you, but you have to leave that woman." Her name was Clarissa.

I told him, "You have to leave Clarissa, if you want me to return with you."

He said, "Yes, I will leave her." But the woman continued to come here to San Miguel. When the woman came to his house, his mother would treat her well − she would even hug her and the woman would bring her presents. But in the end he returned. Afterwards, he told me, "I left her. I love my son and all." And so afterwards, like after three or four months, I went back to him and so he said that he would change. He stopped going around with other women. After that I got pregnant again with Sara.

His mother still doesn't like me, but she treats me a bit better than before. She brings a little – grudgingly – for the children. She treats me a little better.

He is a cane worker. He only has sixty-seven (cane license). He doesn't have a block. He has it (the cane) on his father's land. He always works together with his father. So since he didn't have a block, his father gave him a little bit and he's working there. Antonio always cuts and drives and his father also cuts and so that is when he takes the truck and goes to the factory. He takes his (father's) truck to the factory.

The way I see it, his father treats him very badly. He (Antonio) takes care of his plants, his animals, of everything and they don't pay him anything. And also when the truck fails, Antonio gets it fixed – his father has never paid him anything for fixing the truck. Nothing, nothing, not even his bus fare. On the contrary, when something is bothering him he tells Antonio stuff, but instead of paying him he scolds him. Only now, during the cane season, he pays him when he drives, but otherwise nothing.

Also his father has bees. Antonio takes the honey out; they go to sell it. Sometimes they get two tambos and some more cubes; sometimes even three tambos. They get eight hundred dollars and Antonio goes and gives all the money to his father. His father only gives him a hundred dollars and keeps the balance – he never takes any more. All the time like that. And many people have told me that it shouldn't be that way: Antonio is the one that does the work; he does everything. Antonio is for the bees, Antonio is for the cane, Antonio is for the truck, for cutting bush. He should get half, and if not half, at least more than he gets now.

In low times, we sometimes only get five dollars a week and I have to figure out what we are going to do with those five dollars. It is nothing. And sometimes I tell him, "Antonio, it shouldn't be like this; look for a place to work. Your father doesn't pay you but we need money." His greatest problem is that he doesn't have any work during the dead season. There is no money and so there is nowhere where one can work.

Right now, there's always some way to earn a few cents, even if little. But that is not a big problem: the problems are greater in the dead season of how to get things for the kids because sometimes he only gives me ten dollars, five dollars and it has to last the week. And sometimes on Sunday he says to me, "Take ten dollars." And with those ten dollars I have to buy two pounds of chicken. We only buy chicken on Sunday and with those ten dollars that he just gave, I go to buy it. I only get six dollars change and with those six dollars I have to last the week. And if it doesn't last the week and I ask him for more he asks what I've done with the money. I have to tell him that – what I did, what I bought and all. I have to give him an accounting for everything that I did. That's the way he is. And if I don't, sometimes he gives me nothing.

Sometimes when I go to Chetumal to buy provisions, he gives me thirty, forty dollars. "Take this", he says, "You have to buy everything we need." Beans, oil, almost all the provisions. If I have to buy anything else, he scolds me.

He says that he is the one who earns the money so everything is his because it was he who earned it. I don't provide money. If I were working and earned a good salary, then it would be mine. But he says that since the money is his, everything belongs to him. He says, "It's your duty. You must take care of the children. And besides, everything is mine because I'm the one who gives the orders. That's the way it is."

The television that I paid off little by little – one day when we were arguing, he said, "If you say that that thing is yours, I'm going to take it away and give it to somebody because I don't want you to be telling people that you are buying things. I am the one who buys things and everything is mine. And the kids – you are the one who has to take care of them."

I tell him, "We two, we're both struggling. You are working. I wash your clothes, I take care of the kids and I also have some rights." Yes, I tell him.

And he says, "No, that has nothing to do with it. All these things are mine and you have nothing."

So I tell him again, "If I help you, if I don't wash your clothes, who is going to do it? So I don't have anything – well, you pay me. I take care of your children, I wash your clothes, prepare your food and you say that I don't have anything. Pay me for doing that. Pay me your food." And he begins to argue.

According to him, I don't do any work. He says that he doesn't see what I do because I do the same thing today as tomorrow and every day. He says that I don't do anything. He says that he works more than I because he gets tired, he returns tired. So according to him, he does more than I do.

I say "You work more than I do because you see the money coming. You work and they pay you. I work and nobody pays me. That is why you say that I don't do anything – because I don't make money, because one does the same thing tomorrow as today. Every day."

Like before – when I washed for my mother – she would pay me sometimes five dollars a week and with that money I would buy something for my little ones. Sometimes I would buy a piece of chicken – I am not the only one who eats it. Even he eats it and when I work and buy a piece of meat, even he is happy.

But if I get something and give it to somebody, he's angry. Yesterday night we were fighting. I went and bought a piece of chicken from his mother and cooked it. I sent Sara with three little pieces to my mother. And he asks why do I take them to my mother. "I am just giving them as a present," I say. "She is my mother." And he begins to complain. But if I take it to his mother he is happy because it is for his mother. I can never give anything to my mother. If I give her something, it is when he isn't here – in secret, so there is no scolding.

He says that he is the man and that he is the one who gives the orders and one must do what he says. Also, he decides if the kids can do things or not – for example, if there is something that Liborio wants to do and he doesn't like it. He says that they have to cooperate with him because he is the one who gives orders. This is the way he is with the kids and with me too. That's what causes the arguments. He tells me that I am supposed to obey him and not do what I want because he gives the orders.

Not once has he hit me, but he has hit the kids when they don't do what he says and he hits them because he says that he is the one in charge and they should do what he says. Sometimes I don't like him hitting the children because it isn't always the case that they are doing bad things. That's what causes the fights between us.

I do it for my kids. Because I, for my part, if there were an opportunity to leave, if it weren't for the kids, I would leave.

Better I had stayed single. To my mind that is better because like you go out when you want and you get work. And the money is your money and you do what you want. If one were left single, one wouldn't look for another man, one wouldn't struggle. One would look for work and raise the kids – because a child is the happiness of the home.

No matter if you are unhappy, they always say "Why are you sad, Mama? Lets play this, lets play that." So one always stays a little happy. No matter what difficulties there may be between man and wife, the child is there and one is content. I wouldn't get married. If I could, I would stay single with my mother – like that I could go out.

I see my little sister. She goes around to the dances and if I were her, I wouldn't get married. I talk with my little sister. She says that she is not going to have many – only two. "It is very hard," she says. "Better only two and like that I can educate them well. If they go to high school, then they go without problems, but when there are a whole bunch, one can't find the money." She wants to be a teacher so that she can teach what she learned.

She is luckier than I because we had a hard childhood, even when she was growing up. My parents are living now just as they have always been. When I was a child, I never learned because I never got a book for school. They never bought us books. Now, yes – they have books and all, so they learn more. She is the last daughter and she has the opportunity. Since I was the first, I don't have it.

One doesn't know how it is going to be. One only knows about ourselves and how we, their parents, are bringing them up and if we are setting a good example for them – how we dress them, provide shoes for them. I believe that it is going to be better because she (my daughter) isn't going to suffer in the way that we did when there was hardly enough to eat. Now, at least, though poor, we always find food. Her life is going to be different than mine. And these days they don't have to carry water to sell. We only have to find food for them to eat.

I don't see that it has changed because what she (my mother) experienced as to the way women are treated – no, I haven't seen any changes. It's the same as it was before.

TWO GENERATIONS OF
AN URBAN GARIFUNA FAMILY

Miss Bird

Miss Bird is a Garifuna and was born in Punta Gorda and moved to Orange Walk in the early sixties. Her children are grown. She and her partner of eight years have a farm on the outskirts of town, where they grow sugar cane and a variety of food crops.

I will tell you about my life.

I grew up in Punta Gorda. When I was growing we lived with my grandmother first and then with my mom. We all did that. We had big family – we lived mostly in the bush. We grew our own foods: potatoes, cocoa, corn, yams and more. We used the cow milk sometimes and we make the tortillas and johnny cakes and eat the cocoa. We didn't drink coffee or milo, just different kinds of herb tea we'd make, like fever grass or lime tea. We never have the trouble with fever – I never have fever.

I liked school, but things were hard and I had to help work on the farm, so they took me out. Nowadays you are free to send everybody to high school – then, no. I wanted to go, I couldn't.

When I was twenty-one, I had my first baby. That one died and I nearly died. The afterbirth gave me a lot of trouble – the midwife, she had to tie stones on the afterbirth to get it out. And I had to blow, blow hard into a bottle and eat the eggs. The baby died, but I lived.

So then, with Lotty and all of my babies after that, I no take chance. I go to hospital.

Those things worked – the old-time ways. Nowadays they don't know what to do – use too many injections.

I moved up to Orange Walk in the early sixties. I moved up here to work. They started to build the factory and they paid good. And the ladies, we wash and we cook for the men at the factory. With that money, I sent my children to school so they can be educated and they can grow different than me and their children can grow different. And then my daughter Lotty went to college.

It was hard to move from Punta Gorda, away from my family. There was work, so it was nice and good. Many people I know came up. We get together, we do Masses, we visit. A lot of people came up then for the cane and a lot of people from Mexico and Guatemala came also. Everybody started to work. We made it good.

And then I got the lot in the San Francisco area and built a house to do boarding. We had three, four, five people boarding then. That was hard, hard work. Saturday, we make bread, fry fish. Sunday – cook, go to church, then serve dinner. Monday morning – get up, serve beans from Sunday, put them on rice and plantains, then get ready for twelve o'clock lunch. Tuesdays, I wash, clean house, cook food. Friday evening, I rest, go visiting. Every day I cook.

By the time I had boarders, my partner was gone. He drank a lot and made nice to other girls. I left him. He thief my money for food and spend it on drinks. He stopped giving me money for food, for the kids. He went. When he left, I kept working, had boarders.

Now I have been with Lester for eight years. I like to work, but you know a women can't live by herself here: you need a partner to protect you from other people. If you stay by yourself, somebody will come after you.

After I was fifty, I had the change of life. The change of life is real hard. I know people have died in it. I get real, real sick – that lasted for four years. I started to go to all kinds of doctor. We used to have good money – yes, good money – but it went to the doctors. I went to many, many doctors. I went to Chetumal, Guatemala. All kind of test. I pay a big price. They said it is something with my glands. They give me treatment, but I get worse. I couldn't take it any more. My whole body got stiff, very stiff from it – nervous, all kinds of pain, can't feel no happiness. I'd go to the bush and I use the herbs, the Liquid of Life: I boil it and drink it. I planted the plants in my garden. I'd take them and eat them or put them into my clothing.

They give me more test. Same thing. I get paralysed. I pray to God that He will help me because I never know nothin' about it. I don't know nothin'. I even don't think that could happen to a person. My body couldn't take it.

The Garinagu, we have old, old, old, old tradition: the Dugu. We knock the drum and when you don't knock the drum for six or seven years you get sick or somebody dies in the family. The family has to knock the drums – they do that to save somebody in the family that is sick. Me – myself, I didn't believe in it until I got sick, sick and I had to have one. If you don't do it to save your life, you die.

This is what happens. [You get sick and you don't get well. Nothing works. You get numb, dizzy – everything get black-out. Then you see the spirit: a grandmother or an ancestor. Then you start to talk. You don't know what you are saying. The others with you, they have to listen. The spirits, they tell you to make the Dugu in Dangriga or Punta Gorda.

The spirits also tell you what to do there, like that you must buy three roosters, three big roosters. They say that you carry the chickens there and then the people go for the fishes and the coconut and the ground food. Then you set the roosters, the rum and everything and the food – you set it out and the ancestors receive them. They have the songs for three day, the old-time songs. They'll have that for three day and for three night.

They knock the drum for three days and the spirit comes. The people dance. People drop down and the spirit is in them. The spirits tell them what to do, what they want. There is a special doctor there, the Buyei. She knocks the drum and wets your head and your body and says a prayer over you. You stay there in the temple. People sing and dance and knock the drum, like in the old-time days. The family, they stay there for nine days].

I always say that if God didn't give me that spirit to go there, I wouldn't live.

257

We cannot live without our culture. Some of the younger generation, they are leaving the culture. They want to abolish it, but they can't. They must not. They have to believe in it or they get sick. My children – they never knew nothing about it, but I carried them down to Dangriga to the Dugu to make sure they know about it. I don't want them to die and not know. I teach them what to do when I get sick and the (medical) doctor can't cure me. They know what to do.

We have to show the children what to do. There are several people who don't believed and have suffered because of it. They get punished, they get sick. There was a man in Belize from Seine Bight and there was a Dugu for his family and he didn't go. He said he didn't believe and he didn't go and he died. A pain struck him in his stomach and he died.

We teach them the language. We talk mostly Garifuna around here (at the farm). My kids, they don't talk the Garifuna too good. Their father was Creole. He did not understand my language. My kids, they speak mostly Creole.

The younger people, they don't take care of the body. They have to learn how to use the bush or they won't live long. I am sick now, but I use the bush: I would die without it. I was sickly sometimes in my life, but I am alive and I have grown up kids that are healthy.

My mom, she died about seven years ago. That is a bad feeling to see your mother die. She was in California for a while, then she came back here because she was sick, with her heart. She took pills. She didn't take no bush medicine and she died. She should have taken both. I believe in the bush and in the doctor.

My mom used to tell me that she would die and we needed to take care of ourselves and each other. And my mom said that after she died she would return back and she did. I had a dream that my cousin was sick. My mom told me in the dream that my cousin was sick and that I had to go to him. I told her that I couldn't go because I didn't have any money. She showed me fifteen cents and said that I must take the money and go for him. I tell my old man, I said, "How can I go on fifteen cents?" He said, "You take the fifteen cents and you go bet on number fifteen in the lottery." He said it was true and I did it and I won. I went to see my cousin. He was very sick and I helped him.

My mom came back to me in another dream: I opened a pack of meat in the dream and gave it to her; she wanted it. So I woke up, opened the pack and gave her a piece of meat. Yes, they return back. She told me she would and she has come three times.

My life is very beautiful now. Things got good and we bought this land here and cut it. We built this house. We buy the board and we build it and now we make the farm. We have cabbage and pumpkins and melons, carrots, plantain, okra and many things. We have three kinds of cane: sweet, bamboo, sooly. We sell the cane. We plant rice, sell it. We have chickens. We have eggs and meat when we want it. People come to buy the yams. When you make the farm, you can live good at the farm. I buy fish and meat. When you live in Orange Walk, you spend a lot, lot of money for food, wood. Here, you don't.

We do things early, so we are done by one o'clock in the afternoon. After one, we rest, sleep, visit. We tend to the farm in the morning. We get up at five. This morning I wake up, cook, bathe, eat – at one, done. Rest.

I pray a lot. I pray to God and the saints. The Jehovah's say that these things are wrong, that you shouldn't pray to saints. I don't believe them. They go to houses, they talk. I tell them that I can't leave my Catholic life. I pray to St. Martin – they had a big day for him in Guatemala. I talk to him and tell him what to do with me and my children. When we go into the bush I pray to him to protect us from snakes.

We go to church, the Catholic one. The Seventh Day Adventists, the Baptists, they are taking over. We need to have a Catholic church back here in this part of town for people to go to, or the Catholics, they'll go to other churches. I love my church, everything about it. When we make Mass for the dead, sometimes Father Cal comes – he is Garifuna. We set the foods out and he blesses it. Then we chew it. Fr. Cal, he is from PG. We are glad to have him here.

Orange Walk has changed a lot. They don't live like in the olden days now. They live a modern life. They used to live in the thatch house and make the hammock, now they don't. They build more buildings. People used to go out and sell things: pumpkins, potatoes. People from the village did. Now they don't – sell only at the market and mostly they grow cane and weed. And people don't do honey like they used to and they don't make the hammock any more.

They are modern now – sit on the sofas and watch TV and do the tapes and listen to the stereo. They don't want to do the old-time life. We make our own hammock. They don't use bicycles – use cars. And they have to trust the banks. Sometimes two thousand dollars, four thousand dollars they lose. We never did that. We had the credit union. Safe. Nowadays the banks will only let you save hundreds, thousands of dollars. Used to be that if you had a dollar you could save it in the credit union. Save a dollar every week and get money that way.

The cane got cheap, cheap and then the farmers started to grow weed. Then they had a lot of money and they don't want to plant no rice, no coconut. They buy the cars, clothes. Then the police started to raid them and spray the fields and people was killing each other.

Now they can not grow as much. They used to grow it a lot, lot, lot, lot. They smoked it a lot. They get crazy. Nowadays they take the cocaine, from a bark. They get real crazy – worse than weed. I see it in the TV. It's very dangerous. We lock our doors good now. Nobody done come here. In the town, you have lot of thief. They thief radios, tapes and so.

I'd like to see betterment. Let the children work. If they work, they wouldn't have the time to do the bad things. Me, a mother, I sit down with my boys to tell them not to go out with those boys who smoke. They say, "No, Bird, we won't smoke. They offer but we no smoke it."

But I tell them, "But they could entice you." So many people smoke. They drink, they smoke.

I want my kids to get married and behave themselves – because when they are married they don't have time for what is out there – and stay good. That is my belief. I prayed when Lotty small that she find a good husband and it is true. I pray to the Lord that none of my kids take the drugs. The drugs destroy a lot of life. Quarter part of Belize they are destroying.

Before I die, I want to get ready, fix up the house and everything so all my kids have something, so they will be okay. I am a very sickly person. I want them to be ready. I don't want to be sick no more. We plant rice and cane. Sell them. I want to open a place to mind babies. The girls, they go to work and they need someone to mind the babies.

I don't want to depend on my kids. When I make money, I save it. I take that money, put it into the bank, then I use it to build this house. I lease this land. We will buy five acres. We use that for our farm. It's a nice life. I love my life.

The brackets indicate that this portion of the text is paraphrased at the request of the narrator.

Lotty

Lotty, the daughter of Miss Bird, was born in Punta Gorda, a member of a Garifuna family. They moved to Orange Walk when she was a young girl. She is married and lives with her husband and young son and teaches high school in Orange Walk.

My family is originally from Punta Gorda. We moved up here when I was very young. My uncle lived here first, in the early sixties. The sugar factory was just getting started. In the south there isn't much industry, so my mom came up here after my uncle to work. At that time, she had only my brother and me. She boarded people who worked at the factory.

I grew up without a dad. I had a step-dad. He worked at the factory. I was the oldest child and the only girl. I have four brothers. We used to live almost in the centre of Orange Walk. We were renting then – we then bought this place. It was all bush then: we were isolated. We lived in a thatch house that we built from palmetto trees and used the palm to build it. Soon after, we built this wooden house and started to have boarders.

We didn't have many relatives up here, but we would always meet with other Garinagu who lived up here. Us kids call all the older people aunt and uncle, but they weren't our real relatives. I liked it when they came to visit 'cause then we could go outside and play. They'd come to visit and talk and my mom would send us outside and we wouldn't have to work for a while. Sometimes they'd come for Mass. The Mass is a special ceremony in honour of a dead soul. You cook all the foods that person liked when they were alive, like the cassava and put it out for them. And sometimes there are drums.

At home I worked hard. My mom was strict, so I could get away with things only when my step-dad was around, but when he wasn't, I was really in for it. I took care of the others when my mom went out. I did the dishes, washing, cleaning house. We didn't have any running water then, so we had to get up early in the morning and go over to another street to pump water. My mom did most of the disciplining in the family. She had a real temper. When I was young and it was time to get a lashing I would run – I'd run as fast as I could away from our house. I'd run all around the park. There were some fellows that were always there and they'd laugh and ask my mom, "Miss Bird, you want us to catch her for you?" And they'd chase me down and bring me home.

My mom would always make sure we were neat and clean and well fed. She was so picky about having things done right. She taught me how to do the washing and the cooking and she told me that if I didn't do it right, there was the possibility that my husband would send me home to re-learn. She knew someone who that had happened to and she didn't want it to happen to me.

My mom knew what she wanted for her kids: education, discipline, respect, love and good values. At that time, I didn't think she always used the right ways of achieving them, but she was right in what she wanted. She tried to take good care of her children. For example, she always had the opportunity to go to the United States to work, but she never did. She preferred staying to take care of us.

Anyhow, I think my mom did a great job of trying to instill discipline and hard work in us. She taught us how to take care of ourselves, how to protect ourselves. She didn't show us love a lot. I mean not *physically:* she cared for us a lot, but it wasn't until recently that she started showing it through hugs and kisses. She would lash us.

Yes, my mom was strict and there were things she wanted me to do. She wanted us all to get educated, even though she hadn't been. In Belize, education is very instrumental and good to have and she wanted us to do the best we could. Education was the key to success.

I always liked school. I used to look forward to seeing my friends and working hard. It was more fun than staying home and working. I remember that the girls played differently than the boys. I was the only one with a doll and I'd really be the boss, deciding who I would allow to play with it. We'd skip rope or play Queen. It's like a fashion show: we'd line up and look pretty and try out to be Queen. I never won because I was too short.

When I came out of Standard Six, I couldn't go to high school so I worked in a store. However, my aunts decided to help me financially, so I went to high school at Muffles. I liked it a lot. It was really fun. I was in the academic class there. I liked English, but I hated math. The fourth-year math teacher would just come in and say, "Lot, you can go to sleep, class is starting." I'd put my head down and sleep till he finished. I couldn't cope with it. It wasn't until later at university that I started liking it. Probably because I *had* to pass it then and I also saw the need for it.

It was a privilege to go to Muffles and I think it really shaped my life. By then, I had enough sense and values of my own to know what I wanted and so I worked towards that. The circumstances, events and situations in my life, they told me what to do. I knew I wanted an education, a nice house, a loving husband and just three or four kids and genuine friends. And I worked for it, with God's help. I'm pretty satisfied, but not all the way. There's always room for improvement.

I came out of Muffles in 1979. It was fun graduating and a real accomplishment for me and my family. We had a prom and all those exciting things. The first time I really spoke to my husband is when I invited him to the prom. He was from Dangriga. I had a friend who knew him. I used to always see him riding by on his motorcycle and I said, "That's the guy I want to take to the prom." I got introduced to him and asked him to go to the prom with me. We got to be good friends. And the rest is history!

After I graduated, I applied for a teaching job at a Roman Catholic school. I taught there until 1981. I didn't get into teaching because I loved it, but because I needed a job. After I got into it, I liked it. However, at first I had thought I'd never have the patience to deal with the students. But I found out I could cope. I liked the kids.

In 1981, I got a scholarship to teachers college in Belize City. That was a LOT of fun and a lot of work. That's where I met some of my very best friends. We got so close – we were a clan. We'd have parties and we were involved in everything: drama, talent shows and so. I had my own little place to live in. We had certain days when they'd come over and we'd cook and study and we'd all just sleep right there. Yes, we were on the go, my friends and I. Even after I got married and moved back here, we stayed together. They are mostly in Belize City or in the south. I don't have too many close friends in Orange Walk, though I have lots of good acquaintances. And I'm real good friends with Sister Grace. I have always admired her. I can tell her about anything and I have trust in her. With my friends, we talk about everything. I know I don't have to pretend with my friends. I can be myself.

One thing I can tell you, if I trust you and love you like a friend, don't do anything to let me down. Don't disappoint me, because it hurts real deep when a friend is not genuine. Unfortunately, I've been hurt real bad. Just once – I was too naive. It's hard for me to pretend that everything is okay when it isn't. I always weigh people out: I analyze them. Sometimes I need to remind myself not to be too critical. I know who I like and who I feel comfortable with. Consequently, it takes me some time to trust a person to the stage of really being friends.

I started teaching at Muffles in 1984. I've always admired the institution. I have great pride in working there. The first year I had a home room of forty-five girls. It was hard, but I enjoyed it. There are times when I don't know how to cope because the teaching and working with young people is so demanding. English is a pressure class because the students have to pass it, so we all get a little tense because if they fail English, they fail the year. That's money for their parents and time for them. English is their second language, so it's hard for them. Sometimes they'll be failing and their parents will get mad at ME for it.

At first we were using books from England, but now we use a lot of books that are donated from the States. The classes at school are geared toward taking the exam and coping with the normal demands of life and Christian expectations.

There are times when I really look forward to going to school and sharing with the students, talking with them. Listening to them and teaching is exciting. It's exciting to teach young eager kids something they don't know and I learn from them. It's rewarding and beautiful. I joke with them a lot, but I don't let them get away with anything. I try to stay around in the afternoons so I can help them.

Sister Grace is the manager of the school, she and Sister Mary. It is a Sisters of Mercy school. They have the final say in everything, but they usually let the principal use his discretion. They trust him. For important decisions, they come in and discuss things. The principal is strict, but I can see why: he wants the best for the school. He is strict with the teachers as well as with the students. He is a pusher: he gets things done. Sometimes he and I don't agree about the best manner to do things. Unfortunately, school has been hit from outside because of politics. The principal is a strong believer in his party and its philosophies. Sometimes people identify the school and its teachers as with that party, which at times isn't good.

I get along real well with the teachers there. Several of them were my classmates and are totally aware of my frankness. And some of them taught there when I was a student. Sometimes when I complain about a kid, Sister Grace will laugh and tell me that I did the same thing.

Since I am pregnant, I will get twelve weeks maternity leave. Before we started the social security programme nine years ago, just the employer would pay part of the benefits, but now social security pays sixty percent of your salary. And you don't have to fear losing your job. But you only get six weeks after your baby is born.

Romel and I got married in 1982. I always wanted to get married someday – I wanted a husband that would be understanding and loving and respectful. I wanted him to have some sort of formal education. I didn't want him to be violent – I'd seen enough of that, not in my home, but in my neighbourhood. I wanted him to be easy going and cool and reliable. I wanted him to have God in his life. Fortunately, I found this person in my husband. I am pretty satisfied. I think it is working out good.

I like my marriage. Romel is real cool, real easy going, laid back – unlike me. He supports me in things I need to do. We discuss things and have a good rapport. I can rely on him: he's strong. And until Jason started needing discipline, I never heard Romel even raise his voice. He's firm, yet gentle and effective.

Romel helps me with the cooking and the cleaning. Now and again he helps me with the laundry. It's not the norm with the men here, but he helps a lot. I help him too. We try to work together and we haven't had any interference from in-laws. They don't tease him for helping me, like some in-laws do. Some people, mostly older people, say that the man has been obeahed if he helps out.

I'm not too crazy about housework. I like to cook, but I really like to just sit around with my family and talk, be with them. I'm not the perfect housewife. It's a whole day's job and I teach all day. I take care of things, though. It's nice to just be at home with my family. I want them to know that there is someone here to take care of them. I really give them a lot of care and attention. I am always here to listen to my husband and my little boy. We always share what is happening to each other.

Right now, my husband and I have several things we want to attack. Right now, we are building our new house. It's small, but it's a big accomplishment for us. We have worked a lot together on the house: making plans, working and making sure the builders are doing their job. We have had to undergo intense budgeting since we didn't want to make a bank loan.

And we also want to prepare for our kids so they can have things a little bit easy, but we don't want them to think that everything comes easy – we want them to know what it is like to struggle. And I'd like to have life easier. I want to continue working, but I'd like to have more time to spend with my family. We both have to work to have what we want. I'd like to have a pick-up truck – our new house is so far away from school – but we can't afford one right now.

We also want Romel to get his degree and me to finish mine. We both went to the States to work on our degrees. I was there for one and a half years. I got a scholarship. It was hard. It was real rough. Jason was about one and a half years old when I left. He stayed here with Romel and my mom. He got so spoiled! It was hard to leave him –he was so young. I felt so bad leaving him, but I did it for him. Maybe I just say that to console myself. But it was rough. I'd never be able to do it again. It took me a long time to decide to take the scholarship. I'd always wanted a college education and everyone told me I should do it. It was hard, but I decided to take it. Romel was real supportive. He had received one the year earlier. Romel and I were in the States for about three months together. I was in Kentucky, he was in Iowa. Then he finished and came back home. We wrote so many letters to each other and they sent me newspapers and tapes and preserves. My family was very supportive.

If I'd had my family with me, then it would have been perfect. I had a lot of fun in the States and I learned so much. I visited about twenty states as part of our programme and through activities I was involved in. I also visited a lot of my aunts and uncles. It was a nice exposure, a good learning experience. I studied English and education, but I still have six more hours to do to get my degree. I also learned a great deal about people and how to take care of myself. Before then I'd always had my mom or my husband to run to, but I was on my own there. Now I am much more confident: I like myself and I trust myself. I can question and challenge –you won't pull any bull on me. I know what I like and don't like, to a certain extent. I don't regret going. I'm glad I went, even though I really missed my family.

My mom and I are close now. We have had very different lives – different circumstances and factors. In those days, going to school after high school was out. She was so busy making ends meet she didn't have the time or money for school. If she had the opportunity for high school, she would have been different. But I think she has had a good life without it: she is energetic and she pushes. She knows how to get things done –she is quite independent.

My life is easier. I don't have to do as much to survive. I can really depend on my husband – she didn't have that. And I won't have as many kids. I have more options because of my education. I have a much more stable job than my mother did. And she helps me a lot. I really trust her with my baby. She didn't have a mother who helped her. Our lifestyles are different, but she knew what she wanted for us – the same way I know what I want for my son. My mom and I, we're both protective, sometimes too much.

Everything is different. There are so many dangers out on the streets now. I've seen Belize change from a place where I felt comfortable leaving my house unlocked, or running around alone at night, to a place that is more dangerous. I think it is because of drugs. It's a big problem – it affects people bad.

There's much more that the politicians and government can do for Belize. We are fortunate now that we've seen both parties at work. What I think now is that the Belize people are waking up a bit and wanting to make the government do things for them instead of doing things just for their friends. And sometimes opposing politicians attack each other verbally on the rostrum. Belize is so small, everybody knows what everybody else is doing and so the politicians get personal. There is too much gossip.

I like politicians who pay attention to the needs of the people and the town and who get involved. A lot of them say they will – its the same old story – they say they'll do a lot of things and that they're really for the people and then they get into office and they don't do anything but help their friends. But there are some good ones and it's getting better. There are improvements.

I do so many things these days: drama, the Rangers, school – and everything always takes more time than you think it will. If I'm not doing something, I feel uncomfortable sometimes, like I've forgotten a meeting or something. I've started easing out of some of these activities, so I can prepare for the new baby and spend more time with my family. I take my little boy along with me sometimes when I go to meetings because I want him to learn that we must give of ourselves to our community.

Fortunately, my husband supports me. He doesn't mind taking me to meetings and such and then he picks me up. People come here and still want me to do things. It's hard to not say yes. Sometimes I say no, when I really need to, but a lot of times people ask me do things that have to be done and are important and I don't feel good saying no.

Another thing I am involved in is Women Against Violence. They had a three day workshop I went to last year. From there on there was no turning back – it is an important group. I became the secretary.

The women down here need that group. There is so much violence and the women are afraid to say anything. They feel alone. The people in Belize City are more outspoken. The people here are shyer, especially the older ladies. The younger ladies don't take as much nonsense. The older ones, because of having more kids and less education, feel more obligation to stay married and in the atrocious situations. What I think they should do is just get up and beat the man back! Well, maybe that's not good advice.

I think the ladies need an outlet. It's a good programme, but we have so much more to do, like organizing and education.

I think to a certain extent (that the differences between men and women) are natural. But it's society that's causing a lot of it. I find myself telling Jason, "Hey, you shouldn't do that because you're a little boy." One day he got hold of some dolls and I said, "Hey, dolls are for girls." One time I was sitting here and gave a good loud laugh and he said, "Mommy, you shouldn't laugh like that because you're a lady!"

It's what we push people to do. Consciously or unconsciously, we start acting the way society wants us to. We get moulded. Like men aren't supposed to cry, but I think that men should cry if they are hurt or whatever. But men aren't supposed to. They need to be "strong."

In the same way, ladies are supposed to stay in the home, but I think that's wrong. I think there are certain things that women can't do because of not being as physically strong. They are a little bit more delicate. But when it comes to taking care of the family and house,

I think that both should help. In my case, I'm lucky, 'cause Romel really wants to help. I don't have to beg him to help.

I don't think that because a person is a man or a woman that it should stop them from doing what they want. But I can't run away from my culture. There are times when I feel myself criticizing a woman for doing things that I wouldn't criticize a man for. I condemn her more than I would a man, even though it's an equal offence. And in the homes, the parents are more strict with the girls. They don't even mind sometimes when their boys do bad things to girls, but they don't want it to happen to their girls. There is a real double standard.

At work, I don't see much discrimination 'cause of sex. Men and women do the same jobs and get paid the same, depending on experience and academic qualifications. When we go on trips or have parties, the men want to stay in a group by themselves and I guess the women do that too. The men teach woodwork and agriculture and the women teach dance and aerobics. And men do the heavier roles for sports. Both men and women teach all the other subjects. We have about the same workload.

Society also expects certain behaviours based on your education, your social and ethnic background and your married life. People in your community dictate you sometimes, but after a while people accept what you do – that is, if it's your community. Even if they accept you, they might still talk about you. If it's not your community and you do something strange, they don't accept you as easy. But if you are from another country and do strange things, sometimes they think that's okay. If the gossip affects you, then you change. If people see that you're not going to change, then they stop talking. I am usually affected by what people say about me, though I ignore it sometimes.

Here in Belize I think that a woman can make it if she wants to. Society doesn't put too much pressure on her to stay down, but she might have her own problems, her own factors – like her husband and his beliefs. But society admires a woman who is pushing herself, has confidence in herself. There are other prejudices, like social, class or cultural. But we have many women in high posts.

I think there is racial discrimination. It is subtle and we try to hide it, but it's there. Since I grew up here, all of my friends are Mestizos and I feel quite comfortable even though I am a Garifuna. It's because they know me. But I've heard of other Garifunas having trouble, especially in the government. When it comes to giving scholarships, or getting a job, there's discrimination. It's hard. I think it comes from both sides. For example, in Belize City, it's mostly Creoles and they didn't like the Mestizos there earlier on. People called them "yellow-belly." But slowly the Mestizo people have come up.

There are more marriages between people from different cultures than there used to be, but it still turns heads.

Garifuna prefer to be called "Garifuna" instead of "Carib". Both Mestizos and Creoles call us Caribs a lot. Some of the Creoles have an attitude about the Garinagu. I think it might stem all the way back because the Creoles were slaves and the Garinugu weren't. That's why we've been able to save all these customs, like the dancing and drumming. The Creole couldn't do that. We all originated from Africa, but they were slaves and were cut off from each other and inter-married with English. The Creole curse the Garifunas a lot – sometimes they get arrogant.

I like my Garifuna heritage. Since I grew up here and not in Dangriga or Punta Gorda, I have been deprived of doing many of the daily traditional customs. I didn't know much about the deeper traditions until I was older. The entire system of the Garifuna culture has affected me. I look like a Garifuna, my thoughts are Garifuna. I can talk Garifuna but not fluently. And those drums beat within my soul.

The custom that really strikes me is the Dugu, a spiritual healing ceremony. The spirits come to you and ask you to do the Dugu. They talk through you and someone has to listen and tell you what they said. The spirits come when they need something or they're not satisfied and you have to do something. Sometimes they come when you are sick or someone in your family is sick. Then they ask you to do the Dugu. For a Dugu, you invite all your relatives. Everybody

272

contributes. It's expensive. There's the beating of drums and different rituals. Sometimes it pleases the spirits – if it doesn't, you have to do it again.

I have been to a Dugu and it was really an experience for me. It really shook me up. First of all, I met people that I'd never met before who were my relatives and then all the dancing and singing –it was incredible. It made me aware of how rich my culture is.

The spirits do not come to every family. They come to those people that can do something for them. They come to ask you to do certain things, say certain things to people. They get mad sometimes. Like for instance, if you have a party and you serve some of the food they like and you don't set any aside for them, they can get real angry. They would come into a person there and talk through that person to the people. They only communicate through certain people. The person that they are communicating through doesn't know what they are saying. [Sometimes they say things to reassure you or to help you. I can't explain how it works, but it works]. It's something really special. It's not something that should be played around with.

There are some Garinagu who feel like it isn't real, who don't believe in it any more. They believe they don't need it any more. [Sometimes it's dangerous to not pay the spirits mind.] You just can't underestimate the spirits. We have many stories about them. There is the spirit who knocks you down from your chair if you are sitting by the door at twelve noon –especially if there has been a recent death in your family. Newly dead spirits still move around, they are not ready to rest – especially if it was a young person who died, someone who was real active who isn't ready to stop being involved. Noon is their busy time. They'll come and just knock you right down. You can die from that.

My husband tells me this story about this greedy guy from Dangriga – the Garinagu, they don't want you to be greedy. This guy, he would fish for fish and crabs. He would try to occupy all of the space on the pier – he'd get there early and set his nets up. One day he was there real early. He was watching his nets and he saw a big face come up and it said, "Have you seen teeth like these?" And he saw these big teeth and started to run around in a fit. He was all foaming and he was really frightened. I don't know if he ever went out there again. It's just a story.

I really want to pass (my culture) on. I want my little boy to learn the language. Here it's hard because he's exposed to Creole in the home, English at school and Spanish just around. I don't talk Garifuna well. My husband can talk it better. Jason is exposed to the food and dances a lot: he likes to Punta, especially because it's popular now. We take him to Dangriga for celebrations. I want him to be proud of who he is.

The Garifuna make sure the younger people learn about the customs, so if a younger person speaks Creole to an older one, the older person doesn't always like it – she wants to hear Garifuna. And we have our dances and food and customs – it's very, very strong. I don't think it will die because the older people make sure that it continues: they will teach the younger people. And I have my part to play too.

The brackets indicate that this portion of the text is paraphrased at the request of the narrator.

Conclusion
Peta Henderson
and
Ann Bryn Houghton

The women who tell their stories here have lived through a period of rapid and sometimes contradictory change. The sugar industry has offered new opportunities in employment and commerce, but it has destroyed the ancient culture and ecology based on the *milpa* and transformed the lives of the inhabitants. Internationally, Belize has established an independent identity as a Central American and Caribbean nation. However, dependence on United States economic and social aid has increased.

Belize has been evolving a two-party political system which offers opportunities for democratic participation. Yet political partisanship may be hindering the development of common interests based on class, ethnicity and gender. Rising real wages and new employment in both urban and rural areas have led to radical changes in family roles and gender relations. Yet the changes have been uneven and unemployment is reducing the options of many young people.

In undertaking this work, we were interested in exploring how women have been affected by these trends. To what extent can they participate in social and economic development yet preserve what they consider to be important in their traditional culture? How do they see themselves as women? How have gender relationships, work roles and political consciousness evolved in the new Belize? We try to summarize below some of the answers that emerge from these life histories.

In general, economic and political trends express themselves in intensely personal conflicts and contradictions for women. Some of the tensions result from the clash between new social opportunities and traditional cultural subordination of women – from "cultural lag." Many have benefited from an improved standard of living: they do not work as hard or as long as their mothers and grandmothers. Some, especially in the urban areas, are slowly gaining personal and financial independence from husbands and fathers and are beginning to take up leadership roles in public life. Yet the results of "development" are by no means unambiguously beneficial: women face new stresses and unfulfilled expectations as they struggle to maintain traditional female skills and values.

Often, the ambiguity derives from the conflict between expanded social opportunity and restrictive gender conceptions. It is hardly surprising that young women today experience identity confusion. Education emerges clearly as a value in the stories of several women, both those who benefited themselves and those who sacrificed for their daughters. Yet, at least in the rural areas, most young women still leave school at age fourteen and return home to help their mothers in the household until marriage.

The culture places contradictory expectations on the young woman: that she should succeed and compete with men in the labour market but that she should see herself as inferior to men and play subordinate roles ascribed by custom. The double sexual standard still allows certain freedoms to men in establishing relationships outside the family, relationships that are denied to women.

Not all the tensions these women face can be explained by cultural lag. In some cases, economic development and political independence have raised new problems as well as new opportunities. For some women, sugar cane has brought increased financial dependence on men. As the values of the market have penetrated even the more remote villages, the unpaid labour of women is seen as having diminished value. Women in public life face new pressures to compete with men. Moreover, where once most women shared a somewhat common social status, class differences in access to education and jobs, as well as in the cultural control of women's sexuality, are threatening to divide women from each other. Rural-urban differences reflect this growing class gap: the stories reveal considerable generational upward mobility in the town but less in the villages.

Women respond in different ways to these conflicts and contradictions. Some find ways to accommodate traditional cultural norms dictating appropriate female behaviour: they make decisions based on a tacit acceptance of the cultural rule which prescribes dependence on men. Faced with oppressive conditions, they find adaptive and non-threatening ways to survive. Others actively seek to overthrow older norms by affirming a new female identity as independent social actors: holding jobs, exercizing joint decision-making authority with their husbands and working with their sisters in lay and religious organizations to end compliance with the cultural rules they find oppressive.

Among those who seek new social roles, some identify completely with development, including the political centrality of the United States and its views on foreign relations; but others are beginning to take a more critical stance and to stress the value of Belizean culture. We think that some of the behaviours or values that seem to represent accommodation to traditional gender rules may reflect a feminine critique of certain aspects of the new society and culture. For example, women who choose to remain in traditional relationships with men despite the opportunity for education or employment may be resisting the expectation that they should play a larger role in supporting the family or that they should receive less financial support from men.

These forces of change, contradiction, accommodation and resistance play out in three areas: gender relationships, work, and political roles and consciousness.

Gender Relationships

Marriage and childbearing, which occupy the bulk of most women's lives in Belize, most decisively shape both accommodation and resistance. Women's experiences in either common-law or marital unions are an integral part of most of the stories. The cultural norm is that women get married in their teens or early twenties and bear children. However, the narratives reveal that the women make a variety of choices.

Some of the women have resisted the cultural norm and have not established primary relationships with men. These women turn to both old and new values to justify their choices and rely on old and new support systems to carry them out. For example, the Catholic Sisterhood has traditionally been one of the ways women could remain single and devote their lives to their work as we see in the case of Sister Grace. Her dedication to teaching and the Sisterhood precluded marriage. Gloria wanted to teach and didn't think it was possible to have both a career and a family. She later resolved the conflict by becoming a nun.

Alternatively, some women draw on new norms to justify their decisions. After one marriage and a common-law union, Susanna found that she could support herself and thus didn't need a husband. "When you have a job, it will replace any husband because when you have money, you don't need a husband," she says. Gabriela chose to remain single after the death of her husband because she was afraid that a new partner would interfere with her relationship with her children and would try to control her. Gabriela, like Susanna, thinks that being single allows greater freedom and is a way of avoiding abuse.

Most, however, decided to marry or live common-law with men. Clearly, they were influenced by the expectations of their families and culture, but they give a considerable range of reasons for entering unions. Several women entered the unions to get, as Clara put it, "something better" than what they had with their families. The "something better" that Clara talks about was to not have to work as hard as she did at home and to "have my own things." Cristina got married when she found out that the reason her father always treated her badly was that he denied he was her father. She thought she would be better off if she wasn't "in her father's power" any more.

In some cases religious values or lack of access to birth control put young women in a vulnerable position which sometimes ends up in unwanted pregnancy and marriage. Magdalena had this experience at the age of fourteen. However, an unwanted pregnancy does not always mean the beginning of a relationship; in some cases, the father denies paternity and the mother's family may agree to take partial responsibility for raising the child.

Many of the women entered unions for financial reasons. The development of the sugar cane industry has created new jobs for women, but many, especially those in the villages, have limited access to jobs. Often they are discouraged from working outside the home by their families and community and are encouraged to be dependent on men. Single mothers have even fewer options. Susanna describes this situation quite bluntly: "I agreed to be with the man because he would support me and everything. Otherwise, how was I going to survive?"

Miss Bird says that safety and companionship were her reasons for entering into a partnership. Though she was single for many years and was the sole supporter of her family, she says, "A woman can't live by herself here. You need a partner to protect you from other people." Her partnership with Lester has also helped her to build and maintain the farm she always wanted.

Some of the women explain that they "ended up" in relationships with men because they were too young to make a good decision or did not really understand what they were getting into. Susanna says, "When you are a young girl, you are crazy. You don't know about life. It is only after that you start sitting down and thinking about what you did." Gabriela recalls that one of her teachers advised her to delay marriage until she was older so she could carry on with her studies and teaching, but she resented the teacher's advice because he was married. A boy started "hanging around" her, and she consented to marry him. Although the marriage worked out well, she reflects that it would have been better to have waited. "But at that time, my mind was not working all together and I didn't understand it that way."

Similarly, Juanita ignored her mother's warnings and got married at a young age; her husband was abusive and the marriage quickly ended while she was still pregnant with her first child.

The women who chose to enter into primary relationships with men all had – and continue to have – expectations of what a good relationship is. Their expectations vary, but all express some ideal about the division of labour between partners, control over money and decision making, childbearing, and how their partners should treat them. When their expectations are not met – as often happens – they employ a variety of strategies to try to gain greater control over their lives. Some of these strategies are adaptive and conservative, aimed at survival and conformity to the cultural norms; others are resistant, making novel and sometimes revolutionary efforts to change existing gender roles and relations in conjunction with changing opportunities.

Some women – Cristina, Magdalena, Clara and Susanna – accept the culturally approved division of labour. Susanna describes the "contract" very succinctly: the duty of the woman when she gets married is to take care of the meals, to wash the clothes and to feed the animals. The duty of the man is to support the woman. He has to find a way to get the money for food. He also has to give her spending money. Another duty for the man is to work on his *milpa* to have corn.

The women conceive of this as a partnership where each person fulfils his or her obligations and respects the other's work. They accept that they may have to engage in small business – such as making and selling bread or tamales – and do most of the child-rearing. Felicia and Bianca (with her first partner) told their partners that they wanted to work outside the home but would remain in charge of house mainte-nance and child-care. Lotty is one of the few married women who resisted cultural expectations and the double day enough to insist that her partner support her career and share the household chores.

The division of authority within the household is an area in which there is considerable tension between the cultural rule and daily practice. Most of the women seem to accept the cultural norm that the man should be the head of the household, have the authority to give orders and exercise the ultimate control over decision-making. Many of the women also think that their partners have the right to restrict their movements and to decide whether or not they can work outside the home. However, most of the women also think that they should have authority over decisions about the household and have at least some input in decisions about the *milpa* or the other work that the man is involved in.

Many women seem to accept the cultural rule mandating male authority, but they do not necessarily subscribe to it as a natural right or believe that the man is inherently superior. Ana was the only woman who said that the man should be the head of the household. "That's the way I grew up and that's the way the Bible says. That's the way God wants." Most of the women accept male authority because that is the cultural norm and most men insist on it. Women therefore need to make the adjustments. As Clara puts it, "Never mistreat your husband. On the contrary, love him, take care of him – give him everything he needs. Thus, if you suspect he is going with another woman, he'll see that she's not your equal – if you take care of him well, it will be hard for him to leave you." Amelia says, "When you want one living (to have a good life), you have to listen to what the man says." Felicia is resigned to the existence of machismo and says that only men who have been to the United States treat women with equality.

Yet many of those who affirm that man is the head of the household also feel there should be more equality between the sexes. Cristina explains, "It should be equal – the same for the woman as for the man. If the woman must obey the man, then the man must obey the woman. But the man wants to say that since he is the man of the house, he orders. The woman has to allow the man to dominate her." Juanita is indignant that her partner claims his right to give the orders because he is the worker who earns the money; she insists that her contribution should give her equal rights. Lotty says that people reinforce the attitude that men should be in control and shouldn't help women with the housework by saying things like, "Men shouldn't cry," or that a man has been "obeahed" (bewitched) if he helps the women with the house-cleaning.

Women who want to see more equality in daily life can act on new values and opportunities in their struggle to gain more freedom. But one side effect of the sugar industry has been increased financial vulnerability due to the seasonality of jobs and fluctuations in the price of cane. The rising cost of living as well as pressures to educate children and to spend money on goods that weren't previously available compound their vulnerability. Many people stopped growing food for subsistence during the period of high cane prices in the seventies. Gabriela, Clara and others comment on the difficulty of no longer having corn to feed their families and the animals. The result is that some women, like Juanita, have become even more dependent on their husbands to give them money for food and other necessities.

In other cases, traditional male sources of power and authority may be undermined by such financial difficulties. Though this erosion of male breadwinning ability may present women like Susanna with new money-generating opportunities such as her store, it may also cause disappointment, as it does Magdalena, who expected that her partner would support her family.

Even when men do not face economic difficulties, they may withhold or threaten to withhold financial support from their families as a mechanism of gender power and control. Some men seem unwilling rather than unable to support their families. Susanna, Magdalena and Juanita's partners denied paternity as a way of avoiding responsibility for supporting the children. Miss Bird, Estella and Magdalena recount how their partners spent most of the money on drink, or on "outside" women and children. Some men insist on having control over money and decision-making. Cristina and Amelia consider themselves lucky that their husbands put the money in their hands and allow them to decide how to spend it. Juanita and Magdalena, on the other hand, think that although they fulfil their marital obligations, they can't count on adequate support or even a say in financial decisions. Rachel's husband can control her activities, to some extent at least, by refusing to buy her a car, knowing that she does not have money herself to buy it.

The stories speak of the variety of strategies women use to gain financial security for their families and control over their lives. Some plant kitchen gardens, or pressure their partners to plant a *milpa* so they will be less dependent on cash. Many women engage in money-making activities: Amelia bakes and sells bread and sweets. When the store went out of business, Susanna and her mother sold ground spices, bread and tamales in the village. Estella resorted to taking money from her husband when he was drunk. Magdalena used to sell coconut oil in Orange Walk until she got tired of what she saw as her partner's failure to share his cane bonus with her and her daughter: she left him for some months. And although Felicia quit working at the hospital at the request of her husband, she later embarked on a very public career in politics.

Not all the women are dissatisfied with the division of labour, control, authority and decision making in their relationships. Lotty says that she's very satisfied with the arrangements she and her husband have: they both have fairly well-paying, steady jobs; they share chores and decision-making and they've worked together to build a new house. Bianca and Ana seem to have a similarly gratifying relationship with their partners. Gabriela says that her short-lived marriage was almost ideal. Rachel says that being the stay-at-home mother she and her husband thought she should be was the best choice, and now that her kids are grown, she has time to do a lot of volunteer work in the community. She is fortunate that her husband has a good job.

Tensions between partners also typically centre on reproduction. When women marry, they expect that they will have children. Child-rearing is still the major source of personal fulfilment and cultural status for most women. Children are loved and wanted, and in the past, especially in the villages, ten or more children were not uncommon. Amelia and Cristina bore seventeen each, although not all are living. Contraception is still not an option for some, because of religious reasons or the opposition of husbands and partners. Control over reproduction has been a major source of male power over women. After nine children, Cristina's doctor suggested a tubal ligation, but her husband opposed it, insisting that she must accept God's will in this matter and that he could support them. So she bore eight more children. Amelia, Cristina, and Clara speak eloquently about the hardships of giving birth to and caring for many children. In their mid-forties, Cristina and Amelia are still raising children under five while hoping fervently that, as Cristina puts it, "God isn't going to give me any more gifts."

To some degree it is development rather than traditional cultural norms that determines women's reproductive strategies. Some of the younger women, such as Lotty, are determined to limit the number of children they have because they remember how difficult their mothers' lives were. Juanita first had monthly contraceptive injections and when these failed had her tubes tied after bearing her sixth child. Her younger sister who attended high school and Sixth Form says she plans to have only one or two children so she can educate them properly. Felicia, who is in her fifties but learned about birth control methods when she worked at the hospital, used birth control to plan the size and timing of her family.

In the town and the villages, nuns instruct younger couples about the rhythm method and health care workers, such as Gabriela, advise them about other birth control methods. The younger women's reproductive strategies undoubtedly have an important effect on gender relations. Once women gain control of their fertility, they and their partners can make choices about family size and spacing. These choices are based on their own needs and desires, their perceptions of the children's welfare, and the cultural context within which they live. The issue is not reduction of family size but increase in women's autonomy.

While financial and reproductive control may be the most common means of exercising gender power, the threat or the reality of abuse is a theme that runs through many of the life stories. Not all the women have experienced abuse: Lotty, Rachel, Gabriela, Cristina and Amelia say that they have been satisfied with the lack of abuse in their relationships. But the possibility looms large in their life decisions. The threat of abuse – even the knowledge of its prevalence – can be used to control women. Its absence can be enough to make them grateful and willing to put up with other inequalities. In Clara's case, although her husband has never struck her, she devotes all her energy to pleasing him so he will not leave her for another woman.

Of those who have experienced abuse, the type and severity varies from relationship to relationship. The women who have experienced abuse don't always use the word "abuse." Rather, they talk about the disrespectful, controlling or violent behaviour of their partners – behaviour that they don't like or think is appropriate. The group Belize Woman Against Violence (WAV) in which Lotty, Sister Grace and Rachel are involved calls the abuse that happens between intimate partners – whether they're married, living in common-law unions, or dating – "spouse abuse." WAV breaks down spouse abuse into three categories: physical, sexual and emotional. Many of the women whose stories are found here have experienced at least one of these kinds of spouse abuse; some, like Estella, have experienced all three.

Physical abuse is the most easily identified type. It includes pulling hair, hitting, kicking, slapping, biting, pushing and throwing objects at the person. The severity ranges all the way from the slap that precipitated Bianca's leaving her husband, to the push which left Juanita, eight months pregnant, lying helplessly on the floor, to the regular beatings suffered by Estella when her husband was drunk, to the blow to the ribs that killed her mother.

According to WAV sexual abuse includes rape, adultery, making demeaning remarks about women or publicly showing interest in other women. Magdalena relives the tragic story of her partner's rape of her twelve-year-old daughter. Estella, Magdalena, Juanita, Miss Bird and others talk about their partners' extra-marital affairs. Sometimes, as in Magalena's and Estella's cases, the man taunts his partner with the affair and gives all the money to the "other woman." Magdalena also talks about how her father sexually abused her mother by criticizing and violently punishing her for only having female children. When Magdalena was born, he said, "You should have held her nose and killed her."

Emotional abuse, according to WAV, "may be the most difficult to define and recognize because almost everyone does it at one time or another. However, for some people it becomes a habit and a method of control. Some husbands cause their wives emotional stress by: ignoring feelings, insulting values, constant ridicule, driving away friends and family, humiliating the woman in public or in private, controlling all the money and decisions, threatening the woman or refusing to allow her to work."

Some of the women, such as Estella and Susanna, talk about their husbands' insults, perhaps the most poignant being Estella's comment that her husband told her she was ugly, and never called her by her name, causing her to go outside the house to cry. Some forms of financial control, such as those used by Miss Bird's and Estella's partners, can be included in this category, as can the threat of violence that husbands sometimes use if a woman does not do her work or in other ways displeases him.

The women who have experienced spouse abuse are by no means passive victims. They have all developed strategies to cope with, accommodate or resist the abuse. Estella, the oldest narrator, recognizes the abuse that she, her mother and her daughters experienced, but indicates that she coped by accepting it as inevitable although there were constant arguments.

For Estella, that's the way most men are and women just have to put up with it. Estella, like Susanna, Clara, and others, accommodate themselves to their partner's abusiveness by monitoring or changing their own actions, so as not to do something that will make their husbands angry and abusive. Some hide or steal money from their husbands, or ask for help from neighbours or family members. Some leave the relationship either temporarily or permanently. Magdalena left her husband for three months after he had raped her daughter; she did the same again later when she considered that he was not providing enough financial support.

Other women choose to leave the relationship permanently. Bianca decided she didn't want to put up with any kind of abuse: since she was financially independent, she could kick her boyfriend out when he slapped her. None of the women say they use physical violence as self-defense, but Lotty and Rachel both mention it as a possibility. Some, like Rachel, have told their husbands that they will absolutely not put up with abuse.

Work

Women spend the greater part of their lives working. The narratives include many stories about the substance and difficulty of their work. They talk about the work they do in the house and the work they do "outside," paid and unpaid work, the work they do to survive or to earn little bit extra, the work they do for satisfaction or to succeed, or to gain autonomy from their families or partners. In descriptions of their work, they also narrate how they experience and respond to the cultural rules that define what kind of work is appropriate for women.

The diversity in the women's lives is nowhere more apparent than in their stories about work. Some women live lives very much in accordance with the traditional division of labour by sex, while others have had the opportunity and desire to do work that was unheard of in their grandmothers' times.

All the women recall a definite division of labour by gender in their homes when they were growing up. Their mothers were in charge of all the housework and child-rearing, while the men worked *milpa* or had paid employment or both. Gloria remembers that her father and grandfather used to take large sacks of corn to Belize City to sell in the market. None of the women's mothers did paid work outside the home, but most did work in their homes that generated income: Sister Grace's mother ran a small school in their home: Rachel's mother took in boarders: Susanna's and Clara's mothers provided meals for foreign cane workers during the cane season: and several of the mothers raised chickens and pigs or made cooked food to sell.

Many of them worked with their husbands. Magdalena's mother helped her husband make charcoal, Ana's mother cooked for her husband's co-workers when they were in the bush doing chicle and Estella helped with the *milpa*. One of the few exceptions was Lotty's mother, Miss Bird, who as a single parent did the work of both parents.

From a young age, the women were expected to help their mothers with their work. Usually, the division of labour that the parents practised was replicated among the children. Some of the women, like Bianca, Cristina and Gabriela, who are the eldest daughters in their families, say their work-load and responsibilities were sometimes overwhelming. Gabriela, for example, resented that she had to be a mother to her younger siblings. The importance of learning how to do "women's work" is stressed. Lotty says her mother "told me if I didn't do it right, there's the possibility that my husband would send me home to relearn." Ana and Sister Grace were rare in that there wasn't such a strict division of labour in their families. After primary school a girl's productive role in the family increased. Some, like Cristina and Magdalena, were taken out of school so they could help more in the home. Others, like Bianca, Gabriela, Clara and Sister Grace, worked for pay and gave most of their incomes to their families.

In talking about their work, most women acknowledge that their lives are easier than were those of their mothers and grand-mothers. The improved standard of living means a lot to these women. Few deny their lives have materially improved over their lifetime. In the town and some villages, there is electricity and running water, although San Miguel was still awaiting electrification in 1992. Children no longer have to haul heavy buckets from the village well, a painful memory for Clara and even for younger women like Gabriela and Juanita. In the village, access to a corn mill, as well as twice-daily deliveries of factory-made tortillas, make Juanita's life easier than her grandmother's or mother's were. Hunger is no longer a fact of life as it was for Estella and Susanna and their children when their husbands neglected them.

The CARE-sponsored immunization programme that Gabriela helps to organize, has resulted in fewer sick children. There is access to transportation to the hospital in town. As both Cristina and Miss Bird explain, women use both the modern and traditional medical systems flexibly, depending on their diagnosis of the problem. Hospital births have helped to reduce some of the uncertainty surrounding childbirth, although some women still prefer to give birth at home and bemoan the demise of the traditional *partera*. All of these changes are undeniable and the women attribute many of them to the sugar cane industry or U.S. aid or both.

Not all women have been affected equally by the changes brought by the sugar industry. For women in the village and even for older townswomen like Miss Bird, there is a sense that little has changed in women's work. To be sure, the corn mill has relieved village women of hours of grinding corn. But Clara continues to spend every morning standing at her washtub as does her daughter, Juanita, and her daughter-in-law who at age eighteen already has two children. Some women say the task of washing is worse now because men's clothes are dirtier from the burnt cane.

On the other hand, the narratives clearly indicate that sugar cane has resulted in many new opportunities, especially in the town. New stores, schools, banks, offices, restaurants and clinics opened and offered jobs to women like Lotty, Marta, Bianca, Ana and Gabriela. Miss Bird moved up from Punta Gorda where there were virtually no jobs, and could support her family by boarding cane workers. Her daughter Lotty was educated in the U.S. and is now a high school teacher. In the village, cane money enabled Susanna to re-open her father's store. A few women worked as maids for people who had more money as a result of the cane.

The women who work outside the home have had to confront a variety of conflicts. In part, these arise out of the tension between changes in the larger society and customary gender relations, and they often focus on female identity. In addition to having to deal with their family's and community's expectations that women should only do certain kinds of work, women are finding – as their sisters in other parts of the world have discovered – that it is logistically and emotionally complicated to balance education and a career with family life. Women face conflicting values: that they study and compete with men in the outside world: that they be good wives and mothers.

Several talk about how complicated it is to balance a family and a career. Gloria thinks it's impossible to perform both roles successfully and so she has devoted herself to her career. Felicia's overriding goal was to be a nurse, but first her parents and now her husband have thwarted her desire. Felicia acknowledges that no matter how much outside work she is involved in, her husband still expects her to take care of all the housework and cooking. She copes with this by hiring a full-time maid, but says her husband expects her to serve him and she still does a lot of work in the home. Rachel and Bianca also employ maids. Bianca's partner supports her career and helps

289

with the housework, but she still hires a maid to help her. Lotty is the only person without a maid whose husband supports her career and shares housework.

In the village, women are faced with other conflicts and pressures. While working for pay locally to supplement the family income is acceptable, having a paid job that takes the young unmarried woman away from the home for long periods is more controversial. When the girl gets her "big body," as Gloria puts it, her movements are often restricted. Gloria talks about the difficulty village girls face in finding employment, not only because of the scarcity of jobs and cost of commuting but because of culturally-felt fears that they will "fall." Gloria was one of only two unmarried women with a full-time, stable job as a teacher. Although now, as a widow and mother of three children, Gabriela is employed as a community health worker, as a young girl she had to overcome the objections of her father before she was allowed to teach in the village school. Once she had her baby she was forced to quit.

Nowhere are gender identity conflicts more evident than in the debates and pressures that surround education above the primary school level for girls. The value placed on education emerges clearly as an element in the new society and girls are increasingly part of this process. In the past, women like Estella and Felicia were told that the woman's place is in the kitchen. Boys were chosen before girls on the assumption that they needed an education more than girls. Of the older women, only Rachel and Sister Grace were educated after age fourteen. Rachel's family moved to Orange Walk from the village so they would have access to better schools. Her father said that girls need an education because "marriage is like a lottery: you never know what you will get. And if you do not get a good husband, then you can leave him and work." Rachel's father was ahead of his time.

Many of the women emphasize how important it was that their parents insisted on an education for girls as well as boys. Sister Grace, Bianca, and Rachel all talk about this. Gabriela recalls with some regret how she ignored her teacher's encouragement and warnings not to get married until she had finished her education as a teacher. It was Gloria's father's insistence that made it possible for her to go to high school in Belize City when she was not accepted to the high school in Orange Walk. For some families, educating a daughter has meant struggle and sacrifice. Clara, for example, who herself had little education, has only one daughter of an age to help with her large family. Yet she has become totally convinced of the importance of her daughter attending high school and has made many sacrifices to this end. She is motivated in part by the hope that her daughter will have the means to help her when she is old or ill. Sister Grace says approvingly that girls who do go to high school are becoming more assertive in the classroom.

In work as in family relations, though, the tensions that women face cannot simply be attributed to conflict between cultural norms and new opportunities, but must be seen as part of the contradictory reality of development. Although the women do not talk much about class, there is an awareness of the growing gap between those who have access to education and jobs and those who do not, and between families which have benefited from the sugar industry and those which have been left out. In addition, the experience of employing, feeding and housing migrant workers from El Salvador, Guatemala and Mexico, who came to cut cane during the *zafra* in the seventies, has given cane-farming families a consciousness of class difference.

In the stories presented here, rural-urban differences most accurately reflect the growing class gap, although differences are also appearing within the villages as well as in the town itself. In San Miguel, the wealthier cane-farming families tend to share the values and way of life of the urban middle class. Unfortunately, the women's narratives do not offer a clear view of how poor and working class families in the town are faring. Rachel expresses a middle-class "liberal" sense of noblesse oblige when she comments on the need to get to know the sick and the poor, many of whom are refugees from other Central American countries who arrived with only the clothes on their backs. Felicia works with prostitutes to find alternative means of making a living. Unemployment is certainly a growing problem, especially in the non-agricultural sector. Bianca says, "Jobs are very hard to find here now. Labourers can usually get jobs – but a lot of jobs have been taken by immigrants." She comments that Belize needs more industry.

The life histories certainly reveal that some families have managed to improve their socio-economic status in recent years. Marta and Lotty acknowledge the vast difference in their lives compared to their mothers' due to education and job experience.

This difference is also visible in individual lives. Rachel, Sister Grace, and Ana have experienced a move from relative poverty to middle-class status in their lifetimes. Ana's story, in particular, reflects extraordinary upward mobility: she has moved from learning her ABCs from her mother in the bush with the *chicleros* to being an executive of a financial institution. Wealthier families have a better chance of sending their daughters to high school. This growing class gap has the potential for driving a wedge between privileged and underprivileged women as the values of individualism and consumerism take hold, and couples begin to concentrate on saving for lawn mowers and the like.

Women must face other contradictions caused by the new work relations, such as the devaluation of housework. When families relied on *milpa* subsistence farming, no difference in value was placed on the work done by men and women. Both sexes had an equal part to play in growing, harvesting and using the corn. With the advent of cane farming, most men are working for money. Work that earns money is seen as being more important. The work that women do in the house is becoming increasingly less respected than the work men do for pay. Most of the women acknowledge how difficult housework is but say that it's often belittled and taken for granted. Clara says that it is hard to see the results of housework, unlike the work that the men do in the fields. Some men have a hard time believing that housework is really work. Juanita's partner does not believe that the work she does entitles her to authority in household affairs because it does not earn money for the family.

While housewives are facing discrimination at home, some of the women who can work outside the home have to deal with gender-based discrimination and harassment on the job. Lotty believes that although the men and women teachers sometimes teach different subjects, usually their jobs are alike and they are paid the same. However, Sylvia, Felicia and Bianca, who all had jobs that are looked upon as being "men's jobs," had different experiences. They all felt like they were watched much more closely than men and felt pressured to prove that a woman could do their jobs. Felicia and Sylvia said that they were held accountable for other women's actions: because some women before them had made "mistakes," they were expected to do the same and were restricted or criticized and scrutinized for signs of failure. Sylvia talks tearfully of the harassment she experienced when she was in training to be a police officer and also says that the women officers are expected to do different chores on the job: they operate the radio, do most of the clerical work and are rarely sent out on operations "because the men do not think they could handle it."

The stories suggest that women, on the whole, have welcomed the new work opportunities and responded creatively to the conflicts and contradictions generated. Having outside work offers many women satisfaction and helps them avoid the isolation that some homeworkers experience. Gabriela expresses this when she talks about how happy she is now that she is meeting new people and learning new skills. Some women, like Ana, find that working for pay gives them more leverage and decision-making power within their partnerships with men. And as Bianca explains, having an income also makes it easier for women to become independent from their families or to leave their partners when the relationship isn't working out.

By working outside the home, the women are actively resisting and changing their families' and communities' ideas of who women are and what they can do. Felicia's parents told her that a woman's place is in the kitchen. Nevertheless, she chose a career in politics, and after many long and difficult years, she overcame her community's objections to women politicians when she was elected deputy mayor. She is now serving her second term and makes it a point to tell other women to speak out and get involved even if those around them tell them that they shouldn't. She also says that her parents now support her work. Ana, who is the manager of a financial institution, says that she feels that part of her job is to show men all the things women can do. Bianca proved to her fellow workers that she could do a job that was classified as a "man's job." Gabriela rides a motorcycle – a radical departure from the norm for a village woman – as part of her work organizing health workshops and clinics for mothers and children.

Not all women are opting for the new roles, and by choosing to be housewives they may be facing new pressures such as family disapproval. Susanna's daughter had the opportunity to go to high school, but to her mother's and grandmother's anger and dismay, she eloped and is now married to the young man. She lives with her mother-in-law in a traditional household situation, and is the mother of an infant son. Yet in choosing the traditional role of wife and mother, women may be resisting the new pressures of a contradictory development.

Politics and Empowerment

"Everything in Belize is politics." Thus says Felicia, who has devoted her life to the politics of the United Democratic Party (UDP). In 1988, when she narrated her story, the UDP was in power for the first time since its formation in 1973. Since then, the People's United Party (PUP) has regained the leadership that it has held almost non-stop since 1954.

Since 1981, when Belize achieved its political independence, party politics have become a central feature of national life, permeating social relations at all levels. Even in the villages, women are beginning to turn out for party meetings and some are taking on leadership roles in the local party organizations. Susanna, for example, was treasurer of her local branch of the UDP: since she runs her own store, she's considered to have a head for figures.

While participation in political life give some women a chance to be involved in making the decisions that determine the future of their community and country, Felicia's experience illustrates that it is still not completely acceptable for women to be vocal about their political views. Several of the other women, mostly urban women who lead relatively public lives, choose not to even discuss politics because of the danger of being pegged as belonging to one party or the other. To some degree, a cultural lag still makes it difficult for women to assume leadership roles.

Political partisanship tends to undermine the development of strong ties between women based on common interests. Those who are actively involved in politics, like Rachel and Felicia, are participating in divisions that separate women and the working classes from each other, making it more difficult for them to work together towards common goals. Although they have very similar motivations, experience and class backgrounds, these two women find themselves on opposite sides politically. Each wants to "help people" and to make a contribution, particularly to the poor and to women. Yet each is convinced of the essential rectitude of her party and the essential evil of the other.

According to Rachel, the UDP is the "party of the rich," while the PUP has provoked many positive changes. In support of her claim, she cites the achievement of Independence, the improved standard of living and the decreased dependence on the U.S. Felicia, on the other hand, believes that the PUP is infiltrated with communists, that Belize wasn't ready for Independence and that Belizeans should be grateful for whatever they can get from the U.S.

Only Sister Grace clearly articulates concerns about the implications for women of this kind of partisanship – which she compares to that between the Democrats and Republicans in the U.S. She says, "I would like to see us become more mature politically, like being able to belong to a political party and not be the sworn enemy of everyone in the other party."

Nevertheless, these narratives express strong awareness of the need for solidarity that transcends political divisions and acts to empower women: Lotty and Rachel are active in Women Against Violence (WAV); Felicia works with prostitutes; Marta is in Rotaract which gives scholarships to cane farmers' daughters and donated an incubator to the hospital; Sister Grace works in Girl Guides and many other organizations and actively promotes certain "women's lib" values among her students. She expresses appreciation for being part of the international community of Sisters. Gabriela works for "Breast

Is Best," helping to spread values of good infant nutrition and to oppose the corporate interests which pressure women to spend their hard-earned dollars on baby formula.

Many women, like Magdalena, work with others through their churches. Magdalena describes her work with the Legion of Mary, and Gloria organized a Church group of young girls in her village to do community projects before she became a nun. Ana notes that religion sometimes acts as a conservative force in women's lives, enforcing acceptance of cultural gender roles and norms. But, as we see in the case of Sister Grace, it may also offer avenues for progressive action and an acceptable and accessible network beyond the family through which women can come into contact to help each other and to combat sexism and abuse.

There are also signs of a new critical consciousness of the contradictions entailed in U.S.-style development. On the one hand, years of colonial paternalism have made many people receptive to U.S. aid and to the cold war ideology of anti-communism. Felicia thinks that international aid is necessary but would not accept it from the Soviet Union or Cuba. On the other hand, awareness of the dangers of excessive U.S. influence is also evident in some of the narratives. Gloria fears that excessive dependence on the U.S. will lead to devaluation of the Belizean dollars and stresses the importance of community self-help. Sister Grace also expresses apprehension about the danger of economic dependence: "We need investment, but I am apprehensive about all the aid coming down here – there are so many strings tied – I think about Nicaragua and Vietnam. It might not be as drastic as that, but no nation gives so much without expecting something in return."

Bianca is the most vocal in her criticism of the assumptions behind U.S.-style development schemes. She is scornful of BABCO, the USAID project that "is supposed to teach people how to diversify from sugar," calling it "a joke". She clearly expresses the connection between the failure of her agricultural supply store and the duty-free privileges given to imported U.S. equipment.

Of course, not all the women express such a clear awareness of the contradictory realities that accompany development. With customary politeness, they may be unwilling to criticize the U.S. to U.S. researchers, or may be afraid of appearing "backward" if they do not embrace the new society wholeheartedly.

But there is a further point to be made. Ana says "many women are conservative, mostly the older ones." This apparent conservatism may be not simply "cultural lag" but rather a form of feminine resistance to certain aspects of the new Belize. When Cristina and Miss Bird continue to use "bush medicine" along with "modern medicine" they are making the statement that many aspects of their traditional culture are valuable and worth preserving. When Cristina bemoans her children's disinterest in medicinal plants, she is also making a claim to the value of women's cultural knowledge which must be nurtured and preserved. When Susanna's daughter rejects going to high school in favour of a more traditional role, she may be asserting through her actions what Bianca puts into words: "But I think we still need good housewives to take care of the children – if my mother was a working woman, maybe we would have had more material things, but it wouldn't have been so good."

Belizean women are becoming aware of the possibility of a better life. However, their experience is full of conflicts and contradictions. While some assert greater control over their lives, for others the gender gap has widened and class and political differences are undermining the possibilities for united action by women to improve their situation. Women's customary contributions are being devalued as the old culture is replaced by influences from North America. But as the stories reveal, women find ways to adapt and to resist. The women's life stories reproduced here show that women are neither passive victims of the old repressions nor complacent beneficiaries of development. They are active agents, often working in very personal ways, but playing a role in forcing the pace of the new and adjusting it to meet their needs and those of their families and communities.

Glossary

Assad Shoman   Former senator, minister and representative of the PUP. Founder of Society for the Promotion of Education and Research (SPEAR).

Atole   Corn flour gruel or soup.

BABCO   Belize Agro Business Company. USAID-financed agricultural development company.

Benque   Benque Viejo. A town in the west on the Belizean-Guatemalan border.

Block   A parcel of land owned or rented by individual farmer, usually for cultivating a permanent crop such as sugar cane.

Bonus   Payment by BSI to cane farmers at end of season.

BRWA   Belize Rural Women's Association.

BSI   Belize Sugar Industries, Ltd., a subsidiary of the British corporation, Tate and Lyle.

Cañero   Cane farmer.

CARE   A U.S.-based non-governmental organization that coordinates health care and development projects in the north with Belizean government, funded by USAID.

CFA   Cane Farmers' Association.

Chaia leaves   Chestnut leaves.

Chiclero	A gatherer of chicle, the chief ingredient of chewing gum. Formerly, chicleros worked as contracted labourers in camps for up to six months of the year.
Comadre, compadre	Godmother, godfather of a person's child.
Company	the Belize Sugar Industries, Ltd. (BSI).
Creole	The descendants of African or West Indian slaves, now comprising about forty percent of population of Belize, concentrated in the Belize District.
Cube	A liquid measure the equivalent of a bucket.
Dugu	A Garifuna ritual designed to propitiate ancestors believed to be causing harm to people.
Eye, the	An illness contracted by children exposed to certain harmful influences, such as a drunk person who "eyes" the child, or by the wind of the rain. The illness is not believed to be susceptible to cure by medical doctors, but can be cured by a bush doctor.
Garifuna	Descendants of Carib people from Eastern Caribbean and runaway slaves who migrated to British Honduras in the 19th century. They are concentrated along the southern coast of Belize.
Garinagu	Garifuna.
Jamote	Sweet potato.
Johnny cakes	A kind of biscuit made with white flour.

Libertad	The older of BSI's two cane-processing factories, sold to a Jamaican-based corporation, Petrojam, in 1988.
License quota	The total tonnage of sugar cane that a licensed cane farmer is entitled to deliver to BSI's Tower Hill factory in a given year.
Macal	Yam.
Marriage Encounter	A Catholic organization that sponsors weekend workshops to promote better relationships between married couples.
Maya-Mestizo	The descendants of Spanish-speaking and Yucatecan Maya peoples who migrated to British Honduras in the mid-19th century and are largely concentrated in the north.
Milpa	Land devoted to the subsistence farming of corn and beans, formerly using the slash-and-burn method but now often using more land-intensive methods.
Milpero	Small farmer, mostly Indian and mestizo, growing food crops mainly for personal consumption.
Muffles	Muffles College. A private Roman Catholic high school in Orange Walk Town.
NIP	National Independence Party.
Nixtamal	Corn soaked in lime before grinding.
Obeahed	Bewitched.

Other side	A common expression used by northern Belizeans to refer to Mexico (Quintana Roo) which lies on the other side of the Deep River (Rio Hondo).
Partera	Spanish for midwife.
Pasmo	An illness caused by a draft or by exposure of a part of the body to cold water, especially when the individual is hot.
Pechuinte	Gibnut.
PG	Punta Gorda, the southernmost city in Belize.
Potato pong	A pudding made with sweet potato.
Punta (rock)	A popular dance form.
PUP	People's United Party.
Recado	Ground spices.
Said Musa	Minister and representative of the PUP.
Tamales	A Mexican dish made of corn meal and wrapped in corn leaves.
Tambo	A drum.
Tie-up	Tubal ligation.
Trash house	Creole expression referring to the traditional rural house made of tree poles sealed with mud and often covered by a thatch roof.
UDP	United Democratic Party.

USAID	United States Agency for International Development.
WAV	Women Against Violence.
Wech	A type of animal with a hard shell or armour plate and prohibited from the diet of Seventh Day Adventists.
Wind of the rain	A cold wind that accompanies rain and is believed to cause certain illnesses.
Wongla sweet	Candy made with sesame.
Zafra	The cane season.

Peta Henderson was born in Belfast, Ireland. She is a member of the faculty at The Evergreen State College in Olympia, Washington, where she teaches anthropology and gender studies. She is the editor (with Stephanie Coontz) of *Women's Work, Men's Property: the origins of Gender and Class.* She has been doing community based research in Belize since 1968.

Ann Bryn Houghton was born in Michigan and spent her teen-age years in Georgia. She earned a B.A. in Liberal Arts from The Evergreen State College in 1987, and has had a variety of jobs since then, including waiting tables, landscaping, and counselling. She is currently working on her Masters degree in Intercultural Relations and Conflict Resolution at Lesley College. She lives at the Beacon Hill Friends House in Boston, and is looking forward to returning to the Northwest upon graduation.